MUIRHEAD LIBRARY OF PHILOSOPHY

An admirable statement of the aims of the Library of Philosophy was provided by the first editor, the late Professor J. H. Muirhead, in his description of the original programme printed in Erdmann's *History of Philosophy* under the date 1890. This was slightly modified in subsequent volumes to take the form of the following statement:

'The Muirhead Library of Philosophy was designed as a contribution to the History of Modern Philosophy under the heads: first of Different Schools of Thought – Sensationalist, Realist, Idealist, Intuitivist; secondly of different Subjects – Psychology, Ethics, Aesthetics, Political Philosophy, Theology. While much had been done in England in tracing the course of evolution in nature, history, economics, morals and religion, little had been done in tracing the development of thought on these subjects. Yet the "evolution of opinion is part of the whole evolution".

'By the cooperation of different writers in carrying out this plan it was hoped that a thoroughness and completeness of treatment, otherwise unattainable, might be secured. It was believed also that from writers mainly British and American fuller consideration of English Philosophy than it had hitherto received might be looked for. In the earlier series of books containing, among others, Bosanquet's *History of Aesthetics*, Pfleiderer's *Rational Theology since Kant*, Albee's *History of English Utilitarianism*, Bonar's *Philosophy and Political Economy*, Brett's *History of Psychology*, Ritchie's *Natural Rights*, these objects were to a large extent effected.

'In the meantime original work of a high order was being produced both in England and America by such writers as Bradley, Stout, Bertrand Russell, Baldwin, Urban, Montague, and others, and a new interest in foreign works, German, French and Italian, which had either become classical or were attracting public attention, had developed. The scope of the Library thus became extended into something more international, and it is entering on the fifth decade of its existence in the hope that it may contribute to that mutual understanding between countries which is so pressing a need of the present time.'

The need which Professor Muirhead stressed is no less pressing today, and few will deny that philosophy has much to do with enabling us to meet it, although no one, least of all Muirhead himself, would regard that as the sole, or even the main, object of philosophy. As Professor Muirhead continues to lend the distinction of his name to the Library of Philosophy it seemed not inappropriate to allow him to recall us to these aims in his own words. The emphasis on the history of thought also seemed to me very timely: and the number of important works promised for the Library in the very near future augur well for the continued fulfilment, in this and other ways, of the expectations of the original editor.

H. D. LEWIS

MUIRHEAD LIBRARY OF PHILOSOPHY

General Editor: H. D. Lewis

Professor of History and Philosophy of Religion at the University of London

The Absolute and the Atonement by DOM ILLTYD TRETHOWAN
Absolute Value by DOM ILLTYD TRETHOWAN
Action by SIR MALCOLM KNOX
The Analysis of Mind by BERTRAND RUSSELL
Ascent to the Absolute by J. N. FINDLAY
Belief by H. H. PRICE
Brett's History of Psychology edited by R. S. PETERS
Broad's Critical Essays in Moral Philosophy edited by DAVID CHENEY
Clarity is Not Enough by H. D. LEWIS
Coleridge as Philosopher by J. H. MUIRHEAD
The Commonplace Book of G. E. Moore edited by C. LEWY
Contemporary American Philosophy edited by G. P. ADAMS and W. P. MONTAGUE
Contemporary British Philosophy first and second series edited by J. H. MUIRHEAD 2nd edition
Contemporary British Philosophy third series edited by H. D. LEWIS
Contemporary Indian Philosophy edited by RADHAKRISHNAN and J. H. MUIRHEAD 2nd edition
Contemporary Philosophy in Australia edited by ROBERT BROWN and C. D. ROLLINS
The Development of Bertrand Russell's Philosophy by RONALD JAGER
The Discipline of the Cave by J. N. FINDLAY
Doctrine and Argument in Indian Philosophy by NINIAN SMART
The Elusive Mind by H. D. LEWIS
Essays in Analysis by ALICE AMBROSE
Ethics by NICOLAI HARTMANN translated by STANTON COIT 3 vols
Ethics and Christianity by KEITH WARD
Experiential Realism by A. H. JOHNSON
The Foundation of Metaphysics in Science by ERROL E. HARRIS
Freedom and History by H. D. LEWIS
G. E. Moore: Essays in Retrospect edited by ALICE AMBROSE and MORRIS LAZEROWITZ
The Good Will: A Study in the Coherence Theory of Goodness by H. J. PATON
Hegel: A Re-examination by J. N. FINDLAY
Hegel's Science of Logic translated by W. H. JOHNSTON and L. G. STRUTHERS 2 vols

MUIRHEAD LIBRARY OF PHILOSOPHY

EDITED BY H. D. LEWIS

VALUE AND REALITY

VALUE AND REALITY

THE PHILOSOPHICAL CASE FOR THEISM

BY

A. C. EWING

Litt.D., F.B.A.

Honorary Fellow of Jesus College, Cambridge

LONDON . GEORGE ALLEN & UNWIN LTD
NEW YORK . HUMANITIES PRESS INC

First published in 1973

© George Allen & Unwin Ltd., 1973

BRITISH ISBN 0 04 100037 4

U.S. ISBN 391 00285 6

Printed in Great Britain
in 11 point Fournier type
by Unwin Brothers Limited
Old Woking, Surrey

In Memory of My Father

PREFACE

The present book is the result of reflections that have occupied me in intervals between other work for most of my life and have been my chief concern during the last five years, though I started writing for it as long as twenty-five years ago. My obligations to others for what I have read or learnt in discussion are too numerous to trace, but I claim to have a number of original ideas to offer. The sub-title has been added to bring out the one most fundamental presupposition of a religious outlook, namely that reality is somehow dominated by values.

My special thanks are due to Messrs. Allen & Unwin and to Professor H. D. Lewis, the Editor of the Muirhead Library, for the publication of this work. I am also indebted to them for allowing me to use, with amendments or extensions, material included in my previous volume in the Library, *Non-Linguistic Philosophy*, and to the editors of *Philosophy* and *Religious Studies*, who had previously published the articles, for giving a similar permission. I have to thank the Reverend E. J. Raymond Cook, M.A., B.D., of Manchester for reading the proofs.

I much regret that it has been found necessary in the interests of circulation to cut down the work very considerably, especially the first, epistemological part, but I appreciate the need for this and do not think any vital damage has been done to the central argument.

A. C. EWING

September 1972

CONTENTS

I

PHILOSOPHY AND RELIGION

It must be emphasized at the start and borne in mind throughout, though I cannot without tediousness continually repeat it, that religion is very far indeed from being a merely intellectual matter. It involves a profound and unique experience which at its best infuses a man's whole nature. What I am discussing in this book is not the whole of religion but the intellectual element. This element may well be present in very commendable form theoretically without much affecting a man's emotional life or obviously improving his moral behaviour. This may happen in a field of thought even more closely related to practice than is belief in God, namely ethics. There is however a difference between the two cases. If a man does not live in accord with his ethical beliefs at least to the extent of doing what he thinks right, it is a case of bad will; if he doesn't know what he is doing is really wrong it is a case of intellectual mistake; but in the case of religion a third alternative is more prominent. A man may be irreligious not because he has decided to be so, knowing or believing his decision to be wrong but yielding to the temptation to make it because it was in accordance with his desires, nor because he has made an intellectual mistake, but because he is lacking in the capacity for a certain kind of emotional experience without which the belief in God would never be felt as real even if intellectually accepted. The proportion of people who have asserted belief in God in Gallup polls in this country has been several times larger than the number who went to church frequently, and though I should wish to insist strongly that a man can be very religious without attending public religious worship it would seem to me silly to suppose this was true of more than a small fraction of the people concerned and that their failure to attend church was not rather a matter of indifference. Further, in so far as religious belief is a matter of intuition rather than of argument, the lack of this capacity may be the main cause debarring a man even from intellectual acceptance of religious belief, for the tendency to have the intuitive conviction and the capacity for the emotion are connected. The chief evidence for God seems to lie in an experience which so far from being a special prerogative of philosophers seems not to be possessed by many of them at all.[1] It is true indeed that a man may also neglect to behave morally through lack of a particular kind of emotional capacity, the capacity to have moral feelings, but the apparent complete lack of this capacity is much rarer than in the corresponding case with religion.

On the other hand the religious man may challenge the right of a philosopher like myself who can claim to have had religious experience only in a very attenuated form to claim to make contributions to a topic of this kind at all. The answer is that, while a high degree of capacity for the experience would be an advantage in discussing the philosophy of religion, its relative absence is not by any means a fatal disability. Religious experts can speak or write in a way intended to make what they say quite intelligible to others at least as regards any propositional content supposed to be apprehended as true. The concrete felt nature of the experience cannot indeed be explained to anybody who has in no degree had it except inadequately by the help of analogies any more than can the unique taste of an unknown food. If and in so far as the mystic's experience is really ineffable either in this or in some deeper sense, as is often said, it must be left out of philosophy since it cannot be discussed. But the field of theology teems with propositions put forward by theologians themselves as subject to rational discussion with arguments for or against. In so far as a proposition is based not on argument but on an intuition supposed to be attained in religious experience, the mere philosopher in so far as he is lacking in religious experience is less qualified to pronounce it true, but he may be able to pronounce it false if he can show it conceptually absurd, though if he does so he will, if he is lacking in the capacity for religious experience, be less likely to be able to suggest alternative propositions which escape the objections and yet express something like what was really meant by the original ones. The philosopher can also find out what metaphysical propositions

[1] For a discussion of the contention that they could attain it if they took the requisite steps see below, pp. 142–5.

have to be accepted if the religious attitude to reality is to be rationally defensible and consider whether these are self-consistent and reconcilable with the rest of our knowledge and well-founded belief. Where there is a clash or apparent clash between different departments of our thought it is the function of the philosopher to adjudicate between them. He can also separate beliefs essential to religion from those religiously unimportant ones which have too often been treated as fundamental by the adherents of a given faith: and in any case nobody can object to his qualifications for considering arguments for or against propositions such as that God exists where the arguments are not based on religious experience. I think indeed that he is in a better position to do all these things than a mystic who is not also a philosopher. The critic need not himself be a productive artist. Similarly in religion, while the deity-blind have no title to a hearing, we may expect an impartial judgement from a thinker who possesses a sympathetic understanding of religious experience, even though he may disclaim any pretension to direct inspiration. Here, as elsewhere, the onlooker is often the best judge.[1] No doubt a fairly considerable number of mystics and other religious experts have had a high degree of philosophical ability, and these quâ religious experts will then indeed have advantages over philosophers who are not religious experts, but they will also have some disadvantages. Their religion has commonly involved the conviction that it was necessary to accept on authority a large number of beliefs that their religious experience by no means guaranteed. And, even where this is not the case, the mystical frame of mind is so different from the analytic that, even where they are combined in the same person, it is almost certain that the first will react unfavourably on the second. To a religious expert God matters too intensely for it to be other than immensely hard for him to subject his belief to adequate philosophical criticism, and the more intense his experience the more likely *ceteris paribus* is it to have led to his attaching in his mind the sanctity which belongs to the most fundamental convictions of religion to beliefs which have happened to be associated with them but are of a religiously unimportant kind. Perhaps mystics do see some things that are completely unintelligible to one who is not a mystic himself; if so, I must ignore these particular statements since I cannot discuss them. But the

[1] De Burgh, *Towards a Religious Philosophy*, p. 48.

ordinary doctrines of the Christian religion, for instance, have always
been supposed by their advocates to have a meaning that is not too
recondite to be intelligible to the plain man with a moderate amount
of instruction, and, if so, *a fortiori* to the philosopher. No doubt,
if there is a God, he must be so immensely above us that his nature
is obscure to all human beings, but one can surely still understand
such a statement as that his attitude to men is least inadequately
expressed by talking of his love. If religious experts are the only
people who understand such statements at all, religion is useless to
most of mankind.

I had better say at the start that I do not accept revealed religion
in the sense of a set of propositions held to be miraculously communicated to us by God through the bible or Christ and therefore
exempt from criticism and infallibly true. But there is another sense
of 'revealed theology' or at least 'revealed religion' in which I am
very inclined to accept it, and which it does not seem to me by any
means inappropriate to distinguish from 'natural theology'. I am not
here referring to the still wider sense of 'revealed' in which it has
been said that all theology and indeed all knowledge must be 'revealed'
on the ground that, if God exists at all, we cannot obtain knowledge
of God or of anything else without his cooperation. This is a perfectly
legitimate contention, but there is also a distinction within the content
of our knowledge of or beliefs about God which is of fundamental
importance and which might be expressed by the use of the old
terms, 'revealed' and 'natural'. What I have in mind is that we must
distinguish between theological beliefs based on an experience which
seems to give intuitive insight and theological beliefs put forward
as established by metaphysical arguments which do not use any
intuitively apprehended propositions that are specifically religious in
character. 'Natural theology' may be retained as the term for the
latter and 'revealed theology' utilized for the former. Revealed
theology in this sense must be discussed if we are to give any proper
account of the philosophy of religion at all, and I do not think it can
be altogether separated from natural theology in the sense in which
the latter consists in a study of the arguments for God. But, while I
think that metaphysical *argument* has an important part to play in
theology, I do not think it can strictly prove the existence of God or
even justify the fully confident belief needed for the religious life.

The most it can do, I feel constrained to admit, is to remove intellectual obstacles to belief, a very important task, and give additional support to the intuitions which are the main cause ultimately of religious belief. I think most philosophers who accept a religious metaphysics would today agree with me here.

It must be recognized that some men have a much greater capacity for religious experience than others, and that therefore it is reasonable to attach special weight to what they say in so far as there is a measure of agreement between them. This gives a place for authority in religion, and it may even be best for certain people who do not aspire to think things out for themselves to accept as final authority for most purposes the church in which they were brought up, but increasing education should decrease the number of such people. The authority of religious experts must however be differentiated in two important respects from the authority of scientific experts, to which it has sometimes been compared. For (1) there is serious disagreement on important points between different religious authorities, which is not the case with scientists in most branches of their subject. (2) The scientist puts forward conclusions which can be verified or falsified by sense-perception in a way which religious statements cannot.

While speaking of my own personal attitude to religion and especially the Christian religion I must in honesty mention certain defects which, while they may have saved me from some common errors, can hardly have improved my qualifications on the whole for dealing with this subject. (1) Ordinary church services have relatively little appeal to me though I have not ceased to attend church fairly regularly on that account. A contributory factor here is a purely physical one, i.e. I, being tone-deaf, am unable to appreciate the music which plays so large a part in most services, but it is far from being the full explanation. I do not count myself as by any means a very religious person, but solitary thought is more likely to arouse what very limited capacity I have for religious experience than is corporate worship. (2) The Church as an institution has hardly any emotional appeal to me whatever. I am for instance quite unable to understand the great attraction of the Roman Catholic Church for many very intelligent people, though this is due also to an inability to see any rational grounds for accepting their intellectual position.

It is highly probable therefore that I underrate the value for religion of ritual and church worship, while I cannot help holding the private opinion that the great majority of Christians overrate it. I think, however, it is most important to make a distinction here. It may very well be that a certain kind of ritual, say the Catholic type, and even submission to a certain kind of authority is the best course psychologically for very many people, perhaps for all people of a certain type that could be defined psychologically. But it does not in the least follow that it is the right way for everybody or that the authority is always right.

In the course of this work I shall embark on metaphysical speculation. 'Metaphysics' is not such a disreputable subject as it was thirty or forty years ago, but a sharp distinction is made between <u>immanent metaphysics</u> which makes a system of what is known to us in our ordinary experience and of the concepts we need to organize it, and <u>transcendent metaphysics</u> which goes beyond this. Many philosophers who had no compunction about admitting the former have rejected the latter. Yet suppose human experience itself when adequately studied by its inherent nature drives us to go beyond itself, as the realist holds is the case with sense-perception, which can be explained only by physical things that are not themselves experiences nor analysable just in terms of experiences but exist quite independently of the human mind. The possibility of this cannot be dismissed a priori without further consideration. Nor can the claim of the religious man who likewise holds that our experience leads us beyond ourselves, though in a quite different way, pointing to God and being unintelligible without God.

I have however made an assumption which, while it would indeed have been taken for granted almost universally during the whole previous history of Christianity, is now widely questioned, namely that religious doctrines are statements which make claim to objective truth in the field of metaphysics. There can be no doubt that they have in fact usually been intended as such, but it is suggested that this is a confusion and that religion could fulfil its main function without such unnecessary claims. The most important thing about religion, it is said, is that it should incite and help people to lead an ethically good life, and they may be incited and helped to do this by avowed fictions or by 'stories' which they contemplate without needing to ask whether they are true or false. It would follow from this that we need not have any metaphysical worries or doubts about faith provided only we are prepared to accept as a good ethical guide for life the precepts laid down by the religion we adopt. To many people who hold such a view today and certainly to its best-known contemporary proponent in this country, when he put forward the view[1] it would also not be a matter of objective truth whether the ethical precepts were good but a matter for decision, but I do not want now to go into this question of the objectivity of ethics. This view of religion is allied with a standpoint according to which the non-assertive functions of language are emphasized and religious language is classed as performing a function other than that of making truth claims. Of course theologians have made truth claims, but the suggestion, I suppose, is that this was, at least partly, due to a mis-understanding of the way in which language worked. What was really an expression of emotion or an imperative by means of a 'story', it is supposed, was treated as an assertion of fact and subjected to arguments for or against its truth. It is however hard to believe that such a mistake should occur so widely; even a child does not commonly understand commands as assertions of fact by mistake. But there is one point of view in relation to which such an attitude towards religion might not unreasonably be adopted. If we came to the conclusion that none of the theological doctrines taken as objectively true statements could be defended, we should then have to consider what, if anything, of value still remained in religion, and so what advantage we could derive from religion considered in its non-assertive functions without regarding it as asserting anything. This is in fact the situation of Braithwaite. He must be regarded as a leader in a desperate salvage operation.

Now it can hardly be doubted that a religious man may be very much helped in his moral life by stories about God. He may be prompted to be very much more careful as to what he does and even thinks because he regards God as knowing everything he does and thinks. He may refrain from sins because he feels they would offend God and he is unwilling to offend a being whom he loves and regards as loving him. He may be encouraged to persevere courageously in face of adversity because he believes that God will see to it that

[1] R. B. Braithwaite, *An Empiricist's View of the Nature of Religious Belief*. For a fuller discussion of this article see my *Non-Linguistic Philosophy*, chapter 12.

everything works out for good in the end or even because he simply believes it to be God's will, though this particular story may be developed in a less edifying fashion. He may be more disposed to be charitable and forgiving to others because he thinks of them as all God's children and so his brothers and sisters. At a lower level he may try harder to do right and avoid doing wrong because he thinks he will be rewarded or punished by God according to what he does (though the appeal to this motive is not without its moral disadvantages). But why do these stories help? Is it not only or mainly because they are regarded as objectively true or at least as symbolizing an objective truth? Two accounts may be given here. It may be said, and this is certainly true, though it is not all the truth, that what a person who speaks like this is doing is telling the stories to himself and others as additional reasons for doing one's duty over and above those a secularist has. If we believe in ethical principles, there is no doubt at all that a secularist has also good reason for doing his duty. If we see something to be our duty this is in any case sufficient reason for doing it, though we may require reasons for deciding that it really is our duty. But when doing one's duty is hard, additional reasons why a man should do it may be badly needed to increase the likelihood of his doing it and the religious man may by his stories supply these. A story however cannot provide a good reason for doing anything unless the story or in some cases the set of propositions which it metaphorically expresses is true. No conclusion as to action whatever can be drawn from what is not true. If I believe that I shall offend somebody I love if I do *A*, this is a reason against doing *A*, but if I later discover that I shall not offend him in the least the reason just disappears and it is no use repeating the story as a fiction. If it were discovered that the person did not exist and never had existed, as many people think they have discovered with God, this would be still clearer if possible.

Secondly, however, it may be urged that to talk in terms of reasons for doing one's duty gives an inadequate account of the influence of religion, though true as far as it goes. It may be not so much that the man who has acquired an effective religious attitude has got new reasons for doing right as that his whole emotional attitude to life is changed by the influence of religion so that what would have been impossible or very hard for him before is now relatively easy. This is because religion arouses certain emotions; but emotion, at least except in pathological cases, requires some objective belief about the real, true or false, to support it for long, and if it exists without knowledge or rationally founded belief with which it is in agreement, it is to be condemned as irrational or unfitting, as it would be unfitting to rejoice at something disastrous or be angry with an inanimate thing. Religion is certainly normally regarded by religious people as founded on the nature of reality. They have indeed a very harsh word for worship of what does not objectively deserve to be worshipped – idolatry. Nor is it easy to see how an emotional attitude of worship could long survive the conviction that reality is not such as to warrant it. A man may be at peace because he believes he is in the hands of God, but he will not be at peace because he imagines a God whom he does not believe to exist.

It might be urged that it was not a question of reasons for the religious or the ethical attitude but of a mere empirical fact, namely that the 'stories' do actually have a good effect, even when not believed, and there is no more to be said on the matter. But what is the evidence for this supposed fact? It is hard to see how there could be sufficient data to establish it with any degree of probability, for the people who use the stories habitually and do not believe them are as yet far too rare for a generalization to be possible. Braithwaite implies that he is ethically benefited himself, but different people may be benefited by different techniques. The universal claim of religion has disappeared.

Further, even if it were to turn out empirically that religious stories could be helpful to very many people who intellectually repudiated their truth, this might well be explained in two ways. (1) Religious stories, like many secular stories, commonly depict ethical actions of an exalted kind and so focus one's attention on an ideal. (2) It is not true that a person must either believe all the time or not believe all the time, and I suggest that, in so far as a person who denies that he believes in these stories is helped by them otherwise than in the purely ethical way just mentioned, it may be because, when he thinks of them in a religious way, he is really believing them 'at the bottom of his heart' or at least half-believing them,[1] although at other times he can say quite truthfully that he is not believing them at all. The

[1] H. H. Price, *Belief*, series 2, lecture 4.

effects on his emotions and actions produced by the stories at the times he believed them might persist even at times when he explicitly disbelieved them, as it admittedly can at times when he is not explicitly thinking of them.

It is important not to confuse the view I have been criticizing with the view that religious statements are symbolical expressions of truth.[1] This is very different from saying that they are not expressions of truths at all. Even if they are symbolical and not literally true, they may well be used to convey something that is true or as near the truth as we can get. Even to judge that one symbol comes nearer to conveying the truth than another we must have at least some idea, even if a vague one, of what is objectively true.

But even if we admit that religious language states alleged facts of a non-empirical kind, we must go so far with the modern school of religious linguists as to admit that it also does other things. All the non-assertive functions which modern philosophers have insisted that religious language performs it does perform, I should think, and more, only we must add that it also at least claims to make statements about metaphysical facts, and that some of these statements are foundational in the sense that the fulfilment of the other distinctive functions of religious language depends largely on them. But besides making metaphysical statements religious language also expresses emotion, incites and commits to moral action, emphasizes certain values, expresses and knits social unions, gives voice to the deepest longings of the soul with great subjective and perhaps sometimes objective gain in prayer, and provides an instrument for communion with the highest being and for the expression of our realization of his supreme goodness in worship. But the ability of religious language to fulfil these functions in any way or degree that goes beyond the way in which they are fulfilled by moral exhortations and imaginative art depends on its connection with some factual belief going beyond the realm of science (and pure ethics). 'Belief in' should indeed, as H. H. Price[2] and many others have insisted, be distinguished from 'belief that', but the former presupposes the latter. Unless I believe that God exists I cannot believe in God. It is by no means the case that an intellectual grasp of metaphysical truths is more important

---

[1] See R. B. Braithwaite, op. cit., p. 28.
[2] *Belief*, pp. 426–54.

than a right moral attitude; but if religion cannot contribute much to the latter without some objective beliefs about metaphysical matters, these are of great importance at least as a means. We must also remember that, if God exists, conscious communion with and a right attitude to God must be regarded as of great intrinsic value over and above their value as means to happiness and morality, but we cannot gain this value unless we believe in God as an objective reality.

2

THE POSSIBILITY OF METAPHYSICS

It seems clear then that religion needs a metaphysics,[1] and undoubtedly one of the chief difficulties that prevent the spread of religious belief today is the tendency to take for granted that so such metaphysics can rationally be admitted. This belief has in recent times commonly been based on one or both of two epistemological principles, the verification principle and the principle that all a priori propositions and inferences are analytic, but I shall not here devote much attention to them because I have elsewhere published detailed refutations of both.[2] It at any rate must be admitted that neither can be established by argument since they are not themselves empirically verifiable or analytically deducible and no other means of establishing conclusions have been admitted by their supporters. They are defended as methodological principles, but to establish a conclusion you require not something merely assumed by way of method but a premise known or somehow shown to be true. Nor can they be defended by appealing to their success in solving philosophical problems because no verification by sense-experience and no purely verbal argument could show they had been successful in doing this.

What strikes me as the one at all plausible argument for the view that metaphysical statements have no meaning (other than the expression of the speaker's attitude) is to the effect that the criterion for the meaning of words must be their use in the ordinary contexts of daily life, and therefore they have no meaning when taken out of these contexts. Thus it is argued that the word 'mind' derives its meaning from the criteria we use in ordinary life to distinguish intelligent

---

[1] By a 'metaphysical proposition' I understand one going beyond the realm of science and if true throwing some light on the general nature of the real.

[2] See, for the verification principle, chapter I in my *Non-Linguistic Philosophy* and, for the doctrine that a priori propositions are analytic, my article 'The Linguistic Theory of A Priori Propositions' in *Clarity is Not Enough*, ed. H. D. Lewis.

beings from lower animals or lifeless matter, and is therefore meaning-less when it is applied to a being who is supposed to have no body and to have created the whole universe. The defect of this argument is that it fails to recognize degrees of meaningfulness. It is certainly true that statements about God have not the same clear definite meaning as statements about human beings. If God is conceived as a mind, he is still so different from any other mind we encounter that the word is bound to lose a great deal of its meaning when applied to him, but it by no means follows that it has lost all. There are a number of intermediate degrees between a perfectly clear definite concept and no concept at all. Even with terms for everyday objects this variation is very pronounced. Even a child has some idea of what is meant by calling Einstein clever, but he will have practically no idea of the intellectual processes which constituted Einstein's cleverness. Somewhat similarly we can meaningfully suppose a being possessed of intelligence and will, far wiser and better than we are, without shadow of evil, related to the whole world as Kant suggests[1] in a way analogous to that in which a builder is related to a ship he makes and again to that in which a captain is related to a regiment he commands. It may be argued that the suggestion that there is such a being is groundless, but hardly that it has no meaning at all. Nor do I see any difficulty about what is meant by talking of a dis-embodied spirit, whether such beings exist or not. In our own experience there is perhaps always an element of bodily sensation; but in the first place sensations qualitatively like those we have from our sense organs do not logically entail a body, for it is generally admitted that we can see no a priori connection between our sensations and our bodily organs; and secondly it is surely a meaningful state-ment that there may be beings who have experience of some sort but no feelings of that particular kind. It could surely be significantly said that a being might know many of the things we know and exert will in the sense of coming to decisions and determining his acts, although he did not have the particular feelings we know as 'organic sensations'.

There is, however, a principle somewhat similar to the verifica-tionist's which I do think to be true and to delimit the extent to which empiricism is right. It is the principle that a statement cannot have

---

[1] *Prolegomena*, Book IV, 357, sect. 57.

meaning unless this meaning is constructible in terms of empirical content. This is really the principle put forward by Locke in terms of his (defective) doctrine of 'simple ideas'. But this principle limits us far less than we might have thought. For it does not confine us to characteristics we have actually experienced but acknowledges our freedom also to form concepts derivative from these. The ways in which the concepts of what is not itself given in experience are derived are classified by Locke as consisting in comparing, combining and abstracting from what is given. This formulation indeed puts the mind's capacity too low, for it overlooks our capacity to conceive them as intensified much above any degree we have experienced (though the omission was no doubt a mere oversight on the part of Locke, who certainly recognized our ability to do this in forming the idea of God). Even in such a case we can say that our concept is derived from content given empirically. We can only form the concept at all in terms of what we already know. The extra element is simply an extension of what is given without importation of fresh qualitative distinctions. It cannot be denied that we can form some notion of what a quality is like in a higher degree from what it is like in a lower, but neither can it be denied that where the degree is very different the concept is likely to be very inadequate (unless we have ourselves experienced the higher degrees) except with such a simple property as finite spatial extent.

Kant's attempt to destroy transcendent metaphysics is discussed in my *Non-Linguistic Philosophy*.[1] Here I shall just mention three points. (*a*) Kant's principal argument was that the categories necessary for science can and can only be proved if it is admitted that they are true not of reality but only of appearances. But this argument presupposes both that they have been proved by him for appearances as universal principles and that they are as such necessary for science, and few philosophers would accept either of these propositions today. And Kant's arguments in the antinomies are also thought invalid by all or almost all of those specially expert in dealing with the problem of infinity. (*b*) Kant while denying metaphysics as objectively certain knowledge admits it as belief (if based on ethics). (*c*) Kant's own epistemology is only intelligible if we presuppose the existence of a real self over and above our experiences existing timelessly, for it is

[1] Chapter VII.

this self that synthesizes ultimately the phenomenal world, and this is certainly transcendent metaphysics.

The most characteristic type of metaphysical arguments today would however be put forward not as deductions but as explanations or correlations aimed at unifying the different aspects of our world as experienced and the concepts we have to employ in dealing with it, though no ground has been shown for ruling out the deductive method altogether in metaphysics.

A question which has much troubled the philosophers who discuss religion today is that as to the possibility of 'verifying' religious propositions or 'falsifying' them. Even if the verification principle is completely rejected as a theory of meaning, religious beliefs, it is felt strongly, can hardly be divorced totally from empirical beliefs which it is logically at least quite conceivable might be shown false. This applies particularly to any even moderately orthodox form of Christianity with its dependence on historical beliefs about Christ, but any religion that involves belief in the goodness of God is faced with the problem of evil and so with the possibility that after a consideration of the empirical facts the evil might in its quantity or manner of distribution or both turn out so grave as to force us to abandon the belief if we would be rational. And it has been contended that the mere possibility that the world might turn out so bad as to falsify belief in God is incompatible with the certain unconditional faith in God which a theistic religion demands. It seems to me however that we could never trust anybody completely if this required the complete absence of any *theoretical* possibility of empirical disproof of his reliability. There is indeed an important difference between the logic of doubts about God and the logic of doubts about a human being. Doubts about a man are normally not as to his existence but as to his goodness or wisdom, but a doubter about God will usually assume that, if God exists, he is perfectly good and wise, so that the doubt turns into one about God's existence. However this is not relevant to the point I am making here, which is the general one that the mere abstract possibility of a belief being subsequently refuted need not make it psychologically impossible or morally wrong to hold the belief with complete conviction subjectively, as we constantly do in ordinary empirical matters. Faith is generally admitted by theologians not to be the same as certainty but rather incompatible with the latter.

B

That the world is in fact so bad as to make belief in God unreasonable
is contended by many, and this view will be thoroughly discussed
in a later chapter; that it is logically possible that it might be so or
might become so is indisputable. Imagine a world in which everybody
was as miserable as the most miserable inmates of Belsen concentration
camp and as malicious as the most sadistic of their warders, though
knowing their cruelty to be wrong. In such a world it must be
admitted that it would be unreasonable to believe in God, therefore
the belief is empirically falsifiable, though not indeed in the purest
empirical sense of the verification principle since some ethical proposition is also required for the falsification, yet in the sense that anybody who held there was any truth in our ethical views would, if the
world were like that, be justified in rejecting it. Just what degree of
badness and absence of goodness would be required to falsify it is not
clear, but neither is it clear just how much apparently adverse evidence
would be required to render it irrational to maintain faith in a particular
human individual or continue to accept a particular scientific theory.

If capable of falsification, are religious statements capable of
verification? Obviously not in the strictly limited sense of the term in
which the advocates of the verification principle employed it, any
more then they could be falsified in that sense. Could religious statements then be verified in the same sort of sense as that in which they
could be falsified? Some complications arise here. For while it seems
that the world might be so bad as to falsify belief in God in the sense
of making it very unreasonable to hold the belief, even the attainment
of as complete a millennium as is conceivable on earth together with
indefinite progress for everyone in an afterlife would not verify it in
the absence of metaphysical arguments from these empirical circumstances to God. However good things were, one would still need a
further argument to show that their explanation required a God.
(In any case universal progress for ever could not be verified completely, but progressive partial verification is admitted as a ground for
accepting causal laws in science.) It has been suggested indeed that the
belief in God might be verified by the fact that it worked well, or again
by finding that all or at least most of those who carried out certain
courses of thought and training assiduously did come to believe in
God. These modes of verification will be discussed later,[1] but they

[1] See below, pp. 55-7.

hardly come under the heading of verification by 'sense-experience'. This is not the case indeed completely even with the first, since to judge progress is not largely a matter of sense-experience.

If we admit that the properties we experience sometimes entail other properties that are not themselves included in the entailing property, I do not see how we can dismiss any type of metaphysical argument in use just because of the empirical principle, i.e. just because the content or material with which we deal must be itself ultimately empirical in character. All we can say is that, unless the property or entity inferred is of a kind such as we have at some time immediately experienced or such that at least some aspect of it can be partially conceived in terms of what we have immediately experienced, we must deny meaning to the conclusion. Immediate experience need not be limited to sense-experience, that would be a dogmatic assumption. To be aware of necessary connections is itself an experience, and so is ethical and religious experience.

It seems to me that the opponents of metaphysics in general agree in making metaphysical assumptions. Kant assumes a real self, that synthesizes phenomena; the argument of Wittgenstein's *Tractatus* from the structure of language assumes that truth consists in making a kind of copy of reality; the argument against synthetic a priori propositions by recent philosophers assumes that the real consists of logically independent, only externally related facts or entities of some sort, ('logical atomism') since otherwise one fact could entail another. Perhaps if we could neatly separate all different facts from each other the analytic view would be true, but we cannot analyse one fact adequately without bringing in others. We should indeed expect antecedently that in order to show knowledge or rational judgements in metaphysics impossible on principle we should need first to have some a priori knowledge that the nature of reality was such as to exclude this, i.e. to know metaphysics; and if so, the task of disproving metaphysics so to speak en masse is impossible. What I have said is quite compatible with most of the metaphysical arguments that have actually been used being quite wrong. How far we may go in metaphysics can only be settled *ambulando*.

In fact, I think by far the most influential argument against metaphysics is the old, old one from the disagreement between metaphysicians. Certainly this disagreement is very striking. Yet if a metaphysical conclusion seems true to oneself after due thought and reasoning, such general arguments cannot prevent one from believing it, at least as an approximation to the truth (we cannot in fact help believing what seems evident to us), and if the chances of error in metaphysics are great so is the prize of truth. For, if knowledge has any value in itself, the attainment of knowledge or even justified belief about such high matters must be in itself, even if not in its effects, of far greater value than the knowledge of detailed scientific propositions, to which many of the best minds are yet prepared to devote their lives. And, even if one's metaphysics is wrong, it will, if consistent and logical, still be some contribution to knowledge, because it will give hypothetical knowledge as to what would follow if certain assumptions were true. After all pure mathematics is only hypothetical, and though we cannot expect metaphysics to have the applicability of mathematics, it is on any view of philosophy and its history far from unknown for one philosopher to progress by learning through the mistakes of another. Further, and this is a point often overlooked, there is almost as much disagreement in analytic or critical as in metaphysical philosophy. If metaphysics is therefore dismissed on that account, it will be hard to defend against a like treatment the epistemological theories which up-to-date antimetaphysical philosophers advance today. There are often equally great differences of opinion about the interpretation of what a philosopher said, though he no doubt did mean something or another.

However, we must add that, although disagreement among metaphysical philosophers cannot possibly be explained away, its extent may well be exaggerated. Here a suggestion made by Wisdom may be used not only for dealing with some of the disputes between analytic but also some between metaphysical philosophers. When two philosophers contradict each other, he suggested that what at least often happens is this. Each philosopher uses a different word, neither word is quite appropriate, but either, if the philosophers are competent, conveys valuable suggestions, and what they call their arguments for their different views are really statements of the respects in which their words are more appropriate. One philosopher asserts the truth of P and another the truth of Q, P and Q being apparently quite incompatible. Now P and Q would be statements couched in words having an ordinary meaning outside philosophy, but it is very unlikely that words could be applied in metaphysics in quite the same sense as they bear in ordinary talk. Yet the facts are likely to be such that some of the criteria required if we are to assert P are present and also some of the criteria required if we are to assert Q, otherwise there would be no temptation to assert either. There will be a tendency to assert P and a tendency to assert Q. Both tendencies will have some justification but neither a complete one. We cannot say without reservation that either side is right, because all the criteria required to justify its assertion are not present; but both sides still express truths, and not merely hypothetical truths, in so far as either is really appropriate in certain respects.

If we combine the two rival sets of arguments we shall thus have not indeed an authoritative decision as to which side is right but a much better account of the senses in which the words used by either are applicable than we could have had from either side alone. It must not be said that this solution of differences is merely verbal, far from it indeed. For to decide in what sense or senses a word can be rightly used of something in answer to a question is just to decide what is the right answer. It would indeed then not matter much which word we used provided we made clear all the reservations which the arguments on the other side showed to be required. It would not much matter whether we called ourselves monists or pluralists, said the world was one or many, provided, if we were monists, we limited our statement by adequately explaining the ways in which our use of the word 'one' when applied to the whole cosmos differed from its use when we say 'there is only one person in the house' or 'the earth has only one natural satellite', and, if we were pluralists, we limited our statement by corresponding reservations. The monist says that reality (or at least the world we experience) is one because P and Q are true, e.g. everything is related to everything else, there are all-pervading causal connections, etc.; the pluralist says it is many because R and S are true, e.g. there are different human beings so sharply separated that they cannot know directly each other's experiences, many of the relations a thing has are quite irrelevant to its internal nature, etc. The solution suggested is that we should say the world really is one in senses P, Q and really many in senses R, S and leave it at that.

I think this account can easily be pushed too far. It is as it stands too flattering to philosophers. Their arguments do not always consist simply in giving certain respects in which a word indisputably applies. Many arguments used by philosophers have no doubt not done anything so useful at all but have been mere fallacies. Indeed the account suggested by no means does justice to the great amount of real argument, good or bad, there is in philosophy. In the dispute I have taken as an example, for instance, monistically inclined philosophers have produced arguments – I myself think fallacious ones – to show that a relation can never be irrelevant to the internal nature of its terms, and there have been long articles of hard argument about the question whether all relations are thus 'internal'. And in a question such as that of the existence or non-existence of God on a given definition of God it is hard to see how both sides could be right. But I think there is a good deal of truth in the suggestion. Contending philosophers have each a message with something positive in it of truth, and as the controversy develops they tend in self-defence against the objections of their opponents to incorporate into their philosophy more and more of the qualifications that are needed, as a democratic government often inserts amendments in its bills to meet partially the grievances of the opposition, but usually not enough in either case to bring the controversy to a conclusion. I believe that the true philosophy, if it could be produced, would synthesize differences in some such way, and every noteworthy philosopher has done something which could be described as giving an, in some degree original, partial aspect of the truth. Usually the same philosopher will find it psychologically impossible to give an even relatively adequate account of both the complementary opposites to an issue – a great philosopher may indeed very well be more one-sided than those who are scholars rather than original thinkers – and for this reason it is particularly valuable to study different types of philosophers. In this there indeed does seem to be agreement among most philosophers in practice; it is widely admitted by philosophers of most varying views that the great thinkers, however different their tenets, are all worth studying. The justification of this can hardly lie in anything but the supposition that they serve to supplement each other by each giving a partial truth.

But the individual philosopher has to play a curious dual role. (1) When considering his own opinions on their merits he cannot help regarding them as absolutely true as long as he holds them, otherwise they would not be his opinions. No doubt he ought to be trying frequently to criticize them, but when arguments convince him that his view is wrong on a specific point then it ceases to be part of his view. Yet (2), if he has any sense, he will also hold the general view that it is fantastically improbable that his philosophical views should in all respects be exactly right. So in so far as a man expounds his philosophy, he is asserting a series of propositions of which he must, if he is rational, believe that they are not all and not indeed even mostly true. Since it is no doubt the duty of some men to expound their philosophy, it may well even be his duty to do this, as long as he cannot pick out the propositions which are not true and in regard to every particular proposition believes, on consideration of any grounds of which he can think for or against it, that it is true. It may be replied that he ought not to assert them as true but only as the nearest approximation to the truth attainable by him at the time. I indeed heartily make such a qualification as to my own views in general, and only because it would be insufferably tedious do not repeat it as regards most particular statements I make of a positive view. But it must be admitted that it is sometimes impossible to maintain this position in one's own mind with sincerity, for when a man considers the evidence in regard to a particular disputable view as it strikes him he may often feel a conviction in his own mind that it is not only approximately true but true. It is not in a man's power to choose whether he shall believe or not believe what seems to him evident or proved, even though when he gets outside the particular problem and thinks in quite general terms about the likelihood of his particular philosophical views being just right he must admit that it is very unlikely indeed, and even if it seems to him only the most reasonable supposition he cannot help believing it to be the most reasonable, though he may disagree in that with most other authorities. The above remarks apply to all controversial matters, but they do apply to philosophical questions in a particular degree. Some things indeed in philosophy I do claim to know with certainty, namely that some views expounded by other philosophers are, as I understand them, false, but then I cannot be sure that I have understood the other philosophers aright. One should further distinguish between a sure conviction that religious propositions express at least in symbolic form a truth fundamental to the universe and one's precise interpretation of that truth.

Metaphysics is involved in the very substitutes modern philosophers provide for it. Deprived of the old and venerable privilege of speculating about the nature of reality they have cast their eyes about for some job to save the poor philosophers from unemployment and have found it in the analysis of commonsense and scientific concepts or some account of these. Now if all commonsense and scientific propositions were taken to be either false or such that their assertion could not be justified, it would be possible to carry out such a distinction between this merely analytic philosophy and the speculative supposedly pseudo-philosophy which goes further and makes assertions about the nature of reality. But in that case there would be no justification for believing even that anybody holds the beliefs analysed. That people in fact believe so-and-so is itself a commonsense belief. But if the beliefs are true and in so far as they are taken as true, to give an analysis or account of what is believed is already to claim to assert true propositions about mind or matter too general to fall within science, and if this is not practising metaphysics, what is? Contemporary philosophers do not talk as much about 'the analysis of commonsense propositions' as they used to do in the thirties, but an analysis of concepts does entail a corresponding analysis of propositions, and they are analysing concepts if they are doing anything at all. Many philosophers in the past would indeed have said that physical objects, and even, according to some, minds as we know them, were mere appearances, but even they would have had to admit that in talking about them we were still making generalizations about human experience, and human experiences are after all real. We cannot annihilate an experience by calling it a mere appearance. Again, if commonsense propositions are regarded as not wholly but partly true, to give their analysis is at any rate to make partly true statements about the real, and the process of analysis can hardly be separated from the process of sorting out those parts of the propositions of common sense which are true from the remainder.

Analytic or, as it is sometimes called, 'critical philosophy' and 'speculative philosophy' or metaphysics may be distinguished, but they involve each other. One philosopher may be predominantly analytic and another predominantly speculative, but you cannot do analytic philosophy without doing or assuming some speculative philosophy (metaphysics), and you cannot do speculative philosophy, except very badly, without doing some analytic, because speculative philosophy too has to use commonsense concepts which require analysis and criticism. It does not follow that we can have much metaphysics, but it does follow that we must have some, and we cannot possibly say in advance how far we may be able to go in it. It can only be settled *ambulando* whether a major metaphysical system like Hegel's, MacTaggart's or Whitehead's is possible or not.

It may indeed still be maintained that, although we can assert general metaphysical propositions about the physical world and human minds, we cannot have a metaphysics which goes beyond these familiar objects and makes inferences about e.g. God, and this might indeed yet turn out to be the case. But my discussion has, I hope, shown at any rate that we have no right to deny the possibility of this on principle in advance of any consideration of particular arguments for such a metaphysic. We must transcend human experience if we are to reach even physical things, and our own experience if we are to reach other human minds, and perhaps still further transcendence may be needed.

At the same time it would be a great mistake to think of metaphysics solely in terms of the old deductive pattern. A metaphysics needs to include deductive arguments of some kind at certain points, as indeed does a science, but it is more likely to bear on the whole the nature of very general hypotheses for explaining and organizing the most general features of the world and of human life and knowledge.

One of the main grounds for hostility to metaphysics has been that it normally relies to some extent on 'intuition', a mysterious mode of cognition other than by experience, memory or mediate inference. There seems something 'fishy', especially in the present climate of thought, about saying that a proposition is true because we have an 'intuition' that it is so. Against this current of thought I insist strongly that we simply have to admit intuition somewhere, and that we can show the necessity of this by a quite simple argument. The argument is that inference is quite impossible without intuition. I do not refer mainly to the argument that inference needs premises known intuitively; it might be argued that these premises are always empirical. My main point is this: Suppose we infer from A, therefore B, therefore C. In order to do this we must see the connections between A and B, B and C. It may be that we are only able to do this because there are other terms D and E such that we could argue A, therefore D, therefore B, therefore E, therefore C. But for that we should have to see

the connection between A and D, D and B, etc., and we obviously
could not go on in this way interpolating terms ad infinitum. Sooner
or later we must come to a point where we can give no further reason
for taking a step in the argument except that we see it to follow in its
own right. Here even Ayer comes to my support. 'What makes it
true, e.g., that the conclusion of a syllogism follows from its premises
is that the inference exemplifies a law of logic. And if we are asked what
makes the law of logic true, we can in this and in many other cases
provide a proof. But this proof in its turn relies upon some law of
logic. There will come a point, therefore, when we are reduced to
saying of some logical statement simply that it is valid. Now to be in a
position to say that such a statement is valid we must be able to see
that it is so, but it is not made valid by our seeing that it is. It is valid
in its own right.'[1] He even permits us to call this an 'intuition'. I fully
accept the qualifications which Ayer lays down immediately afterwards about intuition, as I shall make clear later on.[2] The need for
some intuition if we are to have inference thus seems to have been
proved quite rigorously, and it can hardly be maintained that we can
have no inference. We must of course be clear as to the distinction
between mediate and immediate inference; if we know immediately
(intuitively) that A entails B we can know B but we do not thereby
know B intuitively but only by mediate inference.

It is interesting to note that those who deny that we can ever know
by intuition that something follows from something else would have
no hesitation in claiming that they can see that something does *not*
follow. They surely do not merely fail to see that it does follow from
the fact that Heath became Prime Minister of Britain in 1970 that it
will rain tomorrow, but see directly that it does not and could not
follow. Do they want any further premises for this assertion or is it an
immediate insight based directly on what these propositions assert?

It is often said today that the introduction of the notion of intuition
does not tell us anything but is simply a pseudo-explanation of the
useless faculty type. What we want to find out is how we know things,
and it is objected that to say we know something by intuition is no
more an explanation than it would be to say paper burns because it
has the faculty of inflammability. And these critics are quite right: to

<hr/>

[1] *The Problem of Knowledge*, p. 16, Penguin ed. p. 20.
[2] Pp. 18–19, Penguin ed. p. 22; see pp. 43–6.

say we know something by intuition is no *explanation*. What it says is rather that the piece of knowledge in question does not require explanation. To refer knowledge to intuition is to say that it can be seen to be true in its own right independently of argument and empirical observation. To explain how we know it would be to give a proof of it and this *ex hypothesi* cannot be done with intuition. But it is very important to decide which are the propositions that we have a right to hold true independently of experience and argument, and so it is important to ask what we know by intuition. To say that there are propositions which we can thus know is all that is meant by saying we have a faculty of intuition. A 'faculty' simply is a capacity, and nobody objects to one saying that a man has a capacity for playing tennis or seeing the point of an argument in philosophy. There is nothing occult or metaphysical about this.

It is sometimes said that what is called intuition is really implicit mediate inference,[1] and this is no doubt true of many prima facie intuitions, but it cannot possibly be true of all. For even when all the implicit inferences have been made explicit and all the missing stages interpolated, the argument given above will still apply. It will still be true that we must be able to see how each stage in the inference follows from the preceding one and we can now *ex hypothesi* interpolate no further stages to explain it.

The chief stock objection to intuition is the great difficulty in drawing up an agreed list of intuitions and the variety of, often conflicting, propositions which different people have thought they knew intuitively. In view of this it is important to insist that we need not and must not claim infallibility for our intuitions any more than for our inferences. But here a verbal difficulty arises. Philosophers have very commonly insisted on using the term intuition like the term knowledge in such a way that it is not a correct use of language to speak of an intuition as being wrong or even uncertain. In that case intuitions are never wrong for the same reason as that for which treason never succeeds. Treason may be said never to succeed because if it succeeds it is not called treason, and intuition is said never to be wrong because if it were thought wrong or even possibly wrong, it would by many not be called an intuition. It need not follow that there is a particular

---

[1] E.g. W. T. Stace in *Mind*, vol. 54 (1945), pp. 122 ff. He does not however apply this to the intuitions of the mystics on which he places great reliance in later works.

faculty, intuition, exempt so far from ordinary human limitations as to be always certainly right. Our psychological state may be just the same whether what we are intuitively convinced of is true or false. Only, if we must never call ' intuitions' wrong, the question whether an intuition is right or not will have to be replaced by the question whether it is a real or only an <u>ostensible intuition</u>. Similarly there are degrees of certainty or uncertainty in our ostensible intuitions, or if you prefer it degrees of certainty or uncertainty as to whether an ostensible intuition is really an intuition.

<u>The axioms of Euclid</u> are the most noteworthy examples given of ostensible intuitions which were generally accepted as self-evident for very long but which have now been admitted by experts to be by no means self-evident but actually in all probability not true. It should be noted however that <u>they never did seem self-evident to many of the ablest geometricians. Even very soon after Euclid had written doubts were raised as to their self-evidence and proofs sought in vain.</u> The fact that they have seemed self-evident and still would if we did not reject self-evidence on principle or defer to the authority of scientists, is no doubt explained by our inability to perceive or imagine visually any spatial figure as conflicting with the axioms.

But in any case there is no possibility of denying that apparent conflicts of intuition occur. But for the differences and mistakes simple lines of explanation soon present themselves, and while no answer can be given which will enable us to settle every dispute automatically, there are a number of criteria which we can use. Obviously in many cases mistaken intuitions or differences of intuitive conviction can be explained by a mistaken subconscious or almost subconscious inference having presented itself as an intuition or modified the content of what seems to be intuited. A man might have really known intuitively that A was B but have confused B with C or taken for granted that B was C where this was a mistake. In that case he may well wrongly say that he knows intuitively that A is C. In ethics people very commonly differ because they have different views of the factual nature of the actions they approve or condemn and their consequences. It may be that, if the disputants had the same view of these, they would also agree as to the rightness or wrongness of the act. Could one explain in these ways all mistaken intuitive beliefs? It would be surprising if all men's capacities for intuition were equally developed, and it is certainly not in accord with the facts of experience to say that they are so. But we should distinguish between the case of a man merely not being developed enough to see something to be true and the case of one who sees it wrongly. It is the latter case and not the former which seems to want special explanation. It would seem odd if our faculty of intuition sometimes went mysteriously wrong without a cause outside itself. As I have said, mistakes in reasoning or hasty assumptions constitute one kind of cause, mistaken beliefs as to matters of fact another. In such cases we should not really have indeed a mistaken intuition, but a mistake in reasoning, deductive or inductive, or possibly in observation. I should not wish to exclude the possibility of sheer mistakes in intuition, but I feel they would want a cause to account for them. Emotional factors are frequent causes of mistakes in inference and so they may be of mistakes in intuition. A man may easily be too prejudiced to see something or so prejudiced as to 'see what is not there'.

In deciding between conflicting intuitions it is perfectly in order to use arguments. It is true that if the intuition gave certainty arguments would not be needed and vice versa, but this does not cover the case where both intuition and argument give some basis for a view when taken by themselves but neither establishes it decisively alone. In such cases the two may provide a valuable confirmation for each other; and a conflict between intuitions may be often settled by discovering arguments which apply against the one but not against the other intuition in conflict. A situation that may well arise is this: two ostensible intuitions, p and q, may not fit together as they stand but we may find that, if we modify p slightly to $p2$ it will agree quite well with q, and that $p2$ seems as obvious now as p did before and much more in accord with a general line of thought we accepted as right. In such a case it will probably be best to drop p and accept $p2$ as really supported by the intuition which lay behind our acceptance of p.

It may indeed be said that the primary criterion of the truth of an intuition is that we must believe it after an attempt at doubt, following careful reflection on it and all it involves.[1] If we cannot disbelieve it after this, there is nothing left but to accept it as true.

[1] 'If someone thinks that he may have been mistaken in accepting some logical statement which had seemed to him evidently true, there may be nothing for him to do but just look at it again. And if this second look confirms the first, his doubts may reasonably be put to rest.' (Ayer, *The Problem of Knowledge*, Penguin ed. p. 22.)

We must not reject and ignore an intuition altogether because it is not clear. We can only use inductive arguments because we have some confused intuition that even the most expert logicians have not yet succeeded in making adequately clear something like the principle of causality or uniformity of nature. We are thus dependent on a confused metaphysical intuition at the heart of physical science, and it has served us well. There is a certain type of philosopher of whom, I suppose, Whitehead, Hegel, Heidegger and the best of the 'Existentialists' are examples, whose merit consists in bringing forward intuitions which they can never make anything like clear but of which they can yet give an impression to a sympathetic reader that is of some cognitive value. And the intuitions of the religious man are mostly far from being very clear-cut except where he is unwisely dogmatic. It is also an important part of the value of much great poetry that it expresses intuitions which cannot be made clear, at our present stage of development at any rate. For such intuitions poetry, or 'myth' as Plato held, may easily be a more suitable vehicle than prose.

A criterion sufficiently distinctive and important to be given a separate place is what I might call the 'fundamental character' of an intuition, though I hesitate to use the term 'fundamental' because it has been so grossly abused by the 'fundamentalists' in religion. What I have in mind is that it sometimes can be seen that, unless a certain kind of intuition is admitted, a whole important sphere of thought is invalidated and this puts such intuitions in a different position from others. Thus the whole of empirical science would be invalidated if our intuitive belief in the truth of the necessary presuppositions of induction should be fundamentally mistaken. It seems to me that it is a very strong argument for the essential truth of an intuition if it is necessarily presupposed in the justification of a whole department of human thought, as it is a conclusive proof if it can be seen to be presupposed in all thought.

Most of the objections that have been brought against intuition could equally well be brought against memory. In the case of memory, as in the case of intuition, something is accepted as true simply because we seem to see it to be so. Yet this subjectivity does not prevent our all being quite convinced that the fact that we seem clearly to remember something is at least strong evidence in favour of its having really happened, and there are a whole host of propositions based simply on memory which I and anybody else would regard ourselves as strictly knowing. Yet, though we may say that there are no false memories because we do not call them memories if they are false, as philosophers have often refused to admit that there were 'false intuitions', we must grant that at any rate many ostensible memories are false, as are many ostensible intuitions, and that there is not always a clear distinction between the experience of having a true ostensible memory and the experience of having a false one. Again memory, like intuition, is a source of knowledge or belief the epistemological nature of which is obscure, liable to dispute and different from other kinds. Are we directly aware of the past? If so, is not the past then present? If on the other hand we are not directly aware of the past but only of representations of it, how do we know that those refer to the past? How do we get the idea of pastness at all? When there is disagreement between different people's memories, we cannot decide conclusively between them in the absence of other evidence any more than with discrepant intuitions. And as we cannot use arguments to help in settling a clash of intuitions that do not themselves involve intuition in the shape of awareness of connection between successive stages of the argument, so we cannot in helping to settle disputes due to dis-crepant memories use evidence that does not itself presuppose memory. The process of applying the evidence takes time and so one has to remember the earlier stages when one reaches the later and even where one appeals to written evidence one must rely on one's memory for the meaning of the words written. Yet nobody would on account of these considerations be sceptical of all memory. Everybody on the contrary takes for granted the evidence of memory in innumerable cases without even bothering about further confirmation and is usually considered right in doing so. I do not recommend people to be quite as ready to accept their ostensible intuitions as they are to accept their ostensible memories, but such thorough scepticism as many profess in regard to the former does not agree with such great confidence as everybody shows in regard to the latter.

The necessity for introducing intuition would not be avoided by accepting the Wittgensteinian suggestion that what is wanted is the recognition of other modes of reasoning besides deduction and induction, or even that every topic has its own logic. For the modes of reasoning introduced or the logic enshrined in each topic would have to be seen to be valid. Whether a given thought process is described by saying that we see intuitively that Q follows from P or by saying that we are using a special mode of logic germane to our field according to which we are entitled to infer Q from P, though there is no formally provable law holding in other fields by which we could make the inference, seems to me of little importance, though I prefer the former account.

Intuition may also be conceived as in some cases crowning inference and going beyond it to something not strictly entailed by the inference itself, or in cases of 'organic unities' as awareness of 'toti-resultant' properties of wholes which cannot be inferred by ordinary logical processes from the parts. Further, there are very frequent cases where we have a number of arguments some in favour of and some against a view but can see pretty clearly that the former outbalance the latter or vice versa, though in most cases this cannot be demonstrated by any probability calculus. Such a consciousness, since it is neither an inference by logical rules nor a purely empirical awareness, can be described only as a case of intuitive insight. Yet it must play a great part in any of at least the less exact sciences, though no doubt its rightness in particular instances is open at least to some doubt in the majority of cases. Analogous cases occur with moral difficulties in so far as it is a question of balancing the good and evil in different courses against each other. We must not view ethical intuition as consisting only in awareness that certain kinds of things are good or bad in themselves or certain kinds of acts prima facie right or wrong. It must also appear as the result of the comparison of the degree of different goods and evils which enables us to decide rationally, sometimes with certainty, sometimes only with much hesitation, which of two things it is better to do in view of the situation including all the foreseeable effects of adopting either alternative. This judgement certainly does not belong either to formal logic or to empirical observation, though either may help it.[1]

[1] See chapter 6 for a more specific account of the function of intuition in religion.

3

CRITERIA OF TRUTH

Some study of the criteria of truth is clearly required as a starting-point for any systematic metaphysics, and it is therefore sure to be ultimately relevant to the philosophy of religion even if it is not at first obvious how it is going to be so. It would be most satisfactory if we could build up epistemology *ex nihilo* from the beginning, establishing the criteria of truth somehow without any presuppositions and then applying them in our thinking. But it would be pretty generally agreed that in epistemology we must proceed in the reverse direction to this, starting rather with what we find we know or must believe in our ordinary thought when confronted with a particular subject-matter. We see the general first in the particular.

I do not feel confident about our ability to draw up a complete list of criteria, but two obvious ones we can mention at once, experience and consistency. The law of contradiction is, I still think, in a peculiar position in that it can be seen a priori to be necessarily presupposed in any thought whatever, but it is applied in particular cases long before we are educated enough to conceive it *in abstracto*. And we can take for granted that conformity with experience, including memory, is another criterion.

But for science, and indeed commonsense knowledge of the physical world and of other minds, some further criterion besides these two, conformity with experience and conformity with the law of contradiction, is required. And, unless we can strictly deduce God's existence a priori from the concept of God, or from the simplest facts of experience, as the cosmological proof was supposed to have done, which I do not think is the case, or are prepared to ground religious faith entirely on an intuitive conviction, the notion of God will have to rank as a kind of metaphysical hypothesis, and it will then be very important to ask what further criterion (or criteria) for a hypothesis are needed. Scientific, and so *a fortiori* metaphysical, hypotheses are not logically entailed by observations nor, in most cases at least, is the negation of hypotheses strictly entailed by the observations which lead to their rejection. The hypotheses must indeed be consistent with empirical facts, but the scientist does not choose just any hypothesis which agrees with these in the sense of not contradicting them, but prefers some to others. An answer which has often been given and which at one time I accepted as final is that coherence is the additional criterion wanted; and in the past many thinkers have gone so far as to make coherence or at least coherence with experience *the* criterion of truth, by 'coherence' being meant not just the absence of logical inconsistency but the presence of a system in which the different propositions that were members of it positively supported each other.

The word 'entail' is here avoided partly because on the usual (I think very perverse and inconvenient) definition of the word a logically impossible proposition entails every other proposition so that any set of logically impossible proportions would by that definition constitute a 'coherent' system! But a logically impossible proposition does not support other propositions because it could not be used as evidence for their truth. 'Support' has also the advantage over 'entail' of covering cases where the truth of the supporting propositions makes their conclusion probable, not certain. We certainly need some third criterion in science, unless we could hold that all valid inductive arguments could be completely vindicated by formal deduction from some axiom or axioms the denial of which could be seen to be self-contradictory, a view which it would take a bold man to put forward today. <u>Could the third criterion be 'coherence'?</u> There are at least three characteristic applications of the coherence theory which call for attention.

(1) Coherentists have sometimes spoken as if the mere coherence of a number of propositions in a system provided positive evidence for the truth of any one of them even without empirical evidence for the truth of any. It has been said indeed that it is some argument for the truth of a whole elaborately worked-out theory that no incoherency has appeared in the course of its development, since it is unlikely that it could have been worked out without developing such an incoherency if it were false. But this would not be to make the

coherence theory ultimate but to give an argument for accepting it based either on the laws of probability or the experience of system-makers in the past. <u>The question with which I am concerned is not whether coherence is a criterion of truth but whether it is an ultimate one valid in its own right.</u> It would however more usually have been said that the criterion, for us at least, is not mere coherence but coherence with experience. But if all this means is that, when the truth of P is established by experience and P stands in the relation of entailing or probabilifying to Q, P is evidence for the truth of Q, nobody will question it whether he is a coherentist or not, and the coherence theory loses any distinctive character, unless it is maintained that coherence with experience is the only criterion of truth, a view which must be decisively rejected because (*a*) many empirical propositions may be known without making an inference from others, (*b*) many hypothetical and negative propositions may be known purely a priori.

(2) The coherence criterion has been used to prove the truth of some very general propositions by showing that they are presupposed in all our thought, or follow from something that is thus presupposed. But such an argument does not need a special coherence principle to establish its validity. It is obvious in any case that what is necessarily presupposed by true propositions or follows from what is thus presupposed must itself be true. Coherentists have made a valuable point by showing that axioms can be thus justified and, more generally, that inferences work both ways in the sense that with certain reservations the truth of a conclusion supports the truth of its premises as well as vice versa, but both points can be admitted on any reasonable view of logic.[1] As the reader will see in the course of this book, I myself think it a very important argument for a view that it is presupposed, if not in all, in a whole set of our beliefs which it is very hard to abandon altogether.

(3) Scientists always much prefer, other things being equal, a theory which explains a complex set of facts by a single principle to one which explains them by a number of unconnected laws or ad hoc hypotheses, each assumed to explain one particular group of facts; and certainly one of the things that may be meant by saying that a

---

[1] Note how scientific hypothesis are 'verified' by the conclusions which follow from them.

theory conforms to the coherence criterion is that it deals with facts in the former way rather than the latter. But what is the ground for this preference? Is it not simply that the theory which does this explains more? For it explains all the different laws which the other theory assumes by reference to a single law and so leaves only one law and not a number unexplained.

If coherence is put forward as an ultimate criterion of truth, the question should be asked how we know that it is one, let alone the only one or the only one besides experience. It was often based on a definition of truth in terms of coherence, but we may object to this as follows. (1) Since we never have a system which comes completely up to the coherence ideal, such a definition of truth must entail that truth is a matter of degree. Yet it is surely obvious that a great many judgements, e.g. '2 = 2 + 4' and 'London is larger than Cambridge' are absolutely true.

(2) It is very hard to see how coherence itself could possibly be defined without presupposing the notion of truth.

(3) If truth is defined simply as coherence, then the empirical element in our knowledge is completely ignored; if it is defined as coherence with experience, there is again a vicious circle because 'coherence with experience' can only mean coherence with 'true propositions based on experience'.

(4) It seems quite obvious to me that judgements are true not because of their relation with other judgements but because of their relation to something objective which is not itself a judgement.

Could coherence be the criterion or at least an ultimate criterion of truth without being the definition of truth? A difficult question arises as to the sort of argument by which this could possibly be established. The dilemma is this: if it were based on the use of the coherence criterion, the argument would be circular; if it were established by some other criterion, this and not the coherence criterion would be ultimate. The doctrine might for instance be put forward on metaphysical grounds, basing it on the metaphysical doctrine that reality is a coherent system. But this would not really be compatible with making coherence an ultimate criterion of truth at all. For you would need other criteria to establish the metaphysical doctrine in question. You could not at the same time argue that reality was coherent because coherence was a criterion of truth and that coherence was a criterion of truth because reality was coherent.

An appeal to self-evidence would not help: there are many propositions which have a more plausible claim to self-evidence than the proposition that what is coherent is true, unless 'coherence' be interpreted in a sense in which it would altogether lose its distinctive character, e.g. if we interpreted it as just meaning 'being entailed by true propositions'.

The only argument of which I can think that might avoid these objections would be one to the effect that coherence is a criterion which we find ourselves constantly using in arguments accepted by any rational person and that its use could not be explained as instances of the application of some other criteria or as based on some other argument which did not itself use the criterion of coherence. When I wrote *Idealism*[1] and for a long time afterwards I thought that we could justify the coherence criterion by the argument that it was used in all our reasoning, but I now wonder how I could ever have used such an argument. As regards a priori reasoning I do not see how it can be maintained that its validity depends on its being the case that the nearer our system of propositions approaches to a completely coherent system the nearer it approaches to absolute truth. Yet this is what would be required if the ultimate criterion were coherence. All that a priori reasoning presupposes besides the arguments it actually uses and the recognized 'laws of thought' is that, if p entails q and p is true q must be true, a statement which seems to me analytic and is on any view obviously true.

As for inductive reasoning, I used to argue that it depended on the coherence criterion (interpreted as meaning coherence with experience) on the ground that we could only be entitled to accept any scientific hypotheses we did accept either because (1) they were those which could most easily be reconciled with our experience, i.e. cohered best with it, or (2) because they made for coherence by bringing together different elements in our experience and different physical facts under one principle instead of explaining them by different unconnected principles. But is either reason really based on or does it necessarily presuppose the principle that all true propositions must fall into a coherent system? I very much doubt it. Our scientific

[1] *Idealism*, chapter 5, sect. 4.

hypotheses must certainly be reconcilable with our experience, but to say this is simply to say that they must not contradict empirically established propositions and that they must be based on experience, i.e. be justifiable by reference to such propositions; and there is a clear reason for the second ground of acceptance mentioned, that does not involve any appeal to the coherence principle as ultimate, namely that a hypothesis which brings different facts under one law explains more. The hypothesis reduces the unexplained element to a single law instead of dealing in many unexplained laws.

It has been said that we must accept the coherence criterion (and even the definition of truth as coherence) for deductive systems at any rate, if nowhere else. But their coherence is the ground for saying they are worth working out, not the ground for saying that the propositions comprising them are true. The set of propositions deduced are not shown to be true unless the axioms are first accepted not just as postulates but as true statements, in which case the conclusions would have to be regarded as true on any theory of truth; and on the predominant view today according to which the axioms are to be regarded as just postulates, what is established is not the set of propositions connected in the deductive system themselves but the hypothetical propositions that they would be true if the axioms were true. So far from accepting coherence as the criterion of their truth this view really implies that propositions might cohere beautifully and yet not be objectively true. The hypothetical propositions that, if the axioms were true, the various conclusions would be, again only presuppose the obvious proposition that, if p entails q and p is true, q will be, a proposition which certainly does not of itself commit one to a coherence theory of truth.

In view of my criticisms of the doctrine that coherence or even coherence with experience is an ultimate, independent criterion of truth, why is it a virtue at all in a theory to be coherent? (1) 'Coherence' may be used in a weaker sense to signify consistency, and even in its stronger senses it still implies at least that this less rigorous and most essential condition is fulfilled. There is no difficulty here. Plainly logic requires consistency on any view. (2) A view which is coherent in a stronger sense will be, other things being equal, in a stronger position against critics because it will be supported by different converging lines of argument and will cover more facts so that it is less likely to be overthrown by something that has fallen outside the net. (3) As I have said already, even the most characteristic applications of the coherence criterion, in so far as they are valid at all, can be justified by other arguments not dependent on this criterion as an ultimate principle of thought.

What ultimate criterion are we then to accept in place of coherence? A criterion that has often been put forward is practical utility. It has been very commonly held that the fact that a belief worked was a strong argument for its acceptance, and practical working has even been elevated to the rank of sole criterion of truth. I do not deny that working is often a good criterion, but I contend that when this is so it is only because there is some further reason for supposing that in the kind of case we are considering the belief would not work unless it were true. I thus claim that this criterion is not ultimate any more than the criterion of coherence. Why do true beliefs usually work well? Surely because, if your beliefs are true, you will know how to do what is likely to produce the effects you wish to produce, while if they are false you will be likely not to do what is conducive to fulfilling your desires. The former is usually a good thing, though not always. It is sometimes not good because a man's desires may be bad or foolish, and in that case a false belief that prevents him from fulfilling them may work better than a true. But how do we know that a belief works badly in those cases where this can really be regarded as showing that the belief is not true? Presumably because the consequences which should occur if the belief were true do not occur, e.g. the bridge collapses when it should have stood the train. But this is a direct empirical refutation, the validity of which is recognized by every epistemological theory. What shows the belief false is not its practical bearing, i.e. that it injures somebody, but the fact that it conflicts with experience. Such beliefs are not false because they are harmful but harmful because they are false. The criterion of practical utility is again not ultimate.

In the sphere of religion the appeal to practical utility in at least the higher sense of leading to a good life has been and is very common, and though religion has done great harm as well as good in the past I should certainly very strongly oppose the Marxist view that it is on the whole evil in its effects rather than good. But more complications arise here than is usually realized by people who make its practical value an argument for its truth. It is apt to be supposed that, because belief in a particular religion, say Christianity, is liable to produce very good results, that is therefore a vindication of every dogma orthodox in the religion, while it may very well be the case that the good results are due to belief in some of the dogmas only, while belief in others has no important practical effect or even on the whole tends to do harm. People of all major religions or religious sects can no doubt be found for whom as individuals their religious beliefs have worked admirably, but the question may always be asked whether this is due to the particular features of the religion of the individual of whom this is said or to features which it has in common with the other religions such as a belief in a perfectly righteous God. The fact that such people are to be found in different religions supports the second conclusion rather than the first. Or in so far as the benefit seems in a particular case to be tied up with the more specific features of a religion, this may well be a matter of individual psychology.

More fundamentally, unless it is claimed that the principle that what is useful is likely to be true is itself seen to be self-evident, some independent argument is needed to show that this is the case. In the empirical field generally such an argument is, as I have pointed out, to be found in the fact that utility depends on prior truth. A belief that a physical thing was at a certain place or had a certain property would generally not be useful unless the thing was at that place or had that property. But might not the belief in God well be useful even if God did not exist? Even though the belief very often helps people, as I am sure it does, it may be argued that it is by no means clear that its helpfulness depends on God's really existing and not merely on their thinking that God exists.

It would indeed be a strong argument against the belief in the existence of God as a supremely good being who loves us if the belief made no considerable difference for good in anybody's life. Such a God must wish us to enter into communion with him, and such a communion if it occurred could hardly fail to be beneficial. But then it is plain that the negative proposition mentioned is not true; a great number of people have derived great help and moral benefit from holding the belief. The contrary argument that because they have done so the belief is true has less force. Even if God does not exist, one should expect people who seriously believed in God and vividly realized what this involved to derive great comfort and moral stimulus from the belief. It should be a great comfort to believe that we are under the absolute control of a being whom we can regard as a loving father and a great moral stimulus to think that God sympathizes with us and helps us and that the universe is ordered in such a way that righteousness will triumph over evil in the long run, but a false belief can be just as stimulating and comforting as a true one provided it is believed equally fervently. No doubt many religious people are completely convinced that they derive help from their religious life to a degree which far exceeds any that could be explained by their mere belief in God, and if so it may be argued that it requires the actual existence and action on them of God to explain it, but it would be hard to prove the premise of this argument to an agnostic.

None of all this suggests that practical working is an ultimate criterion of truth, meaning by this that it is itself a ground for supposing a belief to be true, and is not evidence of truth only in cases where there is some other reason for thinking that a belief would only work if it were true. There is no absurdity whatever in combining the belief that an extremely pessimistic view of the universe is true with the conviction that general acceptance of the belief would exercise such a depressing effect as to make our situation even worse than if the view were true but not generally believed.

So the criterion we seek has still not been found. If we want to make no more concessions to common sense than are absolutely necessary, we may try Popper's view and say we cannot establish anything positive by arguments of an inductive kind but only refute false hypotheses by experience (though it may be contended that even this cannot be done in strict logic, because any contrary evidence might theoretically be dismissed as an illusion). But if Popper is right we have to admit that we have no real evidence at all that it is any more likely that I shall die if I leap from the top of a skyscraper than if I remain sitting in my study till I go to bed. All we could consistently admit on Popper's view is that the hypothesis that men will always survive falls from skyscrapers is refuted by experience, a very different proposition. Experience also refutes the hypothesis that men will always survive an evening spent in their study. A refutation of a generalization by experience can itself give us no positive information nor even tell us anything about the relative probability of different occurrences. It could not tell us what we should do if we are to attain a given end, only what not to do, if that. Popper indeed shrinks from the extreme conclusion and while denying the validity of any arguments which establish probability talks about a hypothesis being better or less well 'corroborated', but if to say this is to speak about anything beyond our subjective feelings a valid criterion is needed for corroboration as much it was for 'probability'.

But it does seem to be an ultimate reason for adopting one hypothesis rather than another that it explains more. We do assume in our ordinary thought and in science that what happens requires explanation and are inclined to prefer a theory in proportion to its explanatory power. This, I think, can be the only rational ground for preferring the 'simpler' hypothesis in science. The kind of simplicity scientists seek has little to do with ease of understanding by beginners. Einstein's theory was much more difficult to understand than Newton's, yet it was accepted as preferable. It is rather the simplicity which is given by, for example, preferring a theory which explains phenomena so different as the fall of apples on earth and the revolution of planets round the sun by the same principle to one which postulates a host of separate laws to explain the phenomena which we have now succeeded in bringing together under one heading, 'gravitation'. No doubt it may be reasonable to adopt the principle of trying out the simplest hypothesis available first because it is likely to be the easiest to test, but this would be no argument for its truth or more approximate truth. However it is quite a different matter to say a hypothesis is preferable if simpler because it explains more. It is better if it leaves only one law unexplained and explains by means of it the several laws which the other theory postulated but did not explain. And when a hypothesis seems to be not only a way but *the only* way of explaining something this becomes a pretty conclusive argument for the hypothesis, as is clear not only in the procedure of scientists but in the kind of evidence one would accept in the courts, and which would be loved by the readers of detective stories. As long as capital punishment was in force many a man must have been hanged on the strength of such arguments. Confronted with evidence of this kind doubts may be raised as to whether the explanation given was really the only possible one, but a doubt based on the suggestion that perhaps there might be no explanation would be regarded as absurd except in <u>the cases where there are grounds for supposing that no explanation is intrinsically possible from the nature of the subject-matter, as in the case of human free-will</u>, and according to many, though perhaps with less ground, the motions of sub-atomic particles.

In this demand for explanation is to be found the ultimate inspiration of science. It can hardly be denied that in asking for causes, except where there was an immediate practical need, man was at least all the time up to the last few years, asking for *explanation* of phenomena, however much scientists influenced by philosophical ideas, good or bad, today may theoretically describe causation as simply a matter of regular sequence or deny it altogether in favour of statistical frequency.[1] I say 'theoretically' because I suspect that they may well be really thinking in terms of explanation when they do their actual scientific work. Science can indeed supply explanation at the best only up to a certain point for two reasons: (1) the causal, or statistical, laws referred to are not seen to be true a priori, (2) there is the difficulty of the infinite regress of causes which prevents any scientific explanation being ultimate, whether or not it justifies the theological argument for 'a first cause'. But explanation up to a point is better than no explanation at all. Supposing *A* died in a way which was obviously due to human agency under circumstances in which suicide was ruled out and *B* was shown by clear evidence to have been the only other person in the neighbourhood at the time of death, *B* would be very unduly optimistic if he thought he could escape conviction on the ground that his presence provided no ultimate explanation of the death since no account explaining the circumstances which led to his birth and giving the complete causal chain of events which led from there to his presence in the house had been produced. It does seem that explanatory power is commonly regarded as the major point in favour of a hypothesis, provided it does not contradict empirical facts, or go against general laws based on previous experience, and in the latter case it can be said that the objection is that it would

---

[1] I think that, when a scientist actually denies causation or says that science has no need of it, what he is thinking of really is some conception of causality as intrinsic logical connection of active force, the validity of which is also widely (whether correctly or not) disputed by philosophers. He could not either do science or act practically if he did not assume that there were causal relations in the sense at least of relations between earlier and later events which justified at least probable predictions.

involve the admission of an exception to the general laws itself unexplained. If it could be explained why the accepted general laws did
not apply in this instance in their originally accepted form, as with,
for example, Einstein's amendments to Newton, the objection would
fade out.

Explanation is of two kinds: (1) explanation of particular events by
precedent events and conditions, (2) explanation of relatively specific
laws by more general laws of which the former can be regarded as
specific cases arising because the general law is applied in a particular
field. Objection to what I have just said may be taken on the ground
that the scientist no longer believes in universal laws but only in
statistical probabilities. But to say that A will almost always be followed
by B is already to make an assertion which goes beyond experience
almost as much as does the assertion that it will always be so followed.
Laws as to the proportion of times in which certain kinds of events
occur under given circumstances may be regarded in various ways.
It may be said that they are ultimate laws, but this does not seem to
me plausible. Or it may be held that they are all we can discover, at
present at least, though they are based on some more ultimate laws.
The latter might then be regarded as themselves absolutely universal,
the statistical laws proceeding from their interaction. Thirdly, under
certain circumstances and with the assumption of random motion it
might be possible to deduce a law that something would practically
always occur by a direct application of the laws of probability logic.
For instance, if a dozen mosquitoes were enclosed in a vessel one-
fourth of the internal surface of which had been painted with a lethal
dose of DDT and allowed free movement inside the vessel, assuming,
as I have read is the case, that mosquitoes have no tendency to give
preference in alighting to the parts of a wall not so painted, we may
conclude by a simple probability calculus that the chance of any of
the mosquitoes surviving a day in which each alighted a hundred
times was fantastically small. If we could base a statistical law about
the movements of inorganic matter on an analogous calculation, this
would provide a real explanation of the statistical law without necessarily invoking a universal causal law, but in how many cases we
could do this I do not know.

Failing this we must suppose that either the statistical law is an
ultimate fact, as used to be supposed was the case with the most

fundamental universal laws of nature, or that it depends for its explanation on some universal law or laws which we have not yet succeeded
in discovering. The former alternative strikes me as difficult to accept.
That the number of events of a certain kind tends to the proportion
of m in n seems not the sort of thing which could be true just in its
own right. However, the statistical law could be called an explanation
as far as it goes. The fact that the law of gravitation holds in the vast
majority of cases, even if it be only statistical and not true in all,
could be cited to help in explaining why my pencil has just fallen.

But I do not see what ground we could have for saying that there
are no strictly universal laws because we have not yet succeeded in
finding them. On the contrary it seems to me that the criterion of
explicability requires us to suppose that there is an explanation even
if we cannot find it, unless there be some reason, as I think there is
in the case of free will, for saying that a complete explanation is
intrinsically impossible.

The notion of explicability can be used to remove a difficulty
raised by Russell about the establishment of general laws by inductive
methods. He objected that the empirical evidence for any general
law is always compatible with an indefinite number of alternative
hypotheses. Besides supposing that the general law will always hold
under given conditions we may suppose that it has held up to the
present but will cease to hold either now or at any time in the future,
one might fancy, and any such alternative would, he urged, from the
nature of the case be compatible with the empirical evidence available
now. But we may reply that to make such a supposition is to leave the
supposed termination of the law unexplained or rather to go against
the principle of explicability more positively by supposing it to cease
to hold under the same conditions under which it had held before
and so with *ex hypothesi* no reason for the cessation. The sudden
and permanent abrogation of a law which had apparently held all the
time since scientific observations began would most specially and
urgently need an explanation.

The Uniformity of Nature may itself be regarded as a corollary
of the principle of explicability. If A_2 occurs instead of A_1, the
explanation why it does so can only be found in a difference in the
circumstances in which the two happen. On the other hand, if the
occurrence of given conditions fully explains the occurrence of A_1,

it must always occur under these conditions. The main inductive methods can thus be easily connected with the criterion of explicability. Take the two simplest and most universally used methods, Mill's Method of Difference and the Method of Induction by Incomplete Enumeration. *E* is present in one case but absent in another. The presence of *E* in the first case must be explained, but it can only be explained by circumstances that were not present in the second. *A*, *B* and *C* were present in both cases. Therefore they cannot constitute the whole explanation. *D* is the only relevant circumstance that we can detect which was present in the first case but not in the second. Therefore it is, not indeed the whole cause of *E*, but the explanation why it occurred in the first case when it did not occur in the second. (The argument of course does not show that *A*, *B* and *C* or any one of them were not also part of the conditions necessary for the occurrence of *E*.) But in using this method we assume throughout that the occurrence of *E* needs explanation and look for something that will provide the explanation in what went before. Without making the above assumption we have not the initial premise that *E* has to be accounted for. And so with all Mill's methods or any more subtle reformulation of them which modern logicians find preferable. Now take induction by incomplete enumeration. This assumes that the constant presence of the property *b* in instances of *A*, being too frequent to be plausibly regarded as the result of external accident, requires explanation by something in the generic nature of *A* and that therefore all members of the class are likely to have this property or at least that its absence in any of them calls for special explanation.

There have been interminable controversies among philosophers as to the possibility and method of justifying by argument the belief in independent physical things and great questioning as to how we can justify even the belief in human minds other than our own, and these beliefs are indeed incapable of justification in the most direct inductive manner. It is logically impossible for us to perceive unperceived physical things, yet it is part of the notion of physical things that they exist independently of being perceived by human beings. Again it is probably at least causally, if not logically, impossible to apprehend directly the experiences of other minds. (Telepathy is probably not the direct apprehension of the experience of others but the having of experiences similar to theirs in some respects, combined with a non-inferential belief that the other person concerned was having an experience of that kind.) So it is not possible in these cases to establish the existence of the beings we wish to show exist by using straightforward generalizations based on what we have directly observed in the full sense. In the case of human beings we have each of us only observed one specimen, ourselves, and this is not enough for a generalization. In the case of physical things we have either, on the representative theory, never directly perceived even one, or at least we cannot assume we have without begging the whole question, for even if the direct theory is true, we can at any rate not assert that it is till we have already vindicated the existence of physical objects. But, if we accept explanatory power as a criterion, an argument of an inductive causal type is still open to us after all. We can see that an enormous number of things in our experience are explained by assuming the existence of physical objects and other human minds.

Philosophers have again and again criticized the view according to which the belief in other minds is to be vindicated only by an argument from analogy, and it is only if we take its explanatory force as a very strong point in its favour that we can account for the convincingness of the conclusion. A view which brings in other minds has the great advantage over solipsism of explaining a great deal in my experience which I could not possibly explain by reference to past experiences of my own. Here it is especially relevant, as H. H. Price has pointed out,[1] that such a great proportion of my experiences seem to imply the working of a purpose which cannot be regarded as my own, for example the experiences connected with manufactured objects, and particularly the sight and sound of words which when interpreted according to certain rules have an intelligible meaning. This is not intended as an account of the way in which we actually reached the belief as a matter of psychology. We reached it at too early a stage in life for systematic reasoning to be possible to us. What it gives is a ground of justification for the system of beliefs in other minds which has grown up.

And similarly with physical things. The whole apparatus of knowledge which science gives us about them is the most satisfactory explanation we can yet provide of our experiences in perception. At least that is the case if we interpret physical object propositions in a

---

[1] *Philosophy*, vol. 13 (1938), pp. 425 ff.

realist and not a phenomenalist way. Phenomenalism does not, properly speaking, provide any explanation at all but in giving what are called the causes of an event merely states according to its own account what would have happened if certain conditions had been fulfilled which were usually not fulfilled. For the conditions which are said to 'cause' our perceptions are not normally actual perceptions either of our own or of other human beings. This seems to me one of the two main arguments for realism against phenomenalism, the other being that we really know such propositions as that we have bodies and these propositions have to be analysed in a realist and not a phenomenalist way if the analysis is to give what we really mean at the 'commonsense' level. No doubt our views of physical objects are liable to future alteration, but the present views have on the whole worked so well in explaining our experience that we can be confident that any views which supersede them will to a very large extent coincide with or include as special cases our present views at least at the macroscopic level as regards the 'primary qualities' of ordinary objects perceived. It may be replied that these facts could be explained alternatively by supposing Berkeley's God to have arranged that our experience should go on as if there were independent physical things such as we suppose without there really being any such things, but it may be retorted that this view, while giving a general explanation, does not help at all in explaining our experience in detail. It is logically possible that it might have done so, e.g. if we had found empirically that everything happened in the best possible way that we could conceive, thus giving the hypothesis of a perfect creator and world-ruler detailed explanatory force, or if we had had in some way access to that being's conative dispositions and could use suppositions about them as we now do scientific hypotheses for explaining and forecasting particular events.

No doubt it is by no means the case that every hypothesis which would explain the facts if true is thereby proved or even rendered probable. A hypothesis may have to be rejected offhand as contradicting facts other than those it is intended to explain, and there may be several alternative explanations of a given fact. In such cases the scientist will no doubt, *ceteris paribus*, select the one which coheres best with the most successful system of explanation in the field in question, but this would come under the principle of seeking the 'simplest' explanation because it explains more than do separate *ad hoc* explanations.

The latest book I know advocating the coherence theory seems to identify explanatory power with coherence.[1] But coherence, as I have understood it before, seems to me to have meant something quite distinguishable from and not necessarily involved by explanatory efficacy. It seemed to me to mean that all true propositions constituted a system in which they supported each other and that therefore of alternative hypotheses the one must be preferred which brought us nearest to that goal of mutual support without contradicting experience. Now it may be that one could formulate a logical proof that the hypothesis which had most explanatory efficacy would always also be the one which brought us nearest to the coherence ideal; I do not know. But suppose it turned out that it could. This would not by any means establish that coherence was an ultimate criterion at all. For what it would show would only be that it followed from another criterion of truth. To establish it by deducing it by the application of another criterion is already to imply that it is not ultimate. And of the two criteria, explanatory efficacy and coherence, it seems to me that the former has an evidence which the latter does not possess.

It might be objected that the proposition that we should give preference to those hypotheses which have most explanatory efficacy is, in Kant's words, a regulative and not a constitutive principle, but if that were all it could give no positive ground for accepting a hypothesis as true, and we cannot help thinking that, if a hypothesis is the only one which explains something in a way that accords with experience or is the one which does so best, this is a reason for holding the hypothesis to be true. It must be counted as a 'commonsense proposition' that it is an argument for the truth of a hypothesis that it explains facts of experience better than its rivals, but it is far from being a commonsense proposition that true propositions about the world constitute a coherent system (except in the sense of not actually contradicting each other, which, as we have seen, is much less than what the philosophers mean by 'coherence' when they put forward the 'coherence theory'). The former proposition must therefore be treated with great respect, especially as it is not only a commonsense proposition itself but is presupposed in the grounds for our acceptance

[1] Errol Harris, *Hypothesis and Perception*, pp. 255–6.

C

of a great many other commonsense and scientific propositions, and only rejected if there turned out to be extremely strong reasons against it. At the same time in accepting it we must recognize we are going well beyond what is given in experience or could be proved by strict logic. Metaphysically, I think, the distinction between the view I have put forward and the typical coherence view is very important because the latter connotes a pretty thorough monism which the former does not.

In making ability to explain a criterion of truth I do not mean necessarily to assume a complete determinism, and I in fact reject determinism in chapter 10. If the indeterminist is right, the notion that there can be a complete causal explanation of all human acts must be rejected as incompatible with our moral knowledge or the inherent nature of human action or both. But if some things are inherently inexplicable it is no objection to a theory that it cannot explain them, though one would like an explanation why this kind of thing exists, such as theologians indeed supply when they argue that undetermined free will is a necessary condition of the realization of moral good. All that the principle I have put forward says is that it is an argument for a theory, other things being equal, that it leaves less unexplained. Without this principle I do not think we could legitimately advance beyond our own experience, let alone have any science except pure mathematics.

I have in the past used an argument,[1] ultimately originating from Keynes,[2] to justify induction by means of the notion of inverse probability, and this argument might be used equally to justify the application of the criterion of explanatory efficacy which I have just put forward. It may be said, namely, that the reason for accepting a hypothesis as true because it explains something is that, if the explanation is detailed or is applied successfully in many cases, it would be a most improbable coincidence if it were not substantially true and yet things went on to this extent as if it were. If I successfully predicted on the strength of a meteorological theory of mine whether

---

[1] *Non-Linguistic Philosophy*, chapter VI.

[2] *A Treatise on Probability*, pt. III. I however disagree in holding that the argument need not include in its premises a general assumption about the course of nature such as Keynes's Principle of Limited Independent Variety. This depends on my contention that it can work without presupposing the notion of a prior antecedent probability. (See *Non-Linguistic Philosophy*, pp. 134 ff.)

it would be fine or would rain on every day of the coming month, it might be argued that, assuming, as is near being correct, that in western England the chance of rain on any particular day is about 50 per cent, the odds against my success being a coincidence would be something like 1—365, and that therefore my theory must come at least pretty near the truth. And similarly the argument from probability might be used to justify our preference of a hypothesis which explained a lot of different phenomena by reference to a single law. It would be a very odd coincidence, it may be said, if a number of more particularized laws known to hold in experience would be deduced from a more general hypothesis without the latter hypothesis being substantially true itself. And this may be turned into a general argument to justify induction by means of the contention that certain kinds of events, e.g. those which exemplify gravitation, happen so regularly under certain conditions that it would be fantastically improbable if there were no law connecting that kind of event with those kinds of conditions. Experts in the logic of induction do not usually approve the kind of justification of induction I have suggested, but I cannot help thinking myself that it is indeed valid. But it does depend on some proposition about probability – it is difficult to say just what proposition – being taken as self-evident, and it seems implausible to give this proposition such a fundamental role as to make it the ultimate logical basis of all induction. Perhaps the fact that it seems so improbable that a law which explains in detail a very large number of facts should be substantially wrong is just the obverse of our conviction that the explanatory power of a hypothesis is itself an ultimate ground for belief.

The employment of the criterion of explanatory efficacy gives us a ground for postulating causal laws not merely in the sense of regular sequences but in the sense of real intrinsic connections. For only this would explain the repeated sequences we encounter in nature and save them from being anything but mere incredible coincidences, more unlikely according to the laws of probability than having ten times running a hand in bridge consisting entirely of trumps. Now if *b* has just followed *a* regularly in the past, this gives no ground for supposing that it will continue to so on future occasions any more than that a run of luck will continue in a game of pure chance. But if we admit the possibility that dice might be biased, such a run will be evidence of bias and will eventually make it a highly probable conclusion that the bias is so marked that the run will continue as long as one plays. It will thus be possible now to break through the main barrier which hinders the validification of inductive arguments and jump from reports on what we have already experienced to predictions as to what we have not. And certainly we are entitled to do this in so far as we attain to explanations at all. For if *AB* explains *C* once, *C* must follow *AB* every time, the context being similar. For otherwise we should be without an explanation of the difference between the case when it followed and the case when it did not follow*AB*.

If we accept the criterion of explicatory force as providing evidence in favour of hypotheses in science and are not prepared to deny the possibility of metaphysics on principle, surely it is only reasonable to accept this criterion where it gives support to hypotheses in metaphysics.

4

MIND AND BODY

The importance for religion of the subject of this chapter cannot be denied, and it is especially important for one like myself to whom the doctrine of survival of bodily death seems necessary if we are to have at all a satisfactory religion. The mind–body relation has been much discussed lately and the amount of perverse ingenuity devoted to defence of an extravagant materialism seems to me amazing, but I count myself absolved from spending as much space as I should otherwise have done on the topic because it has been handled so thoroughly by H. D. Lewis in his recent book, *The Elusive Mind*, and because I have also defended 'dualism' in other published writings.[1] Much of the chapter was written before the publication of Lewis's book.

Both of us are much concerned in defending the view that human beings can be divided very sharply into two quite different elements, the mental and the physical, whether these are styled substances or series of events. We both go further in fact to take the former, the 'Pure Ego' view about the mental side, but at the moment I am concerned to defend the view that we cannot regard statements about the mind as just statements about bodily events. Even this is enough to make me liable to the charge of dualism. 'Dualism' used to signify the doctrine that mind and body were different substances, but nowadays Ryle and others would apply this term of abuse to anybody who went even so far as to describe them as two generically different series of events.

Let me add one further preliminary remark. For many philosophers there should be a very simple way available of cutting the knot.

---

[1] See articles on *Mental Acts* and *The Relation between Mind and Body* in my *Non-Linguistic Philosophy*, and on *Professor Ryle's Attack on Dualism* in *Clarity is Not Enough*, ed. H. D. Lewis.

They might just say that statements about physical objects have sense only as statements about human experiences, and therefore to make the mind merely a series of states or qualities of the brain would be to reduce it to an adjective of a small selection of its own experiences or rather the hypothetical experiences a physiologist would have if he looked into our brain, since I think we are not supposed to have sensations of our brain and even if we do it is not these sensations but the sensations got by observing it from outside that a physiologist is talking about when he speaks of the brain. I am however not able to undermine the foundations of materialism in this simple manner because I am not prepared to adopt a phenomenalist view of the matter.

Let us now consider the arguments which the opponents of 'dualism' use. Firstly, it is argued that mind and body as conceived by the dualist are too alien for their interaction to be conceivable. This old argument could hardly justify the view that they are properly conceived as identical, and in any case it seems to me that it depends on two assumptions if it is to carry serious weight, both of which are quite uncongenial to the philosophical temper of most who attack dualism today. One of them is that the causal relation involves a necessary connection such as could conceivably be known a priori, for, if this is not assumed, the fact that such a connection cannot be seen is no argument whatever against a causal connection being present. Now the view of causality I have mentioned seems to myself plausible, but it is a view which none or hardly any of the people who have written against dualism lately would for a moment accept. They would maintain rather that causation is a matter of regular sequence or concomitance, and if so there does not seem to be any reason at all why two things very alien in kind should not be causally connected. Nobody could in that case expect to see a logical connection between them because there is none to be seen. The second assumption is that, if there is a logical connection, it must be in our power to see it; but this surely would by no means follow. There may be ever so many a priori connections which really hold between things and yet are as unknown to us as were the a priori connections of geometry to primitive savages. In any case we do not know the internal qualitative nature of matter, the properties studied by science, though physically objective, being only relational, and if we have no knowledge of this how could we possibly know what it could or could not entail?

The position was very different for a philosopher like Descartes who thought he had a 'clear and distinct' idea of both mind and body, from which it would follow, at least if the words 'clear' and 'distinct' were used in Descartes' sense, that if there were a logical connection between cause and effect we could see it. Descartes was therefore in a real difficulty about the relation between mind and body, but the modern philosophers who do not share his assumptions need not share his difficulty.

The difficulty about interaction has however been revived in a new form in which it asserts that two things can interact causally only if included in the same system, but this seems to be an a priori assumption which wants proof. I do not see how it could possibly be established empirically. It is true that all other causation of which we know occurs in a system, but this simply follows from the fact that every event we know is an event either in a mind, in the wide sense in which any conscious being might be said to have a mind, or in the physical world, since both any single mind and the physical world as a whole is to be regarded as a system. But to argue that, therefore, there could not be causal interaction between mind and body would be like arguing that, because all human relations except international relations were relations between different members of the same state, there could not be international relations because these would not be relations between members of the same state and therefore would not conform to the general nature of all other human relations. And how could we know whether a mind and its body do or do not belong to the same system without first knowing whether they are causally connected? The argument from conservation of energy, though formidable for Victorians, does not seem relevant to modern scientific ideas. The objection to interaction is not that we see it cannot happen but that we do not know how it can happen, but till recently at least we did not know how most things could happen.

The evidence for causal interaction between body and mind is empirical. It consists in such everyday facts as that when we are pricked it hurts and when we decide to move our arm it almost always does move. One might dodge it by adopting some metaphysical explanation to account for the correlation which gives such a convincing appearance of interaction, but surely the *onus probandi* is on the person who does this. The evidence for causal interaction is of such a kind as would lead to its unquestioned acceptance in any other case, and therefore we may judge ourselves here, it would seem, entitled to accept it in the absence of any special, valid argument against it. Indeed the majority of contemporary Anglo-American philosophers who have written on the subject ought to admit that they have really no option but to accept it since for them causation has no significance beyond regular sequence or concomitance and the occurrence of this as between at least some events commonly called mental and some called bodily has never been denied.

To admit causal interaction is not to admit dualism in the sense of a two-substance theory. There is no reason why there should not be causal interaction between different qualities and events in the same substance as in different substances. There is indeed a connection between the denial of interaction and the denial of dualism, for if interaction is denied and some form of an identity or a Rylean theory not adopted, a theory according to which mental and bodily events correspond because they are parallel manifestations of the same substance seems to provide the only plausible means of explaining their correlation. Thus the denial of interaction should, I think, lead us to accept a one-substance view, but the acceptance of a one-substance view should not lead us to deny interaction. If the case against interaction breaks down, one argument for the view that mind and body (or brain) are at bottom the same thing disappears, namely that in the absence of interaction such a supposition is needed to account for the experienced correlation.

Passmore in his work *Philosophical Reasoning* attaches great weight to what he calls the 'two worlds argument', and one of the chief uses made by him of this argument is to raise difficulties not about interaction, which he regards as an obvious fact, but about any dualistic doctrines of mind and body. But the application of the argument to this problem falls in my opinion a great deal below the high standard of the rest of the work. He leaves it obscure what the sense of dualism is against which he is arguing. He opposes it to what in the absence of a better name he calls existence-monism, which he describes as the view that 'exist' has an invariant meaning whenever we say that something exists.[1] A dualist should then be someone who

[1] P. 39.

holds that minds exist in a different sense of 'exist' from that in which matter exists. But the only contemporary philosophers to maintain this about mind and body are Ryle and his disciples, and Ryle puts forward the theory in sharp opposition to 'dualism'. Ryle's view plainly entails that a man's thoughts cannot be said to exist in the sense in which his limbs do. Otherwise he could not deny that there are such things as mental events, nor could he accuse his opponents of having committed a category mistake. The traditional dualist on the other hand asserts normally not that minds and bodies exist in different senses of 'exist' but only that they are different kinds of things. Nor does the two-world argument seem to me very formidable, at least as applied to this topic. No doubt if we define 'mind' in such a way as to imply that the only force that 'the mind has at its disposal is spiritual force, the power of rational persuasion' (unfortunately it must be added that it has at its disposal at least one other force, the power of irrational persuasion but that is irrelevant to the argument), and 'body' in such a way that by definition 'nothing can influence a body except mechanical pressure'[1] mind cannot be conceived as acting on body and by a similar argument body on mind, but need they be defined like this even by the 'dualist'?

Passmore also appeals to the epistemological argument that 'if we suppose the mental life is known in one way and the physical in another, it will be impossible to give any account of our knowledge of the transaction between the two lives'.[2] But the argument can have no force unless it is assumed that they are known only in two different ways; if they are also known in a third way common to both the argument breaks down even if it is the case that each is also known in a different way. Now this is the actual situation; even if the mind is known by introspection and the body by sense-perception and these are quite different processes, we can also know by causal inference of mental processes, even in ourselves, and of bodily processes as well. And would Passmore say that we could never know when a universal was applicable to a particular because universals and particulars were primarily known in different ways?

The connection between mind and body is however so constant and all-pervasive that it seems to many philosophers to put them in a

---

[1] Pp. 54–5.   [2] P. 54.

category quite different from two ordinary separate and merely causally connected objects, and since we admittedly have a body Occam's razor is used to forbid the unnecessary assumption of an additional entity, the soul or mind. But just how far can anyone go on these lines intelligibly and reasonably? It is one thing to assert that mental and bodily states qualify the same thing (substance) and another to say that a mental state itself is identical with what we call the corresponding bodily state, e.g. a pain with a behavioural avoiding reaction (cf. Watson's *Behaviourism*) or a process in the brain (cf. J. J. C. Smart, *Philosophy and Scientific Realism*). To such extreme views there is the obvious objection that the notion of mind is built out of experiences and experiences are plainly different from either outward behaviour or changes in the brain as observed by the physiologist. A throb of pain or a thought about Kant's philosophy are surely at least as different from a physical movement as a sight is from a sound. Attempts to evade this obvious argument I shall not discuss as I think they have been treated adequately by H. D. Lewis.

C. Whiteley[1] has produced an article handling the identity theory in a rather novel fashion. He suggested that, since physical science can only tell us about relations and not about qualities, we might think of any qualities present in our experience as the qualitative terms which the brain relations described in science connected. But very awkward questions then arise. If the relations described in brain physiology are taken as strictly spatial, I should object that our thoughts and feelings would have to be extended in such a way that it would not be an absurd question to ask what the distance was in millimetres between my thought about Whiteley's argument at the moment and my contemporary background thought about some item in the morning newspaper. But it is plain that such a question is unanswerable not because we lack the means of measurement but because they are things that simply could not be related like that. There is however a tendency among modern philosophical scientists to say that we have no idea of what spatial relations in the physical world really are like in themselves, and then all we should be saying is that our experiences are related in a certain order but the nature of the connecting relations could not be specified. In that case the objection I have given could

---

[1] *Philosophical Quarterly*, vol. xx (1970), pp. 193 ff.

not be brought, but if we have no idea of what spatial relations are like we have pretty little idea of the brain as a physical object. The brain indeed, as far as we know anything about it, becomes a group of experiences connected by unknowable relations, which is certainly not what the identity theory wanted to say but resembles rather the view of Berkeley, as Whiteley suggests. The brain would become a way of talking about the system in which experiences are arranged, the experiences being the sole real content we know. This objection is additional to the objections raised in his article about fitting mental events into the scheme of the physiologist.

There seem to be only three alternatives. Either the mental and physical belong to different things; or they are different qualities of the same thing; or one of them must be an appearance not a reality. But 'appearance' itself implies experience. The great majority of philosophers have indeed held that we could not be under an illusion at all as regards our immediate experience, but even if it is admitted that we may be deceived as regards some of the qualities we seem to apprehend immediately, it cannot be an illusion that we are having experiences at all, and short of that we cannot get rid of the mental side entirely in favour of the physical. On the other hand if we say that the physical side is a mere appearance we shall have adopted a view for which the brain is no longer central. The materialist sting of the one-substance theory will have disappeared.

The more subtle and somewhat less immoderate form of quasi-behaviourism adopted by Ryle in *The Concept of Mind* does not go far enough altogether to avoid the admission of two different sets of qualities, although he writes as if he thought he had done so. He does not actually identify pain and other sensations with changes in the brain or behavioural reactions, but he does show that, when we ascribe what we call mental properties, we are in most cases talking in terms of dispositions, though I should insist not in all. While he thinks of the dispositions in question as just dispositions to act physically, I should insist however that they ought to be interpreted also as dispositions to think and feel in a certain way. It may be granted that psychological terms commonly include a reference to outward behaviour as well as subjective experiences, but certainly we cannot eliminate the reference to experience.

I shall not deal with Ryle's arguments in full as space is short and

I have already done so elsewhere.[1] I shall just mention the two I think most influential. (1) It is alleged that, if we take a dualist view, then when we talk of other people's states of mind we are asserting something for which we could have no possible evidence whatever. The answer I make is that, if we really have no evidence for other people's experiences, neither have we any evidence for their bodies.[2] Both sets of explanatory hypotheses are justified by the way in which they make sense of our experience or not at all. Nor would it be possible for Ryle to avoid this criticism by falling back on phenomenalism (which he incidentally repudiates), for he would then be both reducing 'minds' to ways of talking about physical objects and physical objects to experiences of minds.

(2) It may be said that, while it is impossible seriously to rule out the mental events known as pains or other sensations, much more doubt attaches to knowing, believing, willing. If we look inwards to find out what they are like they seem to slip from our grasp as if there were nothing there at all. But the difficulty in introspecting them lies, I suggest, in the fact that the unsuccessful attempts at introspection are attempts to envisage cognitions, beliefs and volitions by themselves in the abstract, whereas knowing or believing or willing are inseparable from direction to an object. We can certainly be aware of ourselves as doubting or believing a specific proposition if not believing or doubting in general, or as willing (deciding or trying to do) a specific action, if not of willing in the abstract. Just as it is a vicious abstraction to separate propositions from the cognizing or considering of them, is it not also a vicious abstraction to suppose that we can contemplate knowing or believing *per se* in abstraction from what is known or believed to be true?

We have just got to live with 'dualism', whether we like it or not, at least if we mean by this that we must recognize two quite different sets of properties, the physical and the psychological. This would be more obvious if the term 'experience' were substituted for 'mental events'. The latter may suggest occult entities of a dubious character postulated to explain observed happenings and subject to the objections

[1] For a fuller discussion of Ryle's book see my account of it in H. D. Lewis, *Clarity Is Not Enough*.
[2] I do not think this proposition can be converted. The intellectual case for physical realism seems to me less strong than that against solipsism.

raised against faculty psychology, but the word 'experiences' can hardly convey such a suggestion, and we can hardly deny that experiences occur.

A view which seems to me about as paradoxical, gratuitous and open to objection as behaviourism is what used to be called epiphenomenalism, the doctrine that 'states of mind' or experiences are always direct effects of physiological causes and never themselves causes. It is hard indeed to see any reason for holding such a theory. Even if causation is not reduced to regular sequence or concomitance, regularity must be regarded as at least the criterion for it; and since there is a regular correspondence between certain mental and certain subsequent physical events, e.g. decisions to move one's arm and the arm moving, as well as between experiences and the physiological events said to cause them, it is quite arbitrary to assert causation in the one case and deny it in the other. (Of course there is no evidence that either kind of causation explains our actions completely.) Further, if epiphenomenalism is true, it follows that nobody can be justified in believing it. On the epiphenomenalist view what causes a belief is always a change in the brain and never the apprehension of any reason for holding it. So if epiphenomenalism is true, neither it nor anything else can ever be believed for any good reason whatever. Further, it is assumed in all practical life, including the devising of experiments or the planning of investigations in physiology itself, that epiphenomenalism is not true. In deciding what we are to do we must always assume that our decisions can affect our actions, and they could not if epiphenomenalism were true.

There remains also the old argument that epiphenomenalism would lead to the conclusion that *Hamlet* or the *Critique of Pure Reason* was produced entirely by Shakespeare's or Kant's physiological brain-processes without the purpose or thoughts of either author being relevant to the results. This argument is sometimes put wrongly as being that on the epiphenomenalist view these works could have been produced without any conscious mental processes occurring in the minds of their authors. This would not be the case, for the epiphenomenalist can reply that even on his view, since mental processes inevitably result when the physiological brain-processes have attained a sufficient degree of complexity, and very complex brain-processes are undoubtedly needed for the production of such works, they could not be produced without complex mental processes also. But since these mental processes are supposed by him to have no effects, he is still subject to the objection that these mental processes, though present, had no influence whatever on the works produced. Causally they would be entirely the product of the brain, and no purpose or intelligence whatever would be concerned in their production. It would just be a coincidence that when interpreted according to the rules of the English language the words produced by cerebral action should express such marvellously subtle thoughts as they do. Could one have a more extravagant paradox?

It has indeed been held that one might give a causal explanation of our experiences and actions entirely in terms of brain physiology and yet admit at the same time another explanation in terms of earlier experiences, desires, thoughts; but this could be admissible only if we took a regularity view of causation. Obviously, if *ACDE* produced *B* entirely, a third factor could have no share in its production, but it might be the case that a *B* always followed the set of conditions *ACDE* and also another set of conditions *FGHI*. But, if we adopted the regularity view of causation we should have in any case to admit causal interaction both ways between body and mind since there is undoubtedly a regular sequence of certain kinds of bodily events on mental as well as mental on bodily.

But it may still be contended that mind and body (or rather brain) are the same thing in the sense of being the same substance, though mental and bodily qualities are quite distinct. But before we can decide for or against this theory there remains a preliminary question which we ought to answer, namely – What is to be meant by 'substance'? There are two main types of theory as to what a substance is, the relational type and the substratum type. Taking the former first, a relational theory is one according to which a substance is a series of events related in a certain way. The vital question then is what is the relation which constitutes one substance. Now it is plain that, if mind and body are rightly to be said to constitute the same substance, the relation which makes different mental events (or, what is the same thing, experiences) part of the same mind and different physical events part of the same body must be the same. Otherwise the mind and the body will not be substances in the same sense of 'substance' and cannot without a solecism be called the same substance. But can the relation be the same? In order to fulfil the condition required it must not be either a relation which holds only between different experiences or mental states or a relation which holds only between different bodily states. What relations would be left? Resemblance will not do: my mental side is far more like mental sides of other men than it is like my own bodily side, and indeed my mental and my bodily side today are less like my mental and my bodily side as they were when I was an infant than they are like the mental and bodily sides of most grown-up men. Mere causation is not enough, for my mental and bodily states are also causally connected with those of other men. No doubt the causal laws which connect different states, mental and bodily, of the same person are different from those which connect the states of different persons; for instance, if you learn something this does not of itself help me to remember it, and one might work out a definition of self-identity in terms of such specific causal connections. But if we did that, the mind and the body would still not be substances in the same sense since the causal laws which connect mental are different from the causal laws which connect bodily states. Further, none of these causal laws is such that the assumption that they sometimes connected the states of different people would be actually self-contradictory. Telepathic influence is not seen to be logically impossible. Felt continuity of experience, which has sometimes been suggested as a relation in terms of which self-identity might be defined, is obviously a relation between mental events and not between physical. Memory will not do because definition of identity in terms of it would involve a vicious circle, since memory just means non-inferential cognition that I, the person who remembers, am the same person to whom a certain event happened in the past. Nor can we cut the knot by saying that the defining relation is attachment to the same body, for the whole question would be thereby begged. The question is just what is meant by 'the same body' and in what sense mental states are 'attached to' the body.

A relational theory might indeed be defended by giving a more complex answer to the question of definition. It may be said that the question whether two sets of qualities or states belong to the same substance or to different substances is not one to be answered by a plain Yes or No, since its answer depends on various criteria not all of which are always present and there is no single relation constituting identity of substance over and above these criteria. In that case whether we are to speak of the mind and the body as one substance or two would become a verbal question or at least one of relative emphasis. But in that case the question whether body and mind were one substance or two would have no metaphysical significance but would merely be an issue between two ways of describing the same empirical facts. We could not for instance possibly conclude – to mention the issue which gives most human interest to this discussion – that the mind could not survive bodily death because for certain purposes it is scientifically useful to treat it as an attribute of the body, whereas if the proposition that it is an attribute of the body were established as a metaphysical truth it would entail that the mind could not survive the body.

Suppose now we drop the relational view and substitute a view according to which the substance is a substratum over and above its attributes, what then? Except on a view according to which a substance is something over and above its qualities it is indeed very difficult to see how such different qualities as the mental and material could be combined in one substance. But against such a view of substance the objection is brought that it makes the concept entirely unintelligible, since a substance can only be described in terms of its qualities (and relations). The substratum becomes a mere x, the postulation of which can give us no help in understanding anything and therefore cannot be justified. And in that case how can we ask the question whether mind and body are one substance or two? How can we possibly say whether there are one or two unknowables? Such an attitude seems to me perfectly justified when we are considering physical things. We could only meet the difficulties mentioned if we could claim an immediate knowledge of the substance, which we certainly have not in the case of material substances. It is indeed widely held that we are immediately aware of physical objects in perception, but this could only be awareness of their qualities and relations and not of their 'substance', if such exist. But there is an important difference between this and the corresponding view of the self as substance. For in the case of the former we have no concept whatever of the alleged substance as something over and above its characteristics, but in the case of the self we do seem to be aware in some way of something over and above though not apart from our experiences, so that to assert it need not be merely to postulate a something we know not what, a quite unknowable and incomprehensible *x* to serve as a paper explanation. And, when we look at the matter further, we do find some very serious arguments for the pure ego view of the self and against the view that just reduces the self to a system of experiences and will see nothing beyond.

The first I might mention is this. Suppose I knew that I was going to cease to exist tomorrow but in dying produce a self which would inhabit my present body, be like me in all dispositions and character traits, inherit my memories so that he fancied he was myself and only change by slow degrees. Now suppose I could also know that this, my successor, would spend most of his life in the intensest suffering, would this make me feel anything like as unhappy as would the prospect that I myself should? No doubt I should feel a certain sympathetic horror at the prospect he would have to face as I do when I hear of the sufferings of others, but this would not be comparable with the terror that would overtake me if I knew I was going to be the victim of these horrors.[1] Or suppose that I knew that a self formerly inhabiting my body and from whom I had originated and whose memories I possessed as clearly as I possess my own, and from whom I had developed by a continuous causal process had committed an utterly inexcusable and revolting murder, should I feel or ought I to feel the guilt that I should feel if I had done the foul deed myself? No doubt if my character, as postulated, had developed out of the character of this man, that would give me ground for thinking that I myself was a pretty poor sort of person morally, but character can gradually improve and the very fact that I had originated from such evil antecedents would provide a good deal of excuse for what faults I have and in so far make me feel less ashamed of what I did wrong and not more. These imaginary illustrations seem to show that self-identity cannot be analysed in the sort of way in which it is on the relational view. We could not possibly say both that being the same self as *A* just means having the same body and/or having causally developed from *A* and yet admit that there is and should be a vast emotional difference between my reactions to the proposition that I am the same person as *A* and the proposition that I have any or all

[1] See J. Knox, *Religious Studies*, vol. v (1969–70), pp. 85 and 273; cf. B. Williams, *Philosophical Review*, vol. 79 (1970), pp. 161 ff.

these relations to *A*. If the knowledge of the truth of one statement would cause me agonizing apprehension or shame, and that of the other does not cause any such emotions, and the reaction in one case and its absence in the other are quite rationally based on the respective meaning of the terms, we cannot possibly hold that the statements mean the same.

Secondly, all or almost all relational accounts of the self have to make identity a relative matter in the sense that it admits of degrees. Similarity in qualities is never absolute but greater or less, causal connection is present between different minds, so that it must be a matter of degree which would settle when it served as a ground for judging that two states of mind differently placed in time belonged to the same mind. Even identity of body is a matter of degree since the body does not by any means remain exactly the same in all respects at different times; and our bodily feelings, which have sometimes been suggested as a main criterion, vary continuously. But surely the judgement that I did so and so or had such and such an experience in the past is not a judgement of degree. It is not a question whether the being who did the deed or had the experience was like enough to my present self to be properly called I. However much I may have changed in character since, however uncharacteristic what I did was of my usual self, it is still equally true that I did it, and I am directly aware that I did it. That I did it is not a statement that could be said to be more or less true, except in the sense that somebody else might have participated with me in doing it or even coerced me into doing it against my will, a different matter. And similarly with the statement that I had a certain experience. Questions of degree might no doubt arise here, e.g. was an experience really so pleasant that it could be properly described as delightful or so unpleasant that it could be described as intolerable? But it is not a question of degree whether I had the experience or I did not but somebody else did. In clear cases I just know by memory without any hesitation or shadow of equivocation that I did. I am then aware of a relation of identity between myself and the past self of which I am thinking, not as a matter of inference but directly. This might indeed be explained by saying that in memory we are aware of an ultimate and indefinable relation connecting my past and present experiences and expressed by saying they are different experiences of the same man, but the relation I apprehend in memory between the present and the past seems to be simply that of being different qualities or manifestations of the same thing. It seems a relation that is to be explained in terms of the self and not vice versa.

Thirdly, there are the difficulties for the relational view of defining self-identity without a vicious circle. My self will no doubt on such a view consist of all the experiences related to my present experience by the defining relation which constitutes self-identity, whatever that relation is. But what is meant by 'my' here? We are just trying to define 'myself'. A line of escape that might be tried is to define 'my present experience' as the experiences connected at present with a certain body. But which body? It cannot be defined as the body which is in such and such a place now because it might have been at a different place and still been the body belonging to me. We can only say 'my body', in which case we have still the vicious circle, or else a body defined ostensively, in which case it means 'the body which I or you (from your point of view another I) are signifying in some fashion'. And I at any rate do not mean by 'myself' the experiences attached to my body; when I remember past experiences I am usually not thinking of my past body at all. And whatever other defining relation we take, it would still leave us with the necessity of defining 'my present experience' as starting point for the definition proposed. If the definition be made in terms of memory itself, it is involved in an additional circle because memory would have to be defined as awareness of a past experience as an experience of mine, for if we defined it merely as non-inferential awareness of past experiences, this would be open to the objection that, if I found I could be without inference aware of the past experiences of other men, I should not say that these other men were identical with myself.

Fourthly, it is generally admitted as a basic truth that at any rate I exist. But on a relational view of the self 'I' can only mean the sum-total of the experiences between my birth and my death connected in a sort of system, and at no moment do these experiences ever all exist. So a relational theory seems to entail the conclusion that I do not now exist. I am aware that the reply might be made that, though 'I now exist' is a true proposition, this must be analysed as meaning 'one (or some) of the series of events which constitutes myself now exist(s)', but it seems quite plain that this is not what is meant by 'I exist'.

Fifthly, there is the well-known argument in Kant's transcendental deduction. To realize the truth of any proposition or even entertain it as something meaningful the same being must be aware of its different constituents. To be aware of the validity of an argument the same being must entertain premises and conclusion; to compare two things the same being must, at least in memory, be aware of them simultaneously; and since all these processes take some time the continuous existence of literally the same entity is required. In these cases an event which consisted in the contemplating of *A* followed by another event which consisted in the contemplating of *B* is not sufficient. They must be events of contemplating that occur in the same being. If one being thought of wolves, another of eating, and another of lambs, it certainly would not mean that anybody contemplated the proposition 'wolves eat lambs', and this would be true even if the three different beings were parts of the same brain. There must surely be a single being persisting through the process to grasp a proposition or inference as a whole. Kant indeed thought that at the phenomenal level all this argument required was a certain unity in our thought processes and not a persistent entity, but I think that this was only possible for him because he after all believed in a single real, though to us unknowable, noumenal self.

Sixthly, the very conflicts that make one dwell on the lack of unity in the self really presuppose an underlying unity. Their very sting lies in the fact that the same self cannot both enjoy the present pleasures of imprudence and escape its subsequent ill results or in general satisfy both of two conflicting desires. (Whether it is ever possible in the course of time for the same self to be split into two must be left an open question however, I think.)

Finally, the most popular argument for the pure ego view is that there cannot be knowing without some being that knows, thinking without some being that thinks, willing without some being that wills. That this can be reduced to saying that thoughts, acts of will etc. can only occur as members of systems of experiences, as it would have to be reduced on the merely relational view of the self, seems to me by no means plausible. It seems to involve the circle of reducing the self to a set of acts all of which in order to be acts already have to presuppose the self which it is intended to reduce to them.

It will easily be seen that these arguments, if valid, establish not the existence of a series of momentary subjects but of a substance-self which retains its identity through a period of time.

Objections to the opposed 'Bundle Theory' (I have called it the 'Relational Theory') have recently been admitted even in most unlikely quarters. D. M. Armstrong in his book, *A Materialist Theory of Mind*, which defends either the identity theory of mind and brain or at least something very like it, insists that the bundle theory would entail that a single perception or thought could exist by itself without anything that perceives or thinks, and he declares this impossible.[1]

Strawson also admits that a non-ownership view should be rejected but makes the subject not the mind but 'the person' including the body.[2] From this the mind is an abstraction and not a primary existent at all, though survival, even disembodied survival, of bodily death is regarded by him as logically possible. But I have already argued that we cannot give an intelligible account of the view that mental qualities are qualities of the body;[3] and I cannot either see in what other sense, except that of being joint effects causally of mind and body, they can be properties of a complex substance, mind–body. The arguments I have just given are in any case arguments for a substance-self and not a substance-body.

Actually on a relational theory perhaps the least implausible candidate for a definition of the relation which constituted self-identity might be a certain causal continuity in change. After all the chief criterion for the identity of a piece of matter is causal continuity between its successive states whether in motion or rest. And it is ultimately causal continuity through gradual change which leads to our identifying a man as the same person as he was years before. But there is at least one fatal objection to making this the relation which constitutes self-identity. I know directly in memory that I, the same person as I know now by introspection, am identical with the person who did so and so at a certain past time, but what I am immediately aware of in consciousness of my identity is certainly not some sort of causal connection through many intermediates between my present and my past states.

But if we accept a pure ego theory, we still must not separate the ego sharply from its thoughts and mental states in general. We need

[1] P. 22.   [2] *Individuals*, pp. 96 ff.
[3] I.e. belong to the same substance as the bodily qualities; see above, pp. 73 ff.

not think of this subject-self as having properties of its own beyond those present in our experience, except dispositional properties analysed in terms of conditions. Nor should we think of it as some additional part of the self over and above its properties, as Locke conceived the substratum of substances. We must think of it as not merely manifested in experiences but inseparably bound up with its experiences so that it would be nothing without them and they would be nothing without it. (I include here any sort of mental activities under the term 'experience'.) It is not a being intuited as existing apart from them or postulated to explain them from outside. It must be conceived as something more than the aggregate of mental states which it welds into a unity and something more than a mere sum-total of its qualities, which are abstractions from it; but it could not exist without states and qualities, though the converse is equally true that mental states and qualities, at least at the point where they reach a subtlety such as is found in human beings, require a self to qualify.

I used to raise the objection against the pure ego view that, if the pure ego changes, I am no longer myself, but, if it 'does not change, it is not what I understand by "I", for I certainly always think of myself as capable of changing and, I hope, improving'.[1] The answer I should now give to this conundrum is that the pure ego theory does not commit you to the view that the pure ego does not change. It certainly changes in the sense of assuming new qualities; we must not regard that as a change merely in the qualities and not in the self, for we cannot regard the self as something apart from its qualities; but in another sense it must still be the same self, for otherwise not it but something else would be assuming the new qualities. The self (pure ego) apart from its qualities is only an abstraction, but the qualities apart from what they qualify are also a mere abstraction. Nor should the self be regarded as a bit of unchanging content in its changing experience; this would make it just one of its own qualities or an abstraction from the latter. It is a unique mode of existence, for unconscious matter could not be a substance in the same sense; but we are immediately aware of what it is as that which experiences.

The acceptance of a pure ego does not necessarily entail immortality or even survival. The pure ego might conceivably still in some way be dependent causally on the body for its continual existence. But it

---

[1] See my *Fundamental Questions of Philosophy*, p. 112.

entails that the self is not the same substance as the body, though not implying a two-substance theory, for two reasons; (1) it is compatible with the view that the mind is the only substance and the body (or brain) an appearance of the mind and (2) we cannot properly speak of two substances unless the body (or brain) can be a substance in the same sense as the mind which on the pure ego view it certainly cannot be – and I have argued it cannot reasonably be held to be on any view. 'Soul' is a term which, like most contemporary philosophers, I have generally avoided, but it is perhaps the natural term to use in view of the theory of the self I have advocated. I think that, except for a point which I shall mention directly, my account substantially agrees with that so ably expounded by H. D. Lewis in *The Elusive Mind*, though[1] expressed somewhat differently.

A question that troubles me is what becomes of the self in the event of a dreamless sleep. Assuming that we cannot suppose the ego to exist then as a substance without qualities, we have four alternatives, none of them altogether satisfactory, between which to choose. (1) Lewis is prepared to admit that, when we become totally unconscious, we just cease to exist except in a purely dispositional and hypothetical sense,[2] but I imagine few holders of a pure ego view would be content with this. I am unable to believe that we are just nothing when we sleep and I do not see how, if such a view is held, we can say that we are the same self before and after such periods of sleep, except in a relational sense. To add to this objection, we should have a continual series of creations *ex nihilo*, one every time we woke.

(2) We might say that no state of total unconsciousness ever does occur, that there is present always at least, if not actual dreams, at least some degrees of feeling. This may well be true and is not open, as far as I can see, to any positive objection, but I am sufficiently influenced by the prevailing climate of philosophy to feel a little uneasy about asserting on purely philosophical grounds what looks like a proposition in empirical psychology. It may be replied, however, that if we take this view we are merely saying that an unconscious pure ego is a contradiction, and there is no objection to saying that something self-contradictory cannot exist.

---

[1] I do not myself favour this view since it could hardly be held without the drastic metaphysical assumption that everything physical is the appearance of some mental entity, for which I see no adequate ground.   [2] Chapter 11.

(3) It might be held that the self still retains some actual qualities even in an unconscious state and not merely hypothetical properties; but these qualities being completely unconscious, and yet mental not physical, we can have no idea what they could be like. To make them all purely hypothetical would be really to fall back to the first view and say that the self only exists in the sense that under certain not at present fulfilled conditions it *would* arouse itself and do certain things. But there still may be mental qualities which are neither actualized in experience nor just hypothetical, since we are certainly not in a position to deny that there are any qualities of which we have no idea.

(4) There is a more subtle solution possible connected with the concept of time. Perhaps the periods in which I am completely unconscious should not be thought of as falling within my time at all but only within physical time and within the time of the people who were awake when I slept. The effects on my mind of the occurrence of periods of apparently dreamless sleep in the way of refreshment and ability to think better might be explained by changes in my body. On that view the times of different people could be correlated partly through clocks, etc., i.e. ultimately through their having physical experiences between which there was a certain correspondence, but not completely so, e.g. the period between 1 a.m. and 2 a.m. last night might just not figure in my life as a self but in yours and in the physical system to which both your and my body belong. This is supported by the fact that the same period of clock time may seem much longer to you than to me because you are, for example, bored. But I do not think that this solution either is free from serious difficulties. It seems to involve a thoroughly subjective view of time, and though I have accepted some form of dualism between body and mind I do not feel easy about pushing the dualism so far as to make my mind and my body members of different time-orders. For my body would certainly go through actual processes, for example, breathing and digesting while my mind was not in time-order at all.

But the difficulties would still arise on a relational view of the self. We should still have to say that, when we are, if ever, in a state of 'complete unconsciousness', we either do not exist at all except in a merely potential sense, or we consist of a series of unconscious events, or admit that our mind exists in a time different from that of our body as a series of mental events. The other, and perhaps least implausible solution, namely, that there are no states of complete unconsciousness ✗ is available on either view.

But while a pure ego theory makes survival of bodily death seem more likely than do other theories, we must admit that we are not in a position to decide by philosophical arguments about the relation between mind and body as to whether we shall or shall not survive. Some philosophers have objected that no 'meaning' can be given to the notion of survival, but it is plain that this contention could not be based on an insight into the connection between mind and body. It is held, at least by such philosophers, that we never have a priori insight into causal laws, or laws of concomitance, and of all such laws those connecting mind and body seem the most opaque to our insight, if we can admit here degrees of opaqueness. Survival is however questioned now rather on the ground of the difficulty of giving an adequate criterion of identity, or on the ground that the concept of self presupposes that of other people and we can only know of these others through their bodies. The first argument has been used by, e.g., Geach[1] to support a doctrine of survival which depended on the resurrection of our former body by an act of God, and for many, including myself, it would count as a serious objection to survival if it could be shown that this was the only kind of survival left standing. Geach claims that whatever evidence was given in the shape of alleged memories, independently confirmed, to support reincarnation or another mode of survival, identity could not be established in the absence of the criterion afforded by the existence of the same body.

But it seems to me that we can *imagine* evidence for survival so strong that there could not be much more than a fantastical philosophico-sceptical doubt. This would be the case if we could have as frequent and as coherent conversations with the ostensible spirits of one's dead friends communicating in a characteristic way through mediums as we can now by using the telephone have with absent living friends, and what we heard from them was constantly being confirmed independently where it was capable of confirmation and fitted in with everything else including the personality of those who had died as known to their best friends and conversations with other

[1] *God and the Soul*, chapters 1 and 2.

ostensible spirits. There have been just a few cases where two different people quite unknown to each other consulted mediums in different places who also did not know each other and both encountered in the message received a quite unintelligible sentence but found that the two sentences when fitted together made not only an intelligible message but one which had special associations with the dead person known only to a third party who had never consulted the mediums. It seems to me that the occurrence of a considerable number of such cases would soon make survival far the most reasonable hypothesis, assuming that the good character of the people concerned was sufficiently well known to eliminate fraud. The alternative explanation by telepathy would involve a far too implausible combination of unconscious telepathy between people who had never met normally, unconscious selection of just the one person also unknown who knew the secret and unconscious telepathic combined planning of two messages which would do the trick. That survival might become a hypothesis as well established by empirical evidence as, say, evolution therefore seems to me quite conceivable. Arguments such as those used by Geach might then seem as far-fetched as an argument which might conceivably be brought against any identifications in this life to the effect that it is perfectly conceivable that any man might have an exact physical double, or the philosophical doubts based on Descartes' demon, which have never been really refuted. Nor can I see any impossibility in the receipt of a series of direct telepathic communications from a being whom we could not perceive in bodily form that were yet as intelligible and coherent as any conversation we have with other men and that would give us reasonable grounds for believing in the existence of such a disembodied being. Only the actual situation is vastly different from that pictured. The evidence for survival, though certainly not negligible, is by no manner of means so strong as this, but we are considering simply the question of conceivability, which is all that is needed to meet the objection that 'my survival' is a meaningless phrase because no criterion to determine what surviving spirit was mine could conceivably be applied. Immediate awareness can be a criterion for oneself, and we all in practice assume that memory in many cases gives knowledge even when untested. Criteria are also wanted for the identity of persons other than ourselves, but, as I have just contended, we can well imagine conceivable circumstances in which there was evidence available of a kind which at least made survival of particular persons the most probable hypothesis to deal with the facts.

Some further remarks may be added. (*a*) Geach raises the difficulty that our ability to distinguish between different human beings depends on their occupying different positions in space; but if there is a realm of disembodied spirits, how could we possibly know that there are not non-spatial relations in such a world which serve the distinguishing purpose of spatial relations here?

(*b*) The principle of identity of indiscernibles might be true of disembodied spirits, as it was held to be true of angels, so that they could be distinguished only by their qualities.

(*c*) Need spirits be disembodied if they are not either reincarnated at once in other human bodies or given new bodies created from the old ones by God? May we not after death have a body of a different kind of matter, which need not be regarded as produced by a miracle but might like our present body be a natural growth? The fact that no scientific evidence of the existence of such bodies has been produced does not disprove it. A similar argument might have been used against the existence of dark nebulae a little while ago. How can we possibly know that what does not affect the present apparatus of scientists will not affect the presumably much more delicate apparatus available a few hundred years hence? There are already claims that 'spirit bodies' have been photographed and there is at least no logical absurdity in supposing the claim to be correct.

(*d*) The notion of a disembodied spirit is not necessarily as paradoxical as it sounds, for even in our present state our mind is not extended and can only be said to be in space by virtue of its causal relation to the body. A 'disembodied spirit' too might have a causal relation to some parts of the physical world, but I suppose could still be called 'disembodied' if it was not limited, as we are, to direct action on some one very small part of the physical world.

But when we are thinking of a different order of things quite beyond our experience every account is likely to seem implausible. There is indeed very much in the accepted scientific account of this physical world that would antecedently have seemed enormously so. I am thinking of such facts as the inconceivably great force of atomic explosions and the immense part of the most solid objects we know which is a vacuum according to science as well as the fantastic complexity of our multi-million-celled brains

There is one view of the physical world, namely the phenomenalistic one, on which a further life would be less difficult to envisage because we could then just think of our minds as having different sorts of images, but I should not adopt phenomenalism for that reason.

Even if we could think of no criteria of identity, conditions in a future life as disembodied spirits would be so different that it would be a very big jump indeed from saying we cannot think of any criteria to saying there are none. If I had been an infant prodigy in my mother's womb and speculated about conditions in this life, I should no doubt have had very strange ideas or no ideas at all as to how I could get into touch with other minds. But, whether surviving spirits are disembodied or embodied in some different kind of matter, I do not see why reported memories – the truth of many of which was repeatedly confirmed – and similarity of personality – except in so far as there is an explicable change – might not conceivably serve as criteria in practice adequate to give very strong probability, and of our items of information about other human beings even on earth there is no absolute proof.

Another argument bearing on surival is as follows. It is generally assumed that the formation of the concept of other minds is prior to the formation of a concept of our mind. It is then pointed out that we can identify the other minds, in this life at least, only by reference to their bodies, and concluded that our own mind too must therefore be defined in terms of its body or at least be intrinsically bound up with the conception of body.[1] Strawson does not think that this necessarily excludes survival even as a disembodied spirit, though he gives a very unattractive picture of this kind of survival,[2] but the argument I have given might be used in such a way. To repeat the argument in Strawson's own words, 'One can ascribe states of consciousness to oneself only if one can ascribe them to others. One can ascribe them to others only if one can identify other subjects of experience. And one cannot identify others if one can identify them *only* as subjects of experience, possessors of states of consciousness.'[3]

We may grant that the argument shows we cannot, in this life at least, obtain knowledge of ourselves, even on the mental side alone,

[1] Strawson, *Individuals*, pp. 99 ff.   [2] See below, p. 94.   [3] Op. cit., p. 100.

without some knowledge of the physical. And we may go further and agree with Strawson that the primary concept is that of a 'person', i.e. a being who has both mental and physical qualities and not a mere mind. The distinction between the mind and the body must be sorted out later by analysis and philosophical argument such as I have tried to do in this chapter. But need we go further than this not very drastic conclusion? Does it require us to go on and say we cannot be aware of our mind in distinction from our body? It is significant here that the sense and way in which we can experience our own mind is radically different from the sense and way in which we can experience anybody else's. The former experience is direct and the latter indirect, and this itself gives us ground for saying that consciousness of the intermediate bodily elements necessary for identifying another's mind is not necessary for cognizing one's own. It indeed seems odd to talk of identifying one's own mind, but there is a sense in which one does this in memory. Whenever I remember something, I am conscious of it as something which happened to *me*, and so of identity between myself and the being whose experience is remembered. Now it seems to me very significant that, when I thus recall a past experience, I am not usually at all conscious of what my body was like at that time. No doubt if it was not a very long time ago I *assume* that my body was fairly similar to what it is at present, but I am hardly ever conscious when I have such recollections of having looked at my body at the time and rarely of having had any particular bodily feelings then except in recollections of illness or physical accident. We can therefore very well be in our own case conscious of the identity of the self without being conscious of the identity of its body. Further, granted that we can know others only through their bodily behaviour, we must also admit that we can know anything bodily only through experience and therefore through a mental state of our own. It is true indeed presumably that self-conscious formation of the concept of oneself must be preceded by the formation of concepts of other human beings, but this is not to put the physical always before the mental because knowledge of the physical and still more of other human minds must be preceded not indeed by an explicit idea of the self but by some experience. The Wittgensteinian argument on which reliance is placed is that there is no subjective distinction between genuine and mistaken memories, and so no private criteria for deciding whether statements in a private language are true or false. To this I reply first that the very same difficulty arises if it is sought to confirm the memories by a public physical test. For any such test would take a perceptible time, and therefore it can only be accepted as successful if when we reach the later stages we each rely on our own subjective memories of the earlier. It is no good trying to confirm them by reference to other people's reports of theirs unless we can trust our memory as to what the other people said. We should have also to rely on our memory for the meaning of the words in which they expressed what they remembered. Secondly, from Berkeley onwards especially, perception of ostensible physical things has been shown to be more threatened by the sceptical attack than memory of oneself.

The argument I have just been discussing is connected with the doctrine of Wittgenstein that a private language is impossible. I must say that this argument leaves me quite unmoved. I do not see why I should not give a name to a certain kind of feeling that I did not use in talking to anybody else and which was not correlated by me with any bodily state, except that it would be generally of no particular use.

Strawson, while admitting that the existence of disembodied spirits is conceivable, condemns them to a solipsistic kind of life.[1] He leaves aside as 'a rather vulgar fancy' the supposition that they could initiate physical changes in the world. But, even if they could not do this, I do not see how Strawson knows that they could not act telepathically on other spirits, thus making communication quite possible. Nor is there any reason for excluding the possibility that they were aware telepathically of the states of other such beings. It has been contended that it would be logically impossible to perceive another's experience because the experience would then be one's own, and it must be admitted that I could not literally feel another's pain. But I think this is not the same as to say I cannot be non-inferentially aware that another man has a pain. I can know now non-inferentially that I had toothache yesterday without now feeling the pain. Further, even if one being cannot perceive another's state directly, it might cause one to have ideas of them. There is therefore no reason to suppose that, if there are disembodied spirits, they cannot communicate with each other or indeed with living human beings on earth. They might even have experiences in which they cognized physical objects though

[1] *Individuals*, p. 115.

in a way different from ours. (Indeed we cannot even deny a priori
the possibility that they might have experiences qualitatively like our
sense-perceptions, since we cannot see any logical connection between
our sense-experiences and our physical sense-organs.)

In practice perhaps the greatest source of difficulty in accepting
survival has been our inability to imagine it, but logically this is no
objection against it. Could I have imagined when I was a baby what it
was like to have the experience of writing a book on philosophy?
Even if we should turn out to be disembodied spirits when we die,
the experiences we had might well be much more like those we now
have than we should have been inclined to fancy provided we retained
the capacity for mental imagery.[1] The possession of mental imagery
might indeed explain the more materialistic parts of 'spiritualistic
communications' about the next life, for example, references to having
cocktails and smoking cigarettes, thus removing one influential
objection to accepting spiritualist evidence of survival.

On the other hand it must be admitted that the argument against
survival from the causal dependence on our brain not only of our
sensations but of our memories and thoughts has more force and
certainly lessens the antecedent probability of the belief. But that it
is not conclusive is shown by the reply I have heard that it does not
follow because I can now only see the sky through a window that
I shall be unable to see it when I go out of my house because I shall
have no window to look through. Even the 'instrumental' view of
the brain is not refuted by arguments of this sort, provided 'instrument' is not defined in such a way as to imply that the mind cannot be
affected in itself by what happens to the instrument.[2] Accidents to an
instrument can easily injure the person who uses it.

[1] V. H. H. Price, *Essays in the Philosophy of Religion*, pp. 105 ff.
[2] As seems to be done by C. D. Broad in his refutation of the 'Instrumentalist Theory'
(*The Mind and its Place in Nature*, pp. 533–5).

5

MORAL JUDGEMENTS[1]

We now turn to another kind of judgements which have a special connection with religion and also present many problems of their own, namely judgements as to what ought to be done and indeed value judgements in general. The general type of ethical view which I defend is one towards which the current of philosophical thought, I believe, is now moving, at least in Britain. It agrees with pure emotivism or prescriptivism in holding that 'moral judgements'[2] primarily express practical non-cognitive attitudes, but it disagrees in holding that they are not just expressions of actual attitudes but also involve a claim that the attitudes are rationally grounded. It agrees with naturalism in holding that these judgements are ultimately grounded on empirical facts; but it disagrees in holding that they cannot themselves be reduced to judgements about empirical facts. It agrees with intuitivistic non-naturalism in maintaining that there cannot be any rational reason for action unless there are some reasons for action, namely, intrinsically good ends, which require no further reason to make them a reason, though the greatest reluctance to use the word intuition in describing their view is shown by many by whom what the word stands for is really admitted; but it disagrees with it in denying that we need suppose in order to secure ethics the presence of a 'non-natural' property of goodness or 'non-natural' relation of obligation in the real world.

To take first ordinary emotivism or prescriptivism, this theory has after all to face the fact that we do argue about questions as to

---

[1] This chapter makes use of my article in *The Proceedings of the Congress of Philosophy in Vienna* (1968), by the kind permission of Professor Gabriel of Vienna University.

[2] On such views there are strictly no moral *judgements*, but I have retained the word in inverted commas in the absence of another recognized suitable expression. It means at least what we usually regard and treat as moral judgements, whether they really are such or not.

what we ought to do and that the reasons given are commonly statements of empirical fact, e.g. 'this is taking property which by law belongs to somebody else' or 'this would hurt *A*'. What account can the pure emotivist or prescriptivist give of such arguments? It would be fantastic to suppose that they are all just fallacies. If we are not prepared to say that they give rational grounds for prescribing or condemning certain acts the only alternative seems to be to make them mere tactical dodges, a matter of psychological technique to persuade people to do what we say they ought. Most people at any rate most of the time have a certain kind of feeling, disapproval, when they consider acts which involve hurting others or breaking promises and they dislike performing acts towards which they have this feeling of disapproval, and therefore it is very often an effective method of persuasion to point out that a proposed action involves breaking a promise or hurting another man. But this really cannot be all there is to it. There are various means of persuading people to act in a certain way which can be very effective indeed and yet are far removed from any argument of which a moral philosopher could approve. Brainwashing, clever but fallacious rhetoric, magnetic personality can all compete with real moral arguments as quite efficient instruments in securing such results and they can even result in a person feeling genuine moral approval or disapproval, yet none of these constitute moral reasons. On a pure prescriptivist or emotivist view one cannot distinguish between good and bad moral arguments; in fact there really are no moral *arguments*. Such thinkers could indeed in some sense find grounds for adopting the methods of persuasion used by moral philosophers rather than by brainwashing inquisitors, but the giving of these grounds would still be only a tactical dodge. They may indeed refer to the side-effects of brainwashing methods even if these are successful in attaining their primary object, and give such effects, as a reason for objecting to them, but again this could mean for these philosophers only that they themselves took up a certain adverse attitude to the effects and were urging others to do likewise.

A view like this does seem to me quite definitely to take away the point of ethics, as can be brought out further by asking the question why a person should not do what is wrong. On a pure emotivist or prescriptivist view nothing is admitted except that we actually have feelings and attitudes of a certain kind towards what we call 'right'.

D

Now no doubt if these feelings and motives are sufficiently strong and are not countered by ones felt more strongly they will constitute a sufficient causal explanation (in so far as we can talk of causal explanation in this connection) why we perform the act, but suppose they are not so strong. Suppose on a given occasion we would much rather do something quite different. In that case we must ask what point there is in making the extra effort or sacrifice required to do what we ought, to say that we ought to do it being only to express an attitude towards it not susceptible of rational justification, and this question the emotivist or prescriptivist cannot answer. It may be objected that this shows at the most that the adoption of prescriptivism or emotivism has bad effects and not that it is false, and as we have seen I do not wish to defend the pragmatist criterion as ultimate in general. But this is not merely a pragmatic argument; it is an argument to the effect that the views I am criticizing misrepresent the moral attitude. It is an essential part of the conception of morality that there is a great deal of point about doing what you ought even if you do not want to. But on a pure prescriptivist view why ever should I (except for selfish reasons of prudence)? It has been suggested that once we admit that no reason can be given for a moral principle nothing is added by saying we intuit it. Since we can give no reason for the ultimate principles in any case, all we need or can say is that we adopt them as our principles and leave it at that. But I submit that it makes all the difference in the world. Why should I stick to my principles if it does not suit me unless they are judged by me to be morally binding and not merely arbitrarily chosen? But I have the best of reasons if I see them to be true.

(2)   I am also still convinced by the arguments against naturalism in ethics, which may be summed up as follows. (1) Any naturalist definition of the fundamental term or terms of ethics would have the logical consequence of reducing ethics to an empirical science, but the method by which we reach ethical conclusions is not empirical generalisation. We may use laws thus established to determine the most effective means to a given end, but this is not a method by which we can determine what is good or bad in itself or, without assuming ethical propositions already, what are the moral laws that we should obey.

(2) When we consider particular naturalist definitions of good, it

may be clearly seen that the property could without logical contradiction be conceived as belonging to something which was not good
or similarly something might without logical contradiction be supposed
to be good which had not the property in question. Some kinds of
pleasure may be conceived as bad in themselves and not good, men
may be conceived as desiring something intrinsically bad, *A* might
be really better than *B* though most people valued *B* more, the more
evolved might be less and not more good, what makes for a stable
social order may be bad if the social order it tends to preserve is of a
certain kind etc. The same applies to naturalist definitions of right
or ought. With none of the definitions do we reach the point where we
can say that this is what we really meant by calling something good
or right. It should be noted that in order to refute a definition it is not
necessary to produce an actual example which contradicts it, it is
enough to see that one is conceivable. For example, it seems to me
obvious that men desire what is intrinsically evil since otherwise we
could not account for all cases of cruelty, but this has sometimes been
challenged and another explanation given, yet all that is needed to
refute the definition of 'intrinsically good' as 'desired for its own sake'
is to point out that there is no self-contradiction in supposing that
we might have been so constituted that we sometimes desired what
is intrinscially bad, even if in fact we do not. Again, even if we accepted
the view that all men desired and desired only what is intrinsically
good, the definition could be refuted by pointing out that at least
the degree in which they desire something is not always in proportion
to the intrinsic goodness, real or supposed, of what is desired. (Men
are notoriously liable to desire their own good more than the greater
good of others and a present good more than an equal good in the
remote future.)[1]

(3) When we use moral judgements or value judgements in general
we are certainly usually doing something else besides describing – let
us employ Hare's term 'commending' to signify this extra function
without committing ourselves to its exact nature – and then we can
accept Hare's argument that, if ethical terms were defined naturalistically, we should have no language for commending actions which

[1] This criticism I consider applies even to Blanshard's definition of good as what
satisfies and fulfils, for it is at least conceivable that something bad might satisfy and
fulfil some person (presumably in so far a bad man) more than the corresponding good.

have the natural property or properties given in the definition, yet 'commending' certainly expresses something we want to do and use ethical language for doing.

(4) Naturalism is incompatible with the necessity we find in moral and value judgements.[1] If good and right were natural properties, their connection with the properties which make something good or right would be causal e.g. the connection between approval or desire and the qualities which arouse approval or desire, yet the naturalists would certainly not admit that we can see any necessity in judgements asserting a causal law. But if we see an action to constitute our duty, we see that under the given circumstances it just must be our duty; if we see something to be intrinsically good we see that its goodness follows from its nature and could not possibly be lacking, the latter being what it is.

(5) Any naturalist account must reduce the 'ought' as well as the good to the 'is', and this reduction is impossible. We have here a line of criticism which is valid both against pure prescriptivists and naturalists. They both talk in terms of actual attitudes, whether of the person who makes the 'moral judgement' or of people in general, and seek to give their account exclusively in terms of these, thus committing a category mistake. By falling into this error they commit themselves either to reducing an ought-judgement to a mere expression of the actual attitude of the person who makes it or a statement about the actual attitude of society or ultimately humanity in general. This is most obvious if the naturalist gives his definition in terms of approval making 'good' or 'right' equivalent to 'approved by myself, the speaker' or 'by people in general', but it applies also to the prescriptivist who when saying that something ought to be done thinks that he simply means that he in fact urges it, or the other type of naturalist who defines good as what we desire or as what will ultimately satisfy us, as though it were a tautology that we should desire the right thing if we knew its true nature or that what was really best would ultimately satisfy us most. Even if these propositions are true, they are certainly not true by definition.

The argument against naturalism is complicated by the variety of definitions which the naturalist may offer, some of which might be held to be valid in cases where others fail, so it is important to empha-

---

[1] *The Language of Morals*, pp. 90–3.

size that it is perfectly possible for one to be able to see not only that a particular definition of something is wrong but that a whole class of definitions is; for example, can see clearly that good cannot be defined mathematically without having to examine all the mathematical expressions there are and see that none of them severally can be used as a definition of good. The arguments I have given claim to enable one to see this about the class of naturalist definitions in ethics.

In my criticism of naturalist theories here I have not included some forms of the impartial observer theory. This theory would be naturalistic if it took such a form as that the right act is the act that a person would do if he felt other people's happiness and suffering as much as his own and had full knowledge of the consequences of his act, and it, besides committing one to a hedonist view, would then be open to the objections to naturalist theories given above. If, however, we attach to the definition such conditions as that the observer must be intelligent or be influenced by all the relevant points and only the relevant points in proportion to their relevance we have only said that the right act is the act which a man who judged rightly and did what he judged right would do. The only relevant measure of intelligence here is the ability to judge what is right, and what points are relevant is itself a moral judgement.

Now if moral and value judgements generally (other than merely instrumental ones) are really judgements at all and yet do not consist in the ascription of natural properties, it seemed to me and many others that they must consist in the ascription of other, 'non-natural', properties. I for my part at least assumed that the relations they signified were literally objective relations in the real world in the same way as 'liked' or 'disliked' signify objective relations between different persons, though indeed relations of a very peculiar kind, which was signified by calling them 'non-natural'.[1] Later[2] however I came to the conclusion that this view made an illegitimate assumption, namely, that if moral and evaluative judgements are really judgements capable of truth or falsehood, their function must be to ascribe properties or relations to existing things, as is done by ordinary categorical factual judgements. This assumption I have now abandoned. Of course I do not deny that good is a quality if that means that the word 'good' is

---

[1] In *The Definition of Good* (1947).
[2] See *Second Thoughts in Moral Philosophy* (1959), pp. 50 ff.

grammatically an adjective, nor do I deny that 'obligation' is a
relational word; but it does not follow that, if we can truly say that
something is 'good', there is an actually existent quality of goodness
which the thing has in the sense in which a taste (gustatory experience)
may have the property of being salty; or that if we can truly talk of
objective obligations there is therefore a relation actually existing in
the mental world in the same sense as there is a relation of distance
really existing in the physical world. It now seems to me that the
difference between this kind of judgements and factual judgements is
better expressed by saying that they do not merely ascribe properties
and relations of a different kind but have a quite different function,
say a different kind of thing.

But it is easier to say this much than to describe further what sort
of things they do say. On one point I must first specially insist. The
concessions I have made have indeed brought me nearer to a prescriptivist view, but it seems to me that the objections which I have
brought against this kind of view still hold unless the view is supplemented by admitting that there is a distinction between justified and
unjustified prescriptions the statement of which does not amount
simply to repeating in your own name those prescriptions which you
call justified. In making a moral judgement we do not merely urge
ourselves or somebody else to act in accordance with it; we put forward
a claim that so to urge them is justified. If this is not admitted, we
incur the objections that I have brought against a purely prescriptive
view. My view has now for a long time been that there are two
factors linked in our moral judgements. There is what I have called
an incipient conative attitude in favour of or against the act which
we are appraising or condemning. This psychological attitude must,
I think, be present in some degree in all genuine moral judgements
really experienced as such by us. But it can be justified or unjustified,
rational or irrational, and it is closely linked with a claim that it is so
justified. This is analogous to theoretical belief, which, except where
it is only dispositional, includes always (a) a supposal, conscious
entertaining of a proposition, (b) a claim that the supposal is objectively justified. This claim, I contend, constitutes a judgement in a
full sense and as such is capable of being true or false. It maintains
at least that there is adequate reason to justify the attitude, and this
itself is surely some kind of proposition. A prescription could not be

justified by another prescription unless there were some grounds again justifying that prescription. And a statement of grounds must surely be a judgement in the real sense. Without a claim that there are grounds, even if the grounds are not always specified, a 'moral judgement' would sink to the level of a mere exclamation like 'Damn' or a quite arbitrary command. Its truth claim depends on this and so does the essential element of universality. I mean by universality of course not that the grounds of moral judgements must take the form of simple universal rules like 'Never tell lies', but that if I make a moral judgement about any person's action or proposed action I commit myself to the same judgement about any such action by anybody, including myself, unless I can point to some difference in the circumstances, whether external or in some cases psychological, which is morally relevant.

My introduction of the notion of what I have called an 'incipient conative attitude' as what is expressed by moral judgements brings me nearer to a prescriptivist view but avoids two objections to which the latter is liable. (1) It is objected that moral judgements often refer to the past, and we cannot command or urge a person to have acted differently in the past. This is, I imagine, one of the chief reasons which made Hare avoid the term 'imperative' and talk about a prescriptive view instead, but the nature of a moral reference to past acts is not, I think, made sufficiently clear by him. Even the notion of a prescription, like that of an imperative, seems to me difficult to separate from the notion of prescribing what in future ought to be done. But while we cannot command a person to act differently in the past, we can certainly take up an attitude of sympathy or aversion to a past act, and this is a practical attitude in the sense that it is liable to affect our future conduct if the question arises of acting in such a way in the future or cooperating with or opposing people who should in the future tend or propose to act in a similar fashion. Our future conduct is liable to be very much affected by the cumulative effect of our approvals or disapprovals in the past.

(2) If to make a moral judgement is to issue a sort of command or prescription, what about the case where the judgement relates to an action that I can do now? To prescribe an action to oneself can hardly mean anything but decide to do it if one can. But surely I may judge that I ought to do something and yet decide not to do it or even

not to try to do it, or not try as hard as I know I might. If not there would be no such thing as acting immorally, and – alas – there surely is. <u>Several contemporary holders of non-cognitive theories in ethics have thus involved themselves in the Socratic view that a man cannot willingly do wrong.</u> On their own premises they had a very good reason for this view, since if 'moral judgements' were decisions to do our duty when applied to ourselves, and I do not see what else they could be if they were prescriptions to ourselves about future acts that we might do, it would be self-contradictory to suppose that we could judge A to be our duty and yet decide not do A. Various attempts have been made to get out of this difficulty, but it seems to me that the view is contradicted by the mere fact of temptation, whether we succumb to it or not. For me to be tempted I must at least contemplate the possibility of deciding to act against my conscience, which would mean on the theory proposed the self-contradiction of deciding at once to do A and not A, a course which could not be even seriously considered. The latest attempt by Hare[1] to deal with the case of consciously wrong action by saying that the man who reproaches himself for doing what he knows he ought not to do could not have helped himself would, if universalized, take away all justification for saying his action was morally wrong.

These difficulties are avoided on my view since <u>all my definition requires is that there should be a tendency for a man to do what he thinks right, a tendency which will prevent immoral action, other things being equal, but very often fails to do so,</u> since other things are not always equal and though we desire to do right we have many other desires besides which may conflict or seem to conflict with this one. This at least holds with most people. I do not know if anybody exists who never has had any desire at all to avoid doing wrong because it is wrong, otherwise than a person so feeble-minded that his intelligence does not rise to moral concepts at all, but certainly if a person never has such a desire I should say he was without the basic minimum experience necessary to understand moral terms. There can also be very few people, if any at all, whose desire to do right does not sometimes clash with other desires, and this is quite sufficient to account for people sometimes voluntarily doing wrong. It is

---

[1] *Freedom and Reason*, pp. 78 ff.

quite impossible for a man, with very few exceptions, to feel another's suffering or joy as strongly as his own, and this makes temptation inevitable where there is a conflict of interest except in those cases where the possibility of temptation is inhibited by habits of action so firmly established that the wrong alternative does not present itself as a real option. I am not denying that the temptation may be overcome by the free exercise of our will in whatever sense our theory admits this. But we must remember that to regard what is right with some favour may be very far from deciding to do it. I do not admit that there is anything 'logically odd' about saying that I ought (in the full moral sense) to do *A* but I shall not do it; what I do admit is only that there is something psychologically rather odd because most people do not like to admit that they are acting or going to act immorally, thus losing credit with others.

It seems to me that a similar account should be given of evaluative judgements that do not explicitly introduce 'ought'. I still adhere to my view that good should be analysed in terms of 'ought or 'right' together with a psychological pro-attitude.[1] My main reason for this is that, while I cannot either accept a naturalist definition of good or be clear that I have a simple and irreducible concept of a 'non-natural' property of good, I do think that I have a concept of what is meant by 'ought' which sharply distinguishes statements about what something factually is from statements about what ought to be. Or rather I should say that I have two concepts of 'ought' – one as signifying what is morally obligatory and one as signifying what is reasonable – and would explain the different senses of good partly by differences in the pro-attitude involved and partly by variation between these two senses of 'ought'.

A more important question is that of the truth of moral and evaluative judgements. It has been suggested that the belief that they can be true is not supported even by common sense, on the ground that we rarely use the terms 'true' or 'false' of them even in our everyday speech; but we constantly speak of moral 'beliefs' or of 'knowing' something to be wrong, and this implies that we regard them as

---

[1] This view has been criticized by Blanshard, *Reason and Goodness*, p. 284. For my reply to main criticisms of this type see *Second Thoughts in Moral Philosophy*, pp. 99–101. A fuller reply to his objections will appear in my contribution to the volume on Blanshard in Schilpp's series on *Great Living Philosophers* when the latter is published.

propositions which can be true or false. Further, if my criticisms of a pure prescriptive view are valid, to make a moral or evaluative judgement is, partly at least, to say that a certain practical attitude is not merely actually adopted by me but justified or required, and this is surely something that can be true or false. <u>If my practical attitude is justified, it must be true that it is justified and we have then an evaluative proposition which is true.</u> As I said earlier, a prescription could not be justified by what was merely another prescription. The question is rather in what sense moral and evaluative judgements can be true and whether they are true in anything like the same sense as factual judgements. Even pure prescriptivists have admitted that we can properly say that an ethical 'judgement' is true, while qualifying this by adding that to say so simply means that the person who says it is true has the same emotional or practical attitude as the one who originally made the judgement, but if that were all, the 'judgement' would not even claim justification but be merely a repetition of the prescription. If my argument is valid such judgements must be true in a sense much more like factual judgements than that. It is more dubious whether they are true in exactly the same sense. It may indeed be contended that we have already committed ourselves to saying they are not by rejecting the view assumed both by naturalism and 'non-naturalism' that, if true, they ascribed to things actually existing qualities or relations. It is however also very questionable whether true judgements outside ethics, categorical and hypothetical judgements, straightforward empirical judgements about physical objects and a priori judgements of pure mathematics, are all true in the same sense of 'true'. In my *Second Thoughts*[1] I suggest a distinction between a very general sense of truth which all true judgements in these different spheres have in common and different specific senses each of which would be peculiar to a different general type of judgement. I could not however produce a definition of truth in general from which the more specific senses could be neatly deduced as in the corresponding sense of 'good'. All I could suggest is that all true judgements must somehow refer to and depend for their truth on the real, but different kinds of judgement may do this in different ways. Straightforwardly descriptive affirmative judgements are related to

[1] Pp. 45-7.

reality, if true, in a way which makes the term *correspondence* at least not altogether inappropriate, but this view is discarded for ethical judgements when we deny that goodness is an actual quality, natural or non-natural, or obligation an actual relation existing in the real. But there are other kinds of true judgements which do not correspond to reality in this simple way. A good example outside ethics is to be found in hypothetical judgements. They do not assert what has actually taken place, yet they are dependent for their truth on the real world. It is true that if I jumped from a skyscraper and my fall was not broken I should be killed, but this is not because it describes an event which has actually happened. What it describes is not anything that has ever occurred or, I hope, will occur in the world, but it is yet rendered true by the nature of that world. Similarly with ethical judgements, though I certainly do not want to say that they are in all respects like ordinary hypothetical judgements. The point of resemblance is that they ~~they~~ do not ascribe actual properties but when true assert something that follows from these properties.

It has been objected that on a view like mine or indeed on any view which denied naturalism it could not make any verifiable difference whether an ethical judgement was right or wrong. But we must at any rate admit the concepts of reasonable and unreasonable as applied to factual judgements and it does not either make any verifiable difference whether they are reasonable or unreasonable since, they being only so on the limited evidence at our disposal, they might in either case be true or false. No doubt there is empirical evidence which will either make for or against their truth, though not conclusively, but there is also empirical evidence as to consequences which at least gives some support to ethical propositions. The only ethical propositions to which this does not apply would be the most ultimate ones, but then neither could there be such evidence for the most ultimate propositions of probability theory. In any case the objection assumes the rejected verification theory of meaning.

If asked what ultimately makes something good in itself I should say 'its empirical nature', and if asked what makes an act right I should say 'its empirical circumstances' (including of course under these such facts as that a certain promise has been made). This is not to become a naturalist. For I do not say, as the naturalist does, that moral and other evaluative judgements are reducible simply to empirical judgements; I say they are based on empirical judgements. Thus the truth that I ought not to do certain things to other people is very commonly simply based on the fact that to do these things would hurt.

I may still be attacked on the grounds of Hume's principle that you can never derive an 'ought' from an 'is'. But if this be a valid objection, I do not think it could be met by supposing a non-natural quality of goodness. Either this property already includes the relation of obligation, in which case you have already admitted that an 'ought' does follow from an 'is', since the goodness of something, though different from any or all of its natural properties, is admitted even by the non-naturalist to follow from them. Or it does not, in which case you have still the inference to make if the property is to be relevant to your duties.

There is a sense in which we must be able to argue from the 'is' to the 'ought' if we are to have any rational ethics at all. It is an argument against doing something that it will inflict pain, and this follows from the factual nature of pain. We can infer from the circumstances that we ought or ought not to act in a certain fashion. Some ethical inferences are mediate, some a matter of intuitive insight, some a combination of both, but it is an (immediate) inference to see even that something is in so far bad because it is painful, though it is also an intuition since no mediate step is needed. Attempts have lately been made to ease the transition by arguing that the distinction between factual and normative judgements breaks down. And it might often be hard to frame accurately a purely factual non-evaluative statement from which a particular ethical conclusion could be inferred, but then this would only be because certain kinds of experiences have seemed to men so obviously good or bad that the evaluative notion became inseparably attached to the factual one, and if this is the explanation, it only supports the view that the value of something can follow necessarily from its factual character. But there are hosts of examples where it seems easy enough.

Nor do I feel that there are any strong arguments against saying that moral and evaluative judgements can follow from factual, unless all inference be analytic, a view which I still reject. Hume gives none except that 'ought' stands for a different kind of concept from any included in a factual premise. But I think there are strong reasons against saying that ethical can be reduced to, i.e. identified with, factual concepts. These reasons I have given earlier in this chapter in my attack on naturalism.

It has been suggested that it is not a question of factual premise entailing ethical conclusions or our 'deducing' ethical conclusions from them, these terms being much too strong, but that we can still say that they can provide 'good reasons' for making ethical judgements. This sounds a tempting suggestion, but that necessity is not too strong a word is suggested by the following considerations. Suppose a man wanted to do something which he realized would be very wicked, and therefore came to the following conclusion: 'I want to do this very much but there is one feature of the proposed action which I greatly dislike, namely its moral badness, therefore the reasonable course will be for me to do something which resembles the proposed action in all respects except one, namely its moral badness. In that case I shall be guiltless and yet get what I want.' It is plain that, if he said this, he would be talking nonsense; if he did something which was like the proposed act in all other respects, it would have to be like it in being morally bad also. That surely must necessarily follow, and in maintaining the opposite he would not only have said something unreasonable in the sense in which it would be unreasonable to overlook important consequences likely to follow from an action but have committed an outright absurdity. Whereas if what he had proposed to do had been something different in respect of a particular empirical quality it might have been causally impossible but there would have been no such absurdity. It does not however follow that the necessity need be just the same in kind as that in virtue of which $2 + 2$ must be equal to 4.

But I think there is a simple explanation of the necessity of these judgements which falls outside the ordinary dichotomy between analytic and synthetic and keeps us from identifying it with ordinary logical necessity. Whatever evaluation is exactly, it is clear that if we evaluate something rightly, otherwise than by chance, the evaluation must depend on the nature of A and so must not be different, A being what it is in fact. Otherwise it would not be a correct evaluation. This is obvious with judgements which ascribe intrinsic goodness or badness, but ought-judgements can be described also as evaluating actions either beforehand when we consider what is the right thing to do or afterwards when we consider their merit or demerit. We see that the factual properties by their inherent nature make what has them in so far good. It would not be a proper evaluation of what is evaluated if we did not see this, whether we are talking of moral deeds or of examination papers. But this is very different from the kind of necessity we have in ordinary a priori judgements. It might indeed be contended that the proposition that the evaluation, to be right, must correspond thus to the nature of what is evaluated, was analytic, but the propositions giving the particular evaluations could not be. We may compare the proposition that, if the facts are as a judgement asserts them to be that judgement is true, which is analytic, with judgements as to what the particular empirical facts are in in a given case, which are synthetic.

Particular evaluations, though helped by argument, must at some point involve immediate insight or intuition, I still insist, and my admission of this will make me subject to attack. The objections to the notion of 'intuition' I have discussed in a previous chapter and shall discuss further in the next chapter in reference to religious intuition, but there is one objection recently emphasized with special reference to intuition in ethics that I had better handle here. It is said that a person who appeals to intuition in ethics commits himself to the view that anyone who disagrees with him must be 'morally blind' and that that is surely a most unreasonable claim. But the whole force of the objection depends on the use of extremely strong words to express disagreement. It might be compared to saying that a man who uses an argument in theoretical matters with which some other people disagree is claiming that these people are 'utter idiots', and that therefore the argument must not be accepted. Surely all he need do in either case is admit quite politely that he thinks the others likely to be mistaken. So much is applied in any assertion which is disputed by anybody, and there will be an end to all talk about most topics of interest, and certainly about philosophy, if we refrain from making any assertions that other people will dispute. I do not deny that some people could be rightly called morally blind at least on certain matters – for example, fanatical Nazis – but then some can be called extremely stupid in regard to purely theoretical matters. Often when I express an ethical view I should regard the matter as quite doubtful, though I could not help at present feeling in a certain way about it, and should not wish to condemn morally or adopt an attitude of superiority to a man who disagreed with me.[1]

Attempts have been made to avoid the appeal to intuition by contending that certain attitudes are contained in or excluded by the very notion of morality, but this does not dispose analytically of the position of a sceptic who would say: I grant that e.g. regard to other people's interests is involved in morals, but I do not see why I should be moral if I do not want to be, and I do not want to bother about considering other people's interests. The answer that it will be to his own advantage to do so is not a moral answer and will not cover all cases.

But the role of intuition is not confined to general principles. In any at all dubious moral questions and in many which are not dubious both alternatives will produce some good and also at least the risk of some evil, and in the absence of a way of logically proving or mathematically calculating on which side the balance of advantage lies, to see or judge which alternative is better must be a matter of intuition, at least in the numerous cases where a rational man can be really convinced which is the better thing to do, in other cases we might prefer to call it a matter of sensible guessing.

I have said moral judgements claim to be true. What do they assert when they claim this, it being admitted that they do not assert the existence of actual properties, natural or non-natural, in the real world? This question will come up in a later chapter on Moral Arguments for the Existence of God.

---

[1] It has been made an objection that I inconsistently used the occurrence of differences of opinion in ethics as an argument against 'subjectivism', which is a term I used in my *Second Thoughts* to cover prescriptivism as well as scepticism and the view that ethical judgements are simply judgements about the speaker's subjective state, and yet denied the occurrence of such differences when I had to defend objectivism. To this I should reply that the occurrence of any disagreement in ethical beliefs at all is a fatal objection to the views I was criticizing unless it can be explained away, while in order to have a strong argument against objectivism you have to show, not merely that disagreement exists but that it is much more frequent, fundamental and ultimate than is the case. For my reply to the criticism of objective views on the ground that they are incompatible with the actual differences of opinion see *The Definition of Good.*

6

INTUITIVE CONVICTION AS EVIDENCE IN RELIGION[1]

Arguments for God are under a cloud today, and whether the cloud can be dissipated or not I shall certainly not try to dissipate it in this chapter. As the reader will see later, I certainly do not by any means deny the value of some of the arguments for God, but I must certainly admit in agreement with most modern philosophers that they do not give decisive proof, though I think they do give some considerable intellectual support for the belief. In the absence of a proof it is of very special importance to consider whether those may be right who maintain that men can come to knowledge of God or at least justified belief otherwise than by argument. I am not considering the views of those who base the belief solely on authority: argument would be required to decide whether we ought to accept an authority and, if so, which. What I am referring to is the claim that there are certain 'mystical' and other religious experiences which can without argument adequately and rationally assure one of God's existence. What has been called 'the argument from religious experience' is usually simply an appeal to the intuitive conviction present in these experiences. Obviously from the nature of the case a man who makes this claim for himself cannot *prove* to others that he is right, but can any good reasons be given to support the view that he is wrong? If not, the possibility remains that those who dispute with him are in a similar position to that of a tone-deaf man disputing about the value of music with Beethoven.

A good deal is said about religious emotion, but the experience must be more than a mere emotion if it is to do what is wanted. To have an emotion is not the same as to know or believe something,

---

[1] This is a much expanded version of the article *Awareness of God*, published in *Philosophy*, vol. 40 (1965); and in my *Non-Linguistic Philosophy*.

linked as the two may often be, and a person who makes the above claim is not usually intending to base his belief on an argument to the effect that the emotions he has can only be explained causally by reference to an existent God, though Cook Wilson advanced a by no means implausible argument of this kind.[1] The claim made is on the contrary usually a claim to what is commonly called 'intuition'. It is a cognitive phenomenon, not a mere feeling, though it may be connected very closely with certain emotional feelings. On the other hand it is neither an apprehension of the validity of an argument nor an empirical perception. To intuit God is not to see a vision or hear a voice, nor is it to see a formal proof of God's existence to be valid.

In talking of intuition in religion I am not limiting myself to experiences that would usually be described as 'mystical', still less to trances and visions. To quote such an authority as Archbishop Temple, he points out that the phrase religious experience 'has two distinct meanings. It may be used, as it is by William James, to denote specific moments in which a man passes through what he takes to be direct awareness of God or intercourse with him. The fact that James isolated these "experiences" deprived his treatment of them of half the value that it might have had. The phrase "religious experience" may also mean the constant experience of life and the world that comes to a religious man – an experience which is pervaded and permeated by religion.'[2] He therefore mentions it as an odd fact that philosophers attend mainly to the religious experience of the mystics ignoring the experience of the ordinary Christian believer. I may add that this seems all the more odd as I have never seen Christ himself described as a 'mystic'.

Now I agree with C. D. Broad, a philosopher who was extremely cautious and critical and by no means prejudiced in favour of theology that 'when there is a nucleus of agreement between the experiences of men in different places, times, and traditions, and when they all tend to put much the same kind of interpretation on the cognitive content of these experiences, it is reasonable to ascribe this agreement to their all being in contact with a certain objective aspect of reality unless there be some positive reason to think otherwise. . . . So far as the religious experiences agree they should be provisionally accepted as

---

[1] *Statement and Inference*, vol. II, pp. 859 ff.
[2] *Contemporary British Philosophy*, ed. J. H. Muirhead, First Series, pp. 424 ff.

veridical unless there be some positive ground for thinking that they are not. . . .[1] The claim of any particular religion or sect to have complete or final truth on these subjects seems to me to be too ridiculous to be worth a moment's consideration. But the opposite extreme of holding that the whole religious experience of mankind is a gigantic system of pure delusion seems to me to be almost (though not quite) as far-fetched.'[2]

Is there positive ground for thinking the religious attitude to be fundamentally mistaken? The problem of evil which seems to give such a ground will be considered in chapter 9. Let us now consider various other objections to <u>the view that men can have true cognition[3] of God otherwise than by inference.</u> I have rejected those based on the verification principle and on the contention that the words used in sentences about God are deprived of the contexts which can alone give them factual meaning. I have also defended the concept of intuition.[4]

Let us now ask whether the possibility of veridical religious insight can be disproved by an epistemological argument of any other kind. It seems plain that those who exclude it today are empiricists and therefore should not be in a position to do so a priori. Can their negative proposition then be grounded inductively? Let us put the argument in quite general terms. To refute the possibility of religious intuition in this way we should have to have good reasons for holding a proposition which ascribes some general property x – it does not matter for my purpose what x is – to all kinds of well-accredited cognition, and we must find that this property is not possessed by any alleged religious cognitions. But how could this be established inductively? A universal proposition about a genus can be based adequately on an inductive generalization only if we can establish the proposition inductively for all its species. I shall for the sake of argument waive the difficulty of establishing such a universal episte-mological proposition empirically for any particular kind of cognition. But in any case we are now confronted with a vicious circle. The general property must not belong to alleged religious cognitions, for

---

[1] *Religion, Philosophy & Psychical Research*, p. 197.

[2] Op. cit., pp. 200–1.

[3] I speak of 'cognition' and not of 'knowledge' because the latter term conveys an objective certainty which it is hardly reasonable to claim on this subject, however subjectively certain the believer may feel.

[4] See above, chapter 1.

otherwise the second premise collapses. But if it does not belong to them, we can only accept the first premise if we already assume that no alleged religious cognitions are well accredited, thus begging the question. The first premise cannot be established by generalization without first assuming the conclusion. If we are to discredit alleged religious cognition by an empirically based epistemological argument, we shall then have to adopt a less conclusive form of induction, that called argument by analogy, and contend that, because all other kinds of cognition which are well accredited have a certain property, alleged religious cognition is unlikely ever to be veridical because it does not have this property. But this would only follow if we were entitled to assume that, if it is veridical, religious cognition will be like other kinds of cognition which are veridical. Prima facie we should however expect it on the contrary to be very different, since its object is so different. God, if he exists, is immensely different from any other kind of being, and therefore we cannot expect cognition of God to be anything but very different from any other kind of cognition. This very difference is emphasized strongly by most philosophers of religion and theologians. This makes the argument from the analogy of other kinds of cognition an exceedingly weak one. (Not that we should go so far as to exclude all analogies from the knowledge of finite things as being of no help at all in describing religious cognition of God, but we cannot reject the latter simply because of its differences from the former.)

Some philosophers however think it a fatal argument against the claim to intuition of God that an intuition is something in one's mind and therefore cannot establish a reality beyond us. But the former proposition must be true of every cognitive process. In any sense in which intuition is just in our mind so are mediate inference and sense-perception. For me to have knowledge or justified belief of any sort something must happen in me, but it does not follow that I am aware only of a happening in my mind when I acquire the knowledge or belief and see or think I see it to be true. Nor does it mean that I am establishing what I assert as true by an argument from what happens in my mind; my knowledge that $2 + 2 = 4$ is not an inference from the fact that I feel psychologically certain that it is so.

It has been argued by, for example, McTaggart,[1] that to assert in

_____
[1] *Some Dogmas of Religion*, pp. 38–40.

116   VALUE AND REALITY

favour of a belief that I have an intuition of its truth is always irrelevant
in a discussion on the ground that, if the person to whom I am speaking
has the intuition already himself, my statement is superfluous since
he will then not need to be convinced of the truth of the proposition
said to be intuited, while if he has not the intuition, the mere statement
that somebody else has it will be no ground for accepting its truth.
But suppose this very common situation. A man has a conviction
which is intuitive but falls short of certainty of the existence of God.
He is aware that what seems to him a reliable intuition may really not
be one, and he would certainly not be justified in placing any considerable faith in his intuition if he were the only person who had it.
But if he finds that the intuitive conviction is very widespread and
possessed by a vast number of men through the ages who in other
respects very commonly deserve the titles in a special degree of good
and wise, his attitude may well be transformed. Let us take the analogous case of an intuitive belief in ethics. It seems to me perfectly
obvious without proof that it is wrong to torture another man merely
in order to give oneself the pleasure which some people feel in
watching others suffer. But suppose I never met anybody else who had
this intuitive conviction also. In that case it would surely be only
reasonable for me to suspect that I was under some irresistible delusion
and be very doubtful even about an intuition that is as clear and
convincing subjectively as this one It would not disprove the possibility that I might be right. I *might* have been the first person to see a
fundamental ethical truth – but unless I thought myself a heaven-sent
prophet, I could hardly regard this as likely; and if I was reasonable
I should have to admit – Well, I cannot help thinking instinctively
like this, but I cannot suppose it in the least likely that everybody
else should be wrong and I myself right, so I had better dismiss it
as a psychological 'kink' of mine. But the situation is totally transformed by the fact that I do find that most people agree with me here,
thus confirming my intuitive conviction by theirs. This is the role
of authority in religion, though intuitive conviction here is not so
widely spread as in ethics. No doubt, if we take the case of a man who
has no vestige of intuitive religious conviction, it is unlikely that an
appeal to the intuitive conviction of others will convince him, but
even he will be unreasonable if he takes it for granted because he has
not got it himself that those who have it are necessarily wrong. And,

if a man has the conviction in a weak degree, he is justified in attaching incomparably more weight to it when he realizes its presence in a stronger and more developed form among others whom he respects.

We must not think of religious intuition as by any means limited to a few great teachers. It may well in some, though a much lesser, degree, be possessed by the plain man who says 'I cannot prove but I feel that there is a God'. 'Feel' here does not mean 'have emotional feelings'. If so, it would not be followed by a that-clause. It means 'believe intuitively'.

It may be contended however that, though genuine intuitive cognition cannot be proved impossible, we have no right to admit it because an adequate causal explanation of our religious beliefs has been given by psychologists. In discussing this question we must make certain distinctions. It is plain that the mere fact that a belief can be explained causally is no objection to it. My belief that the Prime Minister is mortal can certainly be explained causally. I believe that all men are mortal and that the Prime Minister is a man, and these two beliefs together cause me to believe that the Prime Minister is mortal.[1] But this explanation does not cast any doubt on but rather validates the belief. There are, however, some modes of causal explanation which, if they could be vindicated, would show that a person was unjustified in holding the belief the occurrence of which they explained, and this would apply to at least some explanations of the Freudian kind. What would invalidate a belief was not that it was caused but caused in a particular way. If it could be proved that a particular man believed in God just because he wanted to, it would follow that this man's belief in God was unjustified, but it would not follow that nobody's belief in God was justified, unless it were proved that every believer's belief in God were due simply to such a desire, and this would be hard indeed to show.

Now the psychologist can point to certain desires and complexes which might give a psychological explanation of such a kind that, if it were the real explanation, it would make religious belief unjustified, but how could he show that the alleged causes accounted for all belief in God? As a matter of fact the situation is much more complex than

---

[1] I do not mean to exclude the possibility that a man's knowledge of or belief in the premises which caused him to hold a certain belief might not itself be indirectly due to acts of free will in the past.

I have yet suggested. Desire could hardly be in a strict sense the *sole* cause of any belief, and it might well be a necessary condition without invalidating the belief. Nobody studies Kant unless he desires to (either as an end in itself or as a means to, for instance, pass examinations), so this desire is a necessary condition of belief in many propositions about Kant's work, but this fact is no reason whatever for supposing that the beliefs are irrational. Similarly, if veridical intuition of God is possible, it may well be the case that no one has the cognition unless they desire to have it, because otherwise they would not think about the matter enough, so that the desire was a necessary condition of the belief, but that would not invalidate the latter. What would normally be meant by saying that a man's belief is caused by his desire is probably that, granted his previous development, which was of course influenced by other causes also, the desire was a sufficient cause for the belief without any influence from the objective side or any reasoning, or that if there was reasoning it would never have convinced the man but for his desire that the belief should be true. The desire then could be said at least to cause the belief indirectly because it causes the reasoning or causes the man to be convinced by reasoning by which he would not otherwise have been convinced. Now, while there are no doubt cases in which a man's belief in God is caused by desire in such a sense, and the particular men of whom this is true are then not justified in holding the belief, it would be hard indeed to refute all claims to intuitive cognition of God by showing that the belief was thus caused in all cases.

No doubt the psychological theories put forward to explain religious belief are not usually as simple as what I have said may suggest, but basically they are similar to my example. The belief is ascribed to a desire or combination of desires (or fears) which are of no relevance to the truth of the belief. The most the psychologist can establish is not that all religious belief is due to the factors he mentions, but only that there are certain factors which *might* conceivably lead a person to hold a religious belief even if it were not warranted and in all probability in *some individual cases* do so. We find such a scientifically inclined, critical, well-balanced philosopher as C. D. Broad, one by no means prejudiced in favour of religion, prepared to say of the psychoanalytic and Marxist theories of religion that 'although the exponents of these theories make a tremendous parade of being "scientific", it is perfectly plain to anyone who has studied any genuine science that they have no idea of the *general* difficulty of proving any far-reaching explanatory hypothesis, or of the *special* difficulties which exist in a field where experiment is impossible,[1] and even the "observations" consist largely of hearsay and tradition. The degree of their confidence is a measure of their scientific incompetence. They seem to have no notion of the importance of confronting their theories with negative instances, or of considering whether half a dozen rival hypotheses would not explain the facts equally well.'[2]

I can indeed think of kinds of evidence on this subject which it is logically conceivable that a psychologist might turn out able to produce that would deal a tremendous blow to the belief in God or any particular religious belief. Suppose he had studied a million or even a thousand cases selected otherwise at random but divided into two halves, one of which was subjected to the causes he mentioned but not the other, and found that those belonging to the former class all held the belief in question and those that belonged to the latter also without exception did not. This might well make it very unreasonable to go on saying that the belief was a valid intuition (or for that matter inference) if those only who had been subjected to these causes had any inclination to think the intuition (or inference) a valid one. There are however some conditions under which I think even this inference would not do the trick. For the argument to work the causes must not be of such a kind as to constitute reasons as opposed to mere causes for belief, for example, we could not call the belief in *B* irrational because only those who had had the experience *A* acquired the belief if *A* were the experience of coming to know premises from which *B* followed. Nor could we if the causes with which he experimented were needed to remove some circumstance that disqualified a person from seeing evidence for *B* or from understanding *B*, for example it would not be an objection to belief in a God of love if it were found that those only could acquire the belief (except mechanically on authority) who had experienced human love.

[1] As what I say on pp. 142–3 shows, I should regard this claim about the impossibility of experiment as somewhat exaggerated, but by no means sufficiently so to weaken much Broad's contention here.

[2] *Religion, Philosophy and Psychical Research*, p. 243.

Thus all the psychologists manage to do in effect seems to me to be to suggest certain causes which might lead people to hold religious beliefs even if they were unwarranted, not to establish the conclusion that these are in fact the causes which make most or even many believers hold the beliefs. To point to certain desires, conscious or unconscious, which may lead to a man being prejudiced in favour of a religious belief is not to show that all religious men are prejudiced by them. The risk of being prejudiced by desire is present in the case of any argument which leads to pleasant conclusions and which is not logically completely compelling, but we are not therefore obliged to abandon all probable arguments which lead to attractive conclusions because of this risk, though when considering the arguments we no doubt ought to do our best not to be prejudiced, and the same should apply to ostensible intuitions. (Since fear, as well as hope, may lead to rash conclusions, we should also on those principles have to abandon all probable arguments which led to unpleasant conclusions.)

Further, the religious man can retort that, if there are some factors which may make a man likely to hold a belief in God even if it is false, there are others which may make him likely to reject it even if it is true. For *prima facie* appearances, at least superficially considered, are very much against it. Even if the problem of evil turns out, as it has done for so many thinkers, on careful reflection not to constitute an adequate refutation of the belief in God, it must be admitted that this world with all the suffering and other evil it contains looks *prima facie* most unlike the work of a perfectly good omnipotent being, and this can well go very far towards explaining the difficulty people have in envisaging a God.[1] There is, further, the total absence of suggestions of God in our ordinary everyday experience as it strikes most people most of the time. The things which occupy our life for the vastly greater part of it for all except people dedicated professionally to a religious life do not, at least in the case of most of us, suggest to us God. It is most difficult for most of us to get away from the material, practical world sufficiently to concentrate our full attention even for a very short time on the attempt to find God, even

---

[1] My argument here assumes that it is possible to deal with the problem of evil in such a way as at least to mitigate the *prima facie* insuperable objection which it constitutes to belief in God, as I try to do in chapter 9. If not, *cadit quaestio*.

if God is to be found, and relatively few people have the zeal to make a practice of doing this. (Probably we should add that of those who have done it very few have failed to attain a genuine religious conviction.) Such circumstances can very readily explain why so many people have no religious belief or one based simply on the authority of others. If the proposed psychological explanation of religious belief is on Freudian lines, we can retort too with the *argumentum ad hominem* that, as Freud explains religion by the father-image, we could equally well explain the widespread rejection of the belief by unconscious 'hate' of one's father.[1] This according to Freud plays such a large part in human life as to make this explanation of the rejection of theism a very plausible one if his psychology has anything much in it; and one does not indeed need to be a Freudian to associate the common revolt against God with the revolt also very common today against parental authority (not only the parent of the same sex as oneself). And the explanation can be used with the greatest ease if we are allowed to postulate that, even if it is never consciously recognized by the man who has it, it can still be there in his 'unconscious'.

So if the agnostic or atheist can explain how people may be theists even if theism is false, the theist can explain at least as easily how people can be agnostics or atheists even if theism is true and to the real believer evident.[2] Thus at the level of psychological explanation the battle seems to be a drawn one. Either side can suggest ways in which the belief or absence of belief of the other may be caused by irrelevant factors, but it cannot prove that it is in fact so caused. At any rate the attempt to disprove religion by psychology has failed. So the religious man who has faced his difficulties and still retained his intuitive conviction in God after having asked himself if it may not be due to his desires and answered in the negative need not be too worried by the psychologist, unless indeed he insists on claiming objective certainty for his views, which is in any case unreasonable. For many such indeed the experience will carry with it its own subjective certainty, which they cannot, even if they will, abandon. I want to emphasize that it seems to be what is best in us rather

---

[1] V. Klausner and Kuntz, *Philosophy and Alternative Beliefs*, p. 262.

[2] I have not included in this explanation the insulting remark that atheists and agnostics do not know God because of their sins. Theists have also committed sins.

than what is worst in us which inclines us to the belief in God. It is a
very strong point in favour of the truth of religious belief if one feels
that all the other higher experiences of life – moral, intellectual and
aesthetic – seem to tend towards it or to put one in a religious state
of mind, but the trouble is that not everyone would admit that they
do, otherwise the case would be pretty conclusive, I think.

It seems surprising that some religious bodies, for instance notably
Roman Catholics, have tended to reject intuition as a source of
knowledge of God. The chief explanation, I think, is that knowledge
connotes for them a certainty, objective as well as subjective, that
short of the 'beatific vision', which is inaccessible to human beings
in this life at any rate, religious intuition cannot give, but which they
thought could be given by the proofs of God supplemental as to his
nature by an authoritative divine revelation. The admission of
intuition as a leading factor would also have undermined the central
position given to the authority of the church, and could not have
provided doctrines so definite as the church wished. It is much less
questionable that the evidence of religious experience supports some
objective view of religious value than that it supports the much more
specific doctrines that Catholics and orthodox Christians in general
would be anxious to defend. Yet I imagine that few religious people
would not admit that 'religious experience' with its intuitive feeling
of his presence was at least of some help in confirming the belief in
God; and if it is impossible to give a fully convincing proof of God by
other means and we have to rely on probability the importance of this
supporting evidence is increased. Certainly we can be sure that it has
been in fact a much more important cause factor historically in
producing belief than the 'proofs of God'. Further, many people who
would say they were convinced by the proofs of God are, it may
well be, convinced only because they have some premise in mind
which is taken as self-evident and which is specifically religious in
character. One of the sharpest religious critics of the view that we can
have intuitive cognition of God is Rashdall, but he lets fall the words:
'That Reality as a whole may be most reasonably interpreted by
Reality at its highest is after all the sum and substance of all theistic
arguments.'[1] What is this proposition if not a religious intuition?
No proof of it is produced.

[1] *Philosophy and Religion.*

The difficulty about intuition in religion, we should also emphasize, is much diminished when we reflect that, if a benevolent God
exists, we cannot but expect him to communicate in some way
knowledge of himself to us, and if, as seems to be the case, logical
proof of the existence and love of God is logically impossible, such
knowledge might be well expected subjectively to take the form of
intuitive conviction; I do not see indeed what other form it could
take.

Now to say that a cognition is intuitive is not indeed necessarily
to deny that it is mediated in some way, though it would contradict
it to say that it is mediate *inference* That is why I prefer to speak of
'intuition' rather than immediate cognition. Thus the cognition could
well be called 'intuitive' in so far as it is not based on argument, and
yet it might be mediated by certain experiences which could help
one to 'see' God. The apprehension of something may well lead one
to the realization of something else without the former being a
premise from which the latter is deduced. There is a distinction
between seeing some truth as the result of seeing others and inferring
it from these others. To say that some being mediates God is to say
that a man may by considering that being be put in a frame of mind
in which he can catch a glimpse of God. The cognition would still be
direct in the sense that it was not an inference. The awareness of God
is commonly held to be mediated by physical nature, the goodness
in other people, many kinds of symbols, and many especially vivid
experiences in life, moral, aesthetic and practical. The relation of
mediation may thus carry us beyond what we could infer.

The concept of mediated cognition that is yet not inferential is
not one which has to be specially invented in order to deal with
religion. It may be argued that it is also needed for the solution of
problems such as that of the knowledge of physical things and of
other human minds. For while our cognition of these is plainly
mediated by sense-perception and by the bodily behaviour of others,
its objects cannot be identified with the mediating factors and even
if they are inferable from them they are known prior to the inferences,
which few formulate and by no means all philosophers accept. Our
knowledge of the past in memory is mediated by our present experience, though it is not inferred from that; insight into universal
truths is mediated by particular illustrations, though not inferred

from them where they are not empirical inductions; moral knowledge is mediated by particular emotional and conative experiences. All or practically all thought seems to be mediated by language or other images.

Now there is something very puzzling about all the cases I have admitted of mediated cognition. We are aware of something over and above the media; this awareness is not just inference; yet if we are asked what it is of which we are thus aware, we can give no definite answer except in terms of the media. Normally at least any knowledge one has of physical things is derived from sense-perception, yet I seem to cognize them directly and not merely infer them from my sense-data;[1] I am not directly aware what my friend's experience or mind is like, yet I do not seem to infer them merely from his speech and apparent bodily states; I seem to be aware not only of the general words I use but of what they mean (even where this cannot be expressed wholly in terms of sensual images); I am conscious of something much more than my present experience when I remember, though I do not immediately feel my past experience, or necessarily even a replica of it (I can enjoy memories of my past misery); there are difficulties about saying what I am aware of beyond 'natural properties' when I make ethical judgements. Yet nobody has yet, in any of these cases ever given a full description of what it is that we are thus aware of which gave general satisfaction or a proof of its reality that seemed to have complete cogency. Hence the temptation to become an extreme verificationist, a road which however leads logically not merely to secularism and naturalism but to solipsism of the present moment. So we see that the puzzle is one of a sort which affects all knowledge and not only religion. I have asked how men can be non-inferentially aware of God without knowing what it feels like to be God; but similarly we might ask how we can cognize physical things directly without being aware of their nature in itself as opposed to their effects on our sensibility, or how we can know other human minds without experiencing how they feel, or our own past experiences when they are no longer there to experience. And it is the reverse of easy to say what we have in view when we think of universals beyond

[1] I am still disposed to hold a representative theory of perception but I should want to combine this, as I did in *Idealism* (pp. 316 ff.) with a direct theory of a cognition of physical objects which is different from but accompanies the sensations they produce.

images and words, and yet surely there is something beyond images and words. In all these cases we are aware of something over and beyond the media; this awareness may even be called direct in the sense that its objects are not just inferred from the media. There is required then throughout most or even all of epistemology the concept of a cognition which is mediated and yet not merely inferential, which can use its media to acquire real cognition of its object in the absence of anything like strict proof and without being directly aware of the latter's internal nature or being face to face with it in all its particularity.

Now religious men seem to have this in the case of God also. It would presumably still be a cognition not of God as he is in himself but of God as he is in relation to us. But by this I do not mean merely 'as the person who has the experience thinks God' but as God objectively is in that relation, i.e. the cognition of God in religious experience might give objective truths about relational properties of God, e.g. God's love to us, though still in a form most inadequate by comparison with the fuller degree of illumination that might be enjoyed by a superior being. We should note however that inner nature may be indirectly partially revealed by knowledge of a relation. Thus direct knowledge of God's love can be conceived as revealing that God is good because such love entails goodness.

Some find the media that specially serve to bring them to God, however inadequately, in images and ceremonies, some in physical nature, some in art, some in special happenings to themselves or those they love, some in the goodness they see in other men, some in philosophical meditation, some in love of particular human beings in its higher forms, some in love of humanity, more in a combination of several of these. We should refer here to two specially important cases of mediation. Whatever view we hold of the incarnation as a theological doctrine, it is a fact that men have had very widely a very special experience of God in contemplating the person of Jesus Christ in thought, and while we must insist that God is partially mediated by goodness in any man, Christ has played a larger part in mediating God for others than has any other single human being. To say this is not of itself yet to say that Christ was God or that we can *infer* the existence of God from a knowledge of Christ.

Secondly, whatever we think of the logical character of the moral arguments for God which we shall discuss in chapter 10, there can be no doubt that moral experience and consciousness of the moral law play a most important part in mediating belief in God. 'The pure in heart shall see God', though we must add that this can be accepted only as a general, not a universal proposition, since many men who are excellent morally do not, consciously at any rate, see God. It is very important to realize that a person who is not consciously religious and perhaps even denies the existence of God in so many words may well be conceived as unconsciously blest by communion with God through these various media.

As regards the cognition of reality as a whole, as distinct from that of a personal God, commonly claimed by the mystic, this might be conceived as mediated by cognition of parts of this whole, which may well be expected to provide a means of revealing the nature of the whole as a whole in various ways and degrees. It is of significance here that mystics stress so much the close interrelation of things, for if things be as intimately interrelated as they think, indeed so closely that the word 'relation' is regarded as inappropriate because it does not express the full depth of their unity, it must follow that the part reveals the nature of the whole.

Religious belief has been so widespread, so dominating a factor for so many who were in other respects among the greatest and best of men and so much the basis throughout history of a whole most fundamental side of life and thought as to make a strong prima facie case at least for the view that 'there is a great deal in it'. In any other sphere overwhelming weight would be given to the conclusions of experts, even if they could not be proved to non-experts, and the great mystics and religious leaders can certainly be described as in their field experts.

But at this point we are brought up sharply by objections based on the divergences beween the adherents of different religious creeds. A very large part of these are admittedly divergences regarding arguments, e.g. about the best authority, and not divergences regarding intuitions, but in so far as there is a conflict of intuitions what are we to say? When two apparent intuitions conflict, we must admit that at least one intuition is mistaken, or, if we make 'intuition' infallible by definition, that a person can think he has an intuition when he really has not. But the fact that conflicts of intuitions, or if we use the latter terminology, apparent intuitions occur, we have seen earlier does not necessarily involve the rejection of all our intuitive convictions. I shall not repeat here the reply I gave to this well-known difficulty in chapter 2.[1] But it must be admitted that the conflicts at least weaken the case for just accepting the authority of the experts. The question arises – Which experts?

It is important however in this field specially to realize that it need not be a case of one intuition being just right and another just wrong, and it may well happen that intuitions which conflict as they stand can be reconciled if one is slightly amended, and that this may be a strong reason for accepting the amendment. Nor must we suppose, especially in the field of religion, that the only alternatives are clear intuitive insight into a definite proposition and no intuition at all. An intuition may, as I have said earlier, be confused and yet give some truth even if we cannot be sure that we have exactly sorted out from it what is true and what is false; and that may be the explanation of many of the obscurities in the remarks of great philosophers and religious teachers and also the excuse for them, though it is no excuse for not carrying careful analysis and inferential thought as far as we can carry them. It is, further, to be expected that most people will interpret any religious intuitions they may have in terms of the religion in which they were brought up, and that they will thus be liable to blend and confuse with true intuitions beliefs based on an authority far from infallible. Seeming intuition may be only a strong conviction based on the teaching of another person of particularly suggestive personality or a church supposed to have special divine authority, but it would be a mistake to dismiss all apparent intuitions on these grounds. They are quite as fertile in producing mistaken inferences as mistaken intuitions, and people have been misled into making dubious inferences hastily through accepting too readily not only the authority of the Roman Catholic Church but that of Marx or even Wittgenstein. On the other hand the fact that a person is already very familiar with a certain view need not exclude the possibility of his being able to verify it later by an intuitive insight which he did not possess when he was first taught it, and in very many cases a man's most distinctive religious experience has led him to embrace views which he did not hold earlier and even to adopt a religion having had

[1] See above, pp. 41–8.

none before, or to change his religion. A view also may be accepted partly intuitively and partly on the strength of arguments, and in the next two chapters I shall deal with arguments which, though not amounting to conclusive proofs, do, I think, especially when combined have some very considerable force. But for the moment the question to consider is how we can distinguish between what on the strength of religious intuition deserves acceptance or at least serious consideration and what does not.

If all religious experts agreed it would be almost as difficult for non-experts to defy them in their own field as it was in the long run for theologians to maintain that the scientific theory of evolution must be rejected on theological grounds. But we must by no means over-estimate the extent to which religious intuitions do diverge. It would obviously be impossible to establish the creed of any particular sect in toto by just appealing to the intuitive convictions of members of that sect, but it does not follow that one could not legitimately appeal to intuition to establish the most fundamental principles of religion in general. Actually on major points the nucleus of agreement between most mystics of different religions and of different civilizations is in fact surprising.

I think that the best way to approach this question is to ask what is fundamental presupposition (or presuppositions) without which a religious attitude could not be regarded as appropriate. For, as I pointed out in the first chapter, it seems quite clear to me that it cannot be appropriate unless certain beliefs about reality are true, and this has certainly been the general view of religious teachers. What is the fundamental religious belief or beliefs? It seems to me that, if we can decide what it is and maintain it in a defensible form, it will be in a much stronger position than any other isolated intuition could be. There is a definite presumption in favour of the substantial validity of whatever is a necessary presupposition of a whole major department of human thought. Now the most fundamental presupposition of religion, you will expect me to say, is the existence of God. But I shall not say this, though this does not signify by any means that I am going to deny the existence of God. However, more important than the existence of God is God's goodness, and the corollary from this that the universe is governed in accordance with a supremely good purpose and is therefore possessed of supreme and overwhelming

positive value, if we could only see it as a whole, including the future
as well as the past; a corollary which is usually derived from the
belief in God but is sometimes held in its own right on the strength
of mystical experience without the belief in a personal God. The
attitude of a person who took this latter view I should consider
religious, but I should not consider somebody had a religious attitude
who believed in God but thought God indifferent to values or actually
bad. So I should agree with Whitehead in making the basic presupposition of religion 'the fundamental rightness of things', meaning
by this not that there is no evil but that the good somehow pre-
dominates. I do not wish to gloss over the tremendous character of the
assumption proposed, and I shall speak a great deal about this in the
chapter on the problem of evil. What seems to me plain is that a
certain view as to the *value* of Reality or of the being on which Reality
is based is the most essential doctrine of religion. I am inclined to say
with W. E. Hocking: 'What I mean by "the true mystic" is simply
the person who in the course of his own experience has in some
moment become aware of the nature of things as supreme good.'[1]
Some religious thinkers prefer to use the term 'holiness' in preference,
but this only seems to me to signify a specially high degree of value.
Otto, who more than any other well-known religious writer has laid
stress on holiness as the fundamental concept of religion, defines
'belief in a divine government of the world' as belief 'in the determination and ordinance of all that is and of all that happens according
to eternal values and eternal purposes',[2] and describes knowledge of
God as the feeling 'which is aware of eternal goodness'.[3]

Now for the ordinary person such a belief is much more intelligible
and helpful if put in terms of a personal God, but it may be held that
this is only a symbol or metaphor without the person who calls it this
ceasing to be religious. But it does seem that the value of religion will
be largely lost if it does not at least stand for some objective truth not
too unlike the plain meaning of the symbols for the latter to be
regarded as some approximation to the truth. And the central concep-

[1] *The Coming World Civilization*, p. 138.
[2] I think we need a reservation to allow for human free will.
[3] *Philosophy of Religion*, pp. 129–30. See also Oman, 'More frequently perhaps than
any other feeling, the sense of the holy follows and depends on its value; and on the
whole this becomes increasingly the case as the mind develops' (*The Natural and the
Supernatural*, p. 66).

E

tion is here value, whether we accept a kind of mystical pantheism or believe in a personal God. If so it is surely a good argument to say 'Religion involves worship. It is plainly inappropriate (most religious people would be inclined to use a stronger word and say "blasphemous" or "idolatrous") to worship what is unworthy of worship. But what is worthy of worship must be supremely good. Therefore, if a religious attitude is to be appropriate at all, the being to whom it is directed must be good, and not just ordinarily good but supremely and incomparably good.' The mystical pantheist may not wish to use the term worship, but he must at least regard it as a supreme good to enter into communion with the Whole, and this could not be a supreme good if the Whole were not essentially good. The value claimed for communion with God in religious experience, whether we identify him with the Whole or just regard him as the supreme being, is obviously inseparably bound up with the idea of the perfect goodness of God. And the experience of peace which plays such an important part in religion surely implies the supreme goodness of that on which the mind rests and the faith that this good will in the end prevail or perhaps has in essence in some way already, or rather timelessly, prevailed. In characterizing God very much commonly is said of his power and his mysterious nature. Now the doctrine of the omnipotence of God is of great religious importance because this gives us a guarantee that his goodness will prevail; and God must indeed be mysterious to beings so much below him as ourselves. But we cannot or at least ought not to worship power and mystery as such. All that matters ultimately is value, and religion in so far as it is of value in itself can only be so because of the value of its object. It was a grievous perversion when some theologians and philosophers (fortunately only a relatively small minority, I think) because they considered it a limitation of God's power that he should be governed by the moral law, made ethical principles the mere outcome of his will, thus making his goodness a tautology.[1]

To say that a certain principle is presupposed if the religious attitude is justifiable is not by any means to say that all religions adopt the principle consistently. A religion may very well be inconsistent with its own fundamental principles in certain subsidiary dogmas maintained by it or by some of its adherents, as has certainly been

---

[1] See below, pp. 185 ff.

very much the case within Christianity, e.g. the doctrine of the damnation of unbaptized infants. Strange to say, people often have inconsistent attitudes without being worried by the inconsistency. My point is rather that it would not be right or rational to take up a religious attitude if we were not justified in regarding the postulates I have mentioned as expressing the truth. If Reality is not regarded as essentially good or dominated by a righteous purpose, the characteristic religious attitude is irrational in the sense in which it would be irrational to feel sympathy with an inanimate thing because it is burnt or to be afraid of the dark.

The central emphasis I have placed on value in the interpretation of religion is not necessarily contradicted by religions which stress the badness of this world, provided they assert or imply the supreme goodness of a more ultimate reality behind this evil world, though it must be remembered that the problem of evil becomes the more difficult the more evil is this world. Even Buddhism despite its pessimism about the world, and (in some forms) atheism, regards the world as at least governed morally, in so far as Buddhism is not viewed as a mere system of moral and emotional training without any sort of metaphysical outlook, as it is by some modern, and perhaps ancient, Buddhists, in which forms I should not call it a religion. For the law of Karma, which is regarded generally as an essential part of Buddhist thought, is a cosmic principle of justice decreeing that all men shall be rewarded or punished in proportion to their deserts, and even if we do not think the concept of punishment as retributive the highest, the doctrine of Karma is certainly one way, if an inadequate way, of conceiving the moral law as inherent in reality. Further, the punishment is treated not merely as an end in itself but as a means of purifying men's character and training them to lead a better life and eventually attain salvation, conceived as an escape from the necessity of rebirth because of our uncontrolled desires. The *Nirvana* of Buddhism has been regarded by most Buddhists not as annihilation but as a veritable heaven, described in negative terms only because it has been conceived as too much above anything we could know in our ordinary life to be describable in positive. To this heavenly goal Karma operating through the world process is held eventually to lead. We cannot therefore say that Buddhism does not make the world order fundamentally ethical, and at least in most of its forms it is optimistic and not pessimistic as to the ultimate destiny of man. The tendency to hold that all men will in the end be 'saved' was strong in Buddhism at a time when it hardly found expression in Christianity. What Buddhism does not give, at least in any of its important forms, is the conception of a single personal God, though in varieties toned down to meet the needs of the un-educated it introduced the conception of personality in the unsatis-factory form of a plurality of gods. But it is a serious objection to making the personality of God a completely essential concept for religion that we should then have to deny the title of 'religious' to so many devoted Buddhists and Hindus.

I am not of course maintaining that all religions teach the principle I laid down, but the consensus of mystics in different religions so contrary to appearances on the supreme goodness of Reality is remarkably strong. The scholar Friedrich Heiler includes among the seven areas common to the world religions of Christianity, Judaism, Islam, Zoroastrian Mazdaism, Hinduism, Buddhism, Taoism that 'there is a transcendent reality; that he is immanent in human hearts; that he is supreme beauty, truth, righteousness, goodness; that he is love, mercy, compassion; that the way to him is repentance, self-denial, prayer; that the way is love of one's neighbour, even of one's enemies; that the way is love of God so that bliss is conceived as knowledge of God, union with him or dissolution into him'.[1]

But what about more primitive religions? Now in considering these one would expect many inconsistencies especially when we reflect on the presence of such a glaring inconsistency even in most of older Christian teaching as the eternal damnation of heretics by a loving God, nor would one expect to find more than faint adumbrations of the principles behind the developed world religions of which I have been speaking. One must further remember that all uses of the conception of God or gods are not religious. Such a concept may be used in lieu of what we should now call a scientific hypothesis to explain particular phenomena. It is plain that the end of an immense proportion of primitive religious rites was simply material advantage and in that case the rite hardly comes under the heading of religion at all. It is no more religious in itself to sacrifice a virgin to a supposed

---

[1] F. Heiler, *The History of Religion as a Preparation for the Cooperation of Religions*, note 6, pp. 142–53, cited by B. Lonergan, *Method in Theology*, p. 109.

more powerful being in order to win a war than to drop bombs on a city, knowing you will kill such people, for the same end of winning a war.[1] And for a primitive man the action of a being more or less like himself but superior in power may seem the most intelligible way of explaining thunderstorms, so that in referring to the god he is really talking science rather than religion, in so far as he can be said to have science. But at least we must suppose there was mixed up with primitive religion the consciousness of the numinous of which Otto speaks, the first intimation of cosmic value. But according to some authorities we can go much further than this. According to such a distinguished anthropologist as Marrett 'the one axiom of savage religion is that gods are good'.[2] And many like Schweitzer have encountered when talking with primitive people the belief that above the strange and mixed plurality of gods their theology describes there exists a single supreme benevolent deity. I thought Marrett's view was now commonly dismissed by anthropologists as old-fashioned, but in a very recent major work on traditional African theology which deals with the beliefs of over 270 tribes and, according to the reviewer G. Parrinder gives 'the most complete overall coverage', an account of their predominant beliefs is presented which might do justice even to Christianity, God being 'both transcendent and omnipotent, just and loving, king and providence, father and mother, anthropomorphic and mysterious', though regular worship of the being is missing.[3] Even if such accounts are exaggerated, there must be in these religions very marked traces of the principle on which I have insisted for there to be evidence that made it at all plausible for any expert to speak as those I have quoted spoke. And this would be enough to bring primitive religion nearer to our developed religions than primitive science is to our science.

On the other hand the immoral character of the Greek and Roman gods is certainly surprising. But even the popular Greek and Roman religions of classical times had another side according to which the

---

[1] The act of human sacrifice might be religious in a genuine sense if it were motivated by a devotion to God which led a man to the mistaken belief that he ought to show it by giving as a kind of present to God what he himself valued most, as in the Abraham story.

[2] *Faith, Hope and Charity in Primitive Religion*, p. 118.

[3] John Mbiti, *African Religions and Philosophy*, reviewed in *Religious Studies*, vol. 7, no. 1, p. 91 (1971).

gods were especially associated with the upholding of the moral law. However they behaved themselves, they wanted men to behave well and punished them if they did not. This element is also very prominent in all the other early religions like the Egyptian which teach a judgement after death.

The tendency to introduce evil gods as well as good or assign to the gods mixed characters is not unnatural in view of the fact that there is much evil in the world as well as good. Indeed evil or capricious gods were liable to be regarded as more important for priestly functions than the good because men needed desperately to propitiate the bad gods who might otherwise harm them, while the desirability of worshipping the good was not so practically obvious. Another factor which helped to make it possible to ascribe actions to the gods which would be immoral if done by men has been, I should think, the idea that the gods were too high a class of beings to be bound by moral laws which were necessary for men but might be (illegitimately but not altogether unnaturally) thought of as inappropriately restricting the freedom of such superior entities. The Greek gods and others were no doubt regarded as in some way great and splendid without being particularly moral. I am talking here of the popular view. By the time of Plato the more educated Greeks had repudiated the immoral stories about them. Further, the more educated Greek or Roman could well be a monotheist with the help of the doctrine that the 'different gods' were really simply different manifestations of one and the same God, as is the case with the educated Hindu today in India. We may therefore think of the conception of value as dominant in the universe as one towards which the earlier religions were at least groping. But the main point I have been making is not this. What I have chiefly in mind is that, if this conception is not true or at least an approximation to the truth, anyone is adopting or implying a mistaken attitude if he is religious.

It may be objected that my definition of fundamental assumptions would not cover a religion which maintained belief in a finite externally limited God like the religion favoured by William James, or again Manichaeism, or perhaps Zoroastrianism. (I have heard there is a division of authorities here as to whether the principle of evil in Zoroastrianism is really independent, but is not an angel created by God but fallen as Satan in orthodox Christianity.) Though it cannot be said that such religions completely satisfy the religious aspirations of man, it must be admitted that they are religions after all. However, as far as I know, the believers in such religions have always envisaged the triumph of the good principle as a possibility and they have no doubt usually believed in it in faith. But if the good principle is ultimately going to triumph, then, the ultimately correct view of the world process will be one which makes it viewed as a whole supremely good. The religious attitude has merely been directed to the future, as it was also by Alexander in a rather different way and by the Jains. We must certainly regard the good as the preponderant factor in the world process if it is to triumph in the end. It is only a view of the world process as a whole that could give a correct idea of its value.

I have not made the belief in a personal God a necessary condition of religion, but this need not debar one from appealing to religious experience to justify the belief in question. The argument can take the form that, though some may think they have a genuinely religious attitude to a non-personal being, they are then really implicitly personifying the latter. For the religious attitude involves love, gratitude, adoration and other emotional attitudes which are intelligible only as attitudes towards a being viewed as personal, or if this should be too much to say about religious attitudes in general, one may contend that the most desirable, characteristic and developed types of religious experience involve just this.

An objection to holding the concept of a personal God to be fundamental to religion is that some mystics who possess an obvious genius for religion have an extraordinarily intense religious experience and have spent most of their energy developing it, yet decline to accept the belief in a personal God. But it is not impossible to have a synthesis of the two rival views. For on the one hand even orthodox Christianity does not claim without qualification that God is personal. One could hardly be more orthodox than St Thomas, yet he denied that any positive attributes are to be ascribed to God except in an analogical sense. The doctrine of the Trinity has itself been commonly interpreted by theologians as implying that God is not a person in quite the ordinary sense, being three persons in one. At the same time Christianity would assert that God contains in his nature all that is of positive value in personality, but exclude the limitations which for a finite person are involved in the notion. Now on the other hand the

mystics who believe in an impersonal God must mostly suppose that
the analogy to personality has at least some application, though they
would insist that it must not be taken literally. For they are constantly
applying it. Mystics in describing their experiences themselves constantly use terms drawn from the field of personal intercourse, and it is
impossible to see how they could express themselves without doing
this (unless they were talking only to other mystics and the mystics
had developed a language of their own). Even the most ' "transcendental" mystic is constantly compelled to fall back on the language
of love in the endeavour to express the content of his metaphysical
raptures.'[1] This does not commit the mystic to saying that God is a
person, but it does commit him to the admission that there is at least
some point in the analogy, and an analogy can have no point without
some degree of similarity in some respect.

This suggests that the difference between regarding God as personal
and impersonal may be looked on as a matter of degree. If we conceive
God as personal we have to admit that he cannot be personal in the
sense in which human beings are personal, which is knit up with their
limitations. But if we try to conceive God as impersonal, we still
have to talk in personal terms of him if only metaphorically, and
unless there is some similarity a metaphor is useless. We may indeed
say that God is 'superpersonal', but the trouble is that, if we try to
think of him as other than personal we cannot, unless we are vouch-
safed some extraordinary experience which very few people would
even claim to have, think of him as anything but sub-personal, as
some kind of unconscious vital force, intrinsically lower, not higher
than ourselves. For of the properties higher than personality which do
not involve personality we have no conception at all. Hence the
necessity of using the concept of personality, excessively inadequate
as it no doubt is, in talking and thinking of God. If we must use
personal terms on the one hand and on the other cannot take their
use as implying that God is personal in quite the same sense as men
are, it is then a question of degree how much we insist on the analogical or metaphorical character of the terms, so that there is no clear
dividing line between a personal and impersonal view of the deity.
This applies whether we think of God as transcendent, or as identical
with the whole, as did theologians influenced by absolute idealism.

[1] Evelyn Underhill, *Mysticism*, p. 509.

I must confess, however, that, while I fully admit the immense difference between the form personality takes in God and in us, I cannot see the sense of denying personality to a being who admittedly has consciousness, thought and will, and these properties seem to be definitely implied both by any argument for the existence of God and by the kind of relation to God which is normally claimed in religious experience. Indeed we should think of God as alone having personality in the full sense and human beings as having it only in a truncated sense. This should be so whether we think of God as the Whole or as creator not actually including the created world in his being.

But the denial of God's personality might be meant as the denial of God as anything but a name for the good there is in the world, and some modernist theologians have sometimes given the impression that that was what they were saying. Now if that is really all, the view put forward falls simply within the sphere of ethics and not religion; it only amounts to the recognition of the value of some parts of life. As we have seen, in order to pass from ethics to religion, we must conceive the good as somehow preponderant. It is certainly logically possible to hold this view without thinking of reality as controlled by a single good being, God. One might adopt a view like MacTaggart's by whom the ultimate reality was regarded as consisting of a plurality of spirits in perfect harmony, or we might think of the cosmic process as just governed by such laws that good must triumph in the end in such a way as to redeem the evil in the earlier stages, though this consummation was long delayed by the abuse of human free will. For since the correct way of evaluating a process must lie in considering it as a whole, if good wins in the end, and it wins in such a way that the good ultimately gained through overcoming the evil immensely outweighs it, we may be able to think of the process as a whole as supremely good, thus enabling us to retain what I took as the fundamental religious postulate. But the organization of the cosmos in such a fashion as to achieve this result does seem to require a mind.

I have suggested that the distinction between those who on the strength of their religious experience assert a personal God and those who, also on the strength of their religious experience, deny such a God, while admitting an impersonal God or 'Absolute', might be one of degree rather than of kind. But there is another very interesting possibility. It might be that the religious experience of one who affirms belief in a personal God and that of one, perhaps equally religious in his way, who has an intense mystical experience but repudiates this idea both have an appropriate real object but that the two objects are different. Philosophical theologians have again and again been involved in difficulties and controversies because of the tendency to identify God with Reality as a whole, since to make God anything less seemed to make him less than the greatest possible and so contradict God's metaphysical, though not necessarily his ethical, perfection, and because of that side of religious experience which points to immanence rather than transcendence. Yet this identification has been more vehemently opposed because it seemed incompatible with the notion of God's personality and raised difficulties involved in making human minds, even the worst, parts or aspects of God. Perhaps the solution may be that we have here a conflict between two modes of religious experience which does not arise because either is illusory but because they differ through each having a different object but are wrongly treated as relating to the same object. There may be a certain experience of the Whole such as the more 'mystical' mystics have in high degree and also a religious experience of a personal God who is supreme ground but not himself all of the Whole, since the beings of the created world are dependent products but not parts of him, and both experiences may be veridical without being incompatible with each other. And perhaps religion could not attain its fullest value without both. This suggestion opens up possibilities for a very interesting though very difficult discussion and may by separating the two concepts help to solve some antinomies about God.

There is however one form of mysticism which does not fit in easily with what I have been saying. This is the negative form of Zen-Buddhism and any other branch of mystical thought which seems to reduce the concept of the reality with which it claims to be in touch to a mere x by denying to it all affirmative predicates without distinction and without qualification. It might possibly be contended that there is still only a difference of degree between this and orthodox Christianity since St Thomas himself denies that positive attributes can be ascribed to God by us in any other than an analogical sense, but if so it is certainly one of the differences of degree that amount very much to differences of kind. A great difference is that, while Christianity makes it clear that even if it is the case that when we ascribe in a positive sense any attribute to God we are not talking adequately, we are talking a great deal less inadequately when we ascribe some than when we ascribe others. If this were not so, it would be no nearer the truth to say God is good than that he is evil, that he is omnipresent than that he is triangular, etc. But the very admission of such a distinction of degrees of inadequacy is incompatible with a purely negative attitude. I cannot myself see what value there could be in religion if its object were eviscerated of content as completely as it is by some mystics. Since to believe we must believe something, a mystic who carries the negative way to such an extreme is really agreeing with the complete agnostic, except that he attributes a very high value, though not a cognitive value, to the religious experience. But how the experience of what is conceived as nothing can be of value, intrinsic or instrumental, is very difficult to comprehend. Or is the value that negative Zen-Buddhists derive from their experience due to their really thinking of God or the Whole as supremely good though they deny it in words? It is not uncommon for a man to think as if something were the case which he does not admit even to himself really is the case. The attitude of Zen-Buddhists to the object of their mystic contemplation must surely at least include some kind of religious awe, and such awe must surely imply some apprehension of value in its object or some at least vague attachment of value, indeed supreme value to its object?

The mystic, even if he does not go to the extremes involved in the 'negative way', and the traditional religious teacher, have each a tendency to a fault of a very different kind. The fault of which traditional religion is in more danger is that of a rigid theological conservativism which is apt to find value only in one set of formulae and has in the past often led to the horrors of persecution. The fault to which the distinctively mystical thinker is liable rather to incline is that of condemning the good in this world as 'worthless trash'[1] and of making the main aim of earthly life the attainment of the bliss of seeing God in abstraction from the world. It is true that God, if he exists, and the 'heaven' which men may be expected to attain in some future state through their devotion to him and of which they may in some cases have premonitory glimpses even in this life must be

---

[1] Cf. W. T. Stace, *Time and Eternity*, p. 126.

conceived as incomparably more valuable than anything on earth, but this does not mean that the right course for the religious man in this present life is to sunder himself from the world. If what is is ultimately governed by values, which seems to me the fundamental doctrine of religion, this world too must have much value, and it must indeed be plain to the most elementary ethical and aesthetic consciousness that there are great values in it, whether or not one doubts if they outweigh the evil, due mostly, we may well think, to abuses of human free will, even though it be much less valuable than some state we may expect to attain in heaven. Archbishop Temple may very well have been right in saying that 'If God made all the world, an "experience" which consists in a "flight of the alone to the Alone" will be less rich in religious apprehension than the "experience" of dependence and devotion which is shared with countless others, and expresses itself through the symbolic use of common material things, and is always conscious of obligation to fufil in conduct the purpose of the God to whom adoration is given. Philosophers have tended to take the mystical experience as typical of religious experience because in it we find religion pure and simple. But if Theism is true, then "religion pure and simple" is a form of religion defective in itself and not specially pleasing to God.'[1] This agrees very well with the suggestion that the cognition of God has to be, at least normally, mediated, but I do not feel myself qualified to deny that some may be privileged to have a special mode of access of God not so mediated and that intervals in which they experience this may be of great value also in helping them to act better in relation to this world, and I do not suppose the archbishop would either. Only he would insist on the Christian principle that love of God must be combined with love of one's fellow men and object strongly, as I indeed also should, to any form of mysticism which led the 'saint' to despise and try to get rid of human attachments or to make the main aim of his life the selfish enjoyment for himself of mystical experience. But no doubt such abuses are the exception rather than the rule among mystics. Both traditional religion and mysticism have been indeed guilty not infrequently of acquiescing in social evils because it was thought that by comparison with eternity the sufferings of this life did not matter, a doctrine which the religious man may use to comfort himself in his

---

[1] *Contemporary British Philosophy*, ed. J. H. Muirhead, 1st series, p. 426.

own troubles but must not apply to his physical and economic dealings with other men. The Marxist doctrine that religion is the opiate of the people, though utterly inadequate and onesided, could not have gained the wide influence it has if religious bodies had not quite often abused their faith in the way indicated, as I understand the Church in the land where the Marxist revolution first broke out did in an especial degree.

Apart from a God, personal or impersonal, including the Whole or an aspect of the Whole, mystics generally seem to themselves to apprehend the following as characteristics of ultimate Reality: (1) immense value or even perfection, (2) a very close unity of all things, so close that the word 'identity' is frequently used instead of 'unity', (3) ineffability, (4) the strange quality to which Otto gave the name 'numinousness', (5) super-temporality. The last claim (5) must certainly be rejected if it implies that time is unreal in the sense that all propositions which contain time-determinations are false, for we can be much more sure of the truth of many common-sense propositions containing such determinations than we can of the interpretation of what the mystic claims to see, but it need not imply that.[1]

We should add that it is important to realize that a person who is not consciously religious and perhaps even denies the existence of God in so many words may well be conceived as unconsciously blest by communion with God through these various media.

I am not claiming to give any fully conclusive reason for accepting a religious point of view. In so far as it was accepted for a reason it would not be intuitive and so discussion of it would not fall in this chapter. In the next two chapters I shall consider arguments for such a view, and while they no doubt fall short of conclusive logical proof they have certainly seemed together with the religious intuition of men to constitute a case for the belief in God sufficiently strong to make it an enormous influence in civilization and particularly on a great number of the best type of men. This being so it cannot be denied that it is a very important task for the philosopher to analyse what this involves, what is to be said for it and whether it can be definitely shown to be wrong. But a question that will be asked is whether anything of the nature of verification is possible.

_____
[1] See below, pp. 279 ff.

Here I find very helpful the suggestions made by Price in the last chapter of his book, *Belief*. It is that the only adequate way of testing fairly whether the belief in God is true is to try to go on in your thoughts for a prolonged period as if it were true. This bears a similarity to the policy of the scientist who, when he is testing a hypothesis, goes on in his thoughts as if the hypothesis were true at least so far as to work out what conclusions would follow if it were true, with a view to verifying or refuting the hypothesis by observing whether these conclusions themselves are true. This must be carefully distinguished from believing or trying to believe that the hypothesis, religious or scientific, is true. There is no lie or attempt at deceiving oneself necessarily involved in the practice. The hypothesis need not be believed but only entertained and considered to the extent of enabling us to see what it would be like if it were true. The worst that can be said is that there is a risk involved that you may eventually come mistakenly to think something true when it is not true, because in carrying out Price's experiment you have too long treated it in your mind as if it were true. There is this risk present even for the scientist, though in a lesser degree. It is by no means unknown for even a scientist to become so attached to his pet hypothesis as to hold it true, even though the balance of evidence is by no means in favour of it, or has ceased to be if it ever was so. No doubt a safeguard is to vary your procedure and from time to time to try thinking as if your belief were not true. And there is a risk on the other side to the one I have mentioned, namely, that if we do not dwell on the hypothesis as suggested, we shall miss the opportunity of attaining a true belief of the greatest value and importance. Between the scientific and the religious case there is indeed the difference that to carry out our test we have to dwell far more persistently on our hypothesis in thought in the latter case; and also, as Price points out, the possibility of verification of the belief depends on subjective dispositions of an emotional kind. We must not press the distinction too far, however, as Price also points out: even the scientist is much less likely to succeed in confirming his hypothesis if he has no real interest in ascertaining whether it is true or false, since he will then be lacking in the motive needed to make the effort involved, and interest is an emotional disposition. Also a man's success as a historian may depend a good deal on his having the emotional dispositions required to understand the motives of people concerned in historical events. For instance, if he is utterly selfish, he may not grasp the possibility of being moved by a disinterested desire for the welfare of others.

But what will verification be like in the religious sphere if and when it occurs? It is pretty clear what it is like in the field of science and ordinary life, but in religion we are handicapped by the absence of any sense-impressions which could as such conceivably verify the existence of God. In an article written rather earlier Price thus describes the verification process in the religious field. 'In the seeking stage we were concerned with propositions all the time. We did not necessarily have to believe them, but our minds were continually occupied with them. In the meditational practices we tried to "realise" the import of these propositions; in the devotional practices we tried to act inwardly as if they were true. These propositions purported to describe someone. We were by no means sure that there was any entity to which these descriptions applied. But now we begin to have experiences of being somehow in personal touch with One whom these descriptions fit. It is no longer a matter of speaking (inwardly) *as if* we were addressing him in a loving and reverent manner, or of voluntarily "assuming" the role of one who does. Instead we find ourselves actually addressing him (inwardly, in the privacy of our own minds and hearts) and now we use these devotional expressions spontaneously without effort, just because it is the natural and appropriate thing to do. . . . We use these expressions because that is how we feel towards Someone in whose presence we seem to be, Someone who seems to be giving us a loving welcome now that we are there.'[1] The success of the verification will presumably depend on the relative number of people who, having tried Price's experiment, have attained assurance of God. There are no statistics available as to this; I should think it would be very high, but then the vast majority of people who have tried the method no doubt already believed in God, and while the confirmation of a pre-existing belief in God by a new and far more vivid degree of assurance no doubt gives some support to the God-hypothesis, it does not give by any means as much as would the attainment of it by those who before they tried Price's method had no belief in God. I do not think the fact that a very large number of people who say they believe in God no doubt

[1] *Faith and the Philosophers*, ed. John Hick, p. 21.

do not have this vivid sense of God's love and presence constitutes a serious objection, because it is very easy to hold the belief luke-warmly on authority and the religious man need not claim that it is easy to attain God's peace. Somebody might argue that a loving God would bestow it on everybody, but it may not be good for us to have blessings too easily without effort on our part. Scientific evidence too is not available to everybody but only to those sufficiently skilled to appreciate its significance and use it. We do not know that the pro-portion of people who followed Price's recommended course for a long period of time and yet failed to attain religious belief would not be smaller in proportion to the total number who try than the pro-portion of students who fail to qualify when taking a university course in science.

To those who would trace any results of this sort to 'autosuggestion' I can only make a reply similar to the one I have already made to the psychologists who argued that religious belief might be explained by irrational causes, a reply similar to that made by Price, namely, that unbelief can equally be explained by irrational causes. Atheism or agnosticism can be explained, if Price is right, by a lack of the desire to love God or experience his love which would result in the experi-ment not being tried or only tried in a most half-hearted fashion, and in many cases by a positive aversion to the idea of there being a God because God had been presented as a merciless taskmaster instead of a loving father, because religion was thought to be tied up with an established order thought to be unjust, or out of a fear of introducing 'unscientific' notions into one's thought.

The issue is one which every man must decide for himself without a clear external test. To some the belief in God, I have heard, presents itself, at least at times, with a force and certainty which hardly allows more scope for doubt than the normal man feels about the, also by no means strictly demonstrable, belief in other human minds. And others without having an absolute conviction of that degree of force may yet well be satisfied that the evidence is strong enough to enable them to hold the belief with a confidence sufficient to act as a major factor in supporting them in the trials and difficulties of life. But, as with all weighing of evidence that falls short of proof, the matter is subjective in the sense that there are no universally agreed standards by which we can measure its degree of force, and each individual can in the last resort after considering the views of others only fall back on the way the evidence appears to himself. For the individual himself the verification of an intuitive belief can only lie in the fact that when he thinks of it with as much impartiality and attention as possible it again strikes him as evidently true.[1]

[1] See Ayer, *The Problem of Knowledge*, p. 16 (Penguin ed., p. 20).

7

METAPHYSICAL ARGUMENTS FOR THE EXISTENCE OF GOD[1]

I do not think the existence of God can be provided in a strict sense, or even that the belief should be based mainly on argument, but I think that two at any rate of the three which have, since Kant at least, been classified as the traditional arguments for God have some force and are worthy of serious consideration. My view of the ontological argument is less favourable, and it surprises me very much that the argument has been revived not only by metaphysicians like Hartshorne[2] but even by a philosopher who has been so much influenced by the linguistic school as Malcolm.[3] As interpreted by them it is given at least a rather less implausible form by making the relevant property not existence but necessary existence. The objection that existence is not a predicate cannot, it is said, be applied to necessary existence, on the ground that the main reason for saying that existence is not a predicate is that a thing must exist before a predicate can be applied to it at all. The same obviously could not be said of necessary existence since many existent things do not exist necessarily. It also seemed obvious that a being whose existence was necessary would be more perfect than a being otherwise equally perfect whose existence depended on something else or who just 'happened to be'.

Now Malcolm and others have urged that the reply that this only shows that our idea of God must include the idea of existence if it is to be consistent and not that God really exists is rendered inappropriate by this amendment. For 'God necessarily exists' is an a priori proposition from its formal nature, as the word 'necessarily' indicates,

[1] This chapter makes use of my article published in *Religious Studies*, vol. 1, no. 1 (1966) and entitled *Two 'Proofs' of God's Existence*, also of my article 'Further Thoughts on the Ontological Argument' in *Religious Studies*, vol. 5, no. 1 (1969).

[2] See *The Ontological Argument*, ed. Platinga, pp. 123 ff.

[3] Op. cit., pp. 131 ff.

and an a priori proposition must either be self-contradictory or true. If the idea of a perfect being is not self-contradictory, Malcolm concludes, God must therefore exist, and while he does not see how the antecedent of this conditional can be proved, he makes rather light of that point, thinking that in view of its place in the language, thought and lives of men there can be no more of a presumption that the idea of God is self-contradictory than there is with the concept of seeing a material thing. Hartshorne's argument also skates too lightly over this.

I find more difficulty. Firstly, nothing has been done to overcome Kant's strongest objection to the proof of a necessary being, namely that there could not be any contradiction in something not existing, because you must ascribe conflicting attributes to something if you are to contradict yourself, but if you merely deny the existence of something you are not ascribing any attributes to anything, so there are no attributes to conflict. This seems to me a fatal objection to the view that the existence of God is logically necessary.

Malcolm indeed himself quotes this argument only to reject it,[1] but his reply seems to me to amount to a mere statement of the contrary without any attempt to counter Kant's precise logical point. Malcolm says that, 'when the concept of God is correctly understood, one sees that one cannot "reject the subject",' but why should we be unable 'to reject the subject'? Presumably because God's existence is by definition logically necessary, but this assumes that there is no contradiction in the supposition of a being of which this is true, and Kant, I think, has shown there is. No doubt there have been thinkers who have given intelligible grounds for saying that God could not be thought away. They may have been convinced by some form of the cosmological argument or by an argument that the existence of God is presupposed in our moral experience or in the whole of our knowledge, or they may have just had an intuitive conviction that God existed of which they could not get rid. But to say that one cannot deny the existence of God on any of these accounts is not to have recourse to the ontological proof, which seeks to show that there is an internal contradiction in denying God, not merely a contradiction with the rest of our knowledge. I therefore still hold to

---

[1] Op. cit., p. 148.

what was generally considered the most unchallengeable doctrine of
the prevailing empiricist and linguistic school, while criticizing them
on many other points, namely the doctrine that <u>there can be no
affirmative a priori existential propositions</u> in the primary and most
natural sense of 'existential'. As Malcolm points out, one can know a
priori such a proposition as that 'there exists a prime number between
17 and 20', but the sense of 'exist' here is quite different. Malcolm
retorts that the sense in which God exists is also quite different from
the sense in which a man exists. But unless we hypostatize numbers
in a Platonic fashion we must admit that propositions in pure arithmetic, even if the word 'exist' does occur in them, are purely hypothetical. And even if we do regard numbers in a Platonic fashion, we
shall not, as theists, wish to say that God exists only in the sense in
which abstract numbers do. Finally, we can only know that there
exists a prime number between 17 and 20 by considering the number
19 not only by itself but in relation to other numbers in the arithmetical
system.

   It will be noted that in arguing against 'the ontological proof' I
have not used the premise that existence is not a predicate. It seems to
me quite obvious that 'existent' fulfils a very different function from
almost all other words used as predicates and that this statement
would cover the predicate 'necessarily existent' since this includes
'existent'. No doubt both terms are predicates in the sense of being
usable as adjectival expressions, but this is only a grammatical matter.

   If we had any means of proving that the idea of a perfect necessary
being was self-consistent, we should then be confronted with an
antinomy, for we should then have proofs both that such a being
existed and that it could not exist. It could not exist by Kant's argument; yet it would have to exist since to say that its existence was
necessary would be to say that it must exist a priori, and we must
grant that any a priori statement must either be true or logically
absurd. But no such proof of self-consistency is available. There are
two arguments which have been used for this purpose in the past,
though not by Hartshorne or Malcolm (as far as I know), and it
seems to me that they are both completely fallacious. One is <u>the argument that self-contradictoriness is an imperfection and therefore could
not be present in the concept of a perfect being</u>. This argument seems
to me to involve a serious confusion of categories, which may perhaps

be brought out best in the following way. To reject a particular account of a perfect being because it included an imperfection is to say that, if such a being existed, it would not really be a perfect being, i.e. it would be inferior to some other conceivable beings. But if the imperfection alleged is self-contradictoriness, we cannot say this since there are no self-contradictory conceivable beings. Self-contradictoriness is not a defect of value in a thing, since it could not exist in anything. It can be regarded as a defect in a concept, but this does not mean that the concept or 'thought' is self-contradictory as a psychological event, for otherwise it could not occur; it can only mean that what is believed is self-contradictory and therefore not true. The argument seems thus to confuse an imperfection in a concept with an imperfection in a thing, which must be a fallacy, however we analyse the notion of 'concept'.

The second argument is the one used by Leibniz. He argues that a contradiction can only occur if one of the terms is negative, and that therefore the concept of a being made up of purely positive terms, as the concept of God is, could not be self-contradictory. Against him I should support Kant's view that positive qualities can be incompatible with each other, e.g. round and square, happy and miserable. Curiously enough, though Leibniz was very much of a metaphysician in the old sense, his crucial argument here is based on the very supposition that has since been used, more consistently, by positivists to disprove the possibility of a priori metaphysics, namely, that all a priori propositions are what Kant later called 'analytic' in the sense that the predicate or whatever is asserted of the subject is part of the meaning of the subject term. From this it would follow that in a negative a priori proposition, S is not p, S must include in its meaning not-p, and since the necessary incompatibility of two properties must be expressible in a negative a priori proposition, this means that, wherever two properties are incompatible, one at least of them must include a negative property. How Leibniz thought this analytic doctrine of the a priori could be reconciled with his own claim to derive a priori new knowledge in metaphysics I am quite unable to see.

Even if Leibniz's argument were valid in itself, it would not however save the ontological argument unless one could show either, in connection with the first form of the argument, that existence was a positive attribute without any negative element, or, in connection with the second, that necessary existence was so. How that could be done in either case I have no idea.

It has been suggested that necessary existence is the same as eternal existence, but the ontological argument plainly does not work unless 'necessary existence' either means or at any rate includes the notion of logically necessary existence. Only if this is so can we use the argument that the proposition that God necessarily exists must be logically a priori and so either self-contradictory or necessarily true.

The fact that God-words have always figured so much in human language may give a presumption in favour of their being really applicable to something, as Malcolm contends, but this certainly cannot be the basis of a strict a priori proof of existence as the ontological argument was intended to be. It appears to me that (a) there is no means of guaranteeing the consistency of a being that united all perfections in itself, (b) at least one perfection commonly ascribed to God, namely that of logically necessary existence cannot be the property of anything because it is internally self-contradictory, (c) the importance of God-language in human life is not even the basis of any presumption in favour of the ontological proof unless it can be shown that the definition on which the proof is based gives the only way of defining God.

The results for theology, we shall see, will not by any means be so disastrous as has been supposed by some. True, we have denied of God a perfection which he is often supposed to possess, and we can no longer say that God is the possessor of all perfections, provided we take these words in such a strict sense as to make them ridiculous. But surely when theologians ascribe all perfections to God they do not mean more than that he has all conceivable perfections, not that he has perfections which no being can have because they are self-contradictory in character. It is generally admitted by philosophers and theologians that it is no reflection on the perfection of God that he cannot do what is logically impossible. Any theist would, for instance, have to admit that it would be an additional perfection in God if he could produce all the good in the world without any of the evil, but we must admit that this is logically impossible if we are to be theists in spite of the problem of evil. And necessary existence I contend is also a perfection the possession of which would be logically impossible.

It has indeed been contended that a being who was not 'necessary' could not be legitimately worshipped, and Findlay once used this argument combined with the argument that no affirmative existential proposition could be logically necessary in order to prove atheism,[1] but he has since changed his mind so far as to admit that God may be a necessary being in some sense which would satisfy the demands of religion.[2] It seems to me indeed that a great part of the religious attitude to God, sufficient reasonably to retain the idea of worship, could be preserved even if we abandoned the notion of necessity altogether. God could still be regarded as supremely good and we could have full faith in his ultimate victory if we retained the notion of omnipotence, which we might do without supposing his existence 'necessary'. Still, it does seem to be a part of fully developed religious experience that God should be regarded as necessary in some sense. But need necessity here mean logical necessity? It is not at all plain that there is any special connection between logical necessity and worship. Logical characteristics do not seem to me suitable grounds for worship, and while a being who was logically necessary, if such a being be possible, and also possessed perfection in other respects might be regarded as a suitable object of worship, some of his perfections, for example love, would seem less good if logically necessary, and I doubt whether any would seem better. I do not see what could be meant by the existence of God being necessary unless at least his fundamental nature were necessary. On the other hand a 'God' who might die and so cease to exist would certainly be thereby a less suitable object of worship, similarly would a 'God' dependent on other beings for his existence or one who was not in an important sense the necessary condition without which nothing else could exist at all. In these senses at least the typical religious attitude to God certainly does imply necessity. I leave open the question what the arguments to which thinkers like Hegel and Collingwood have given the name 'ontological' prove. They certainly do not seem to me to prove anything like what I mean by God.

If we cannot establish the existence of God purely a priori, as the ontological proof was supposed to do, can we establish it by an

---

[1] *Mind*, vol. 57 (1948), reprinted in Flew and MacIntyre, *New Essays in Philosophical Theology*.
[2] *The Transcendence of the Cave*, pp. 86 ff.

inference from premises at least one of which is empirical? The two best-known arguments intended to do this are the cosmological (or first cause) argument and the argument from design.

Let us then turn to the 'cosmological proof'. In dealing with it I had better say at the start that I am not conscious of any intuitive awareness that the contingent entails a necessary being.[1] If this is indeed intuitively known, as has been claimed by some philosophers, the existence of God can be regarded as following a priori from the single empirical premise that I, or any other person or thing, exist, but I am afraid it is not so simple as this. As you have seen, I am very far from wishing to deny that there may be intuitive awareness of God in the sense of a trustworthy cognition otherwise than by sense experience or inference, and I do not think this claim incompatible with the cognition yet being mediated in some way by the natural world. But this religious consciousness has not usually been claimed to consist of insight into a logical connection, and unless it is this I do not see how it can provide the link without which the cosmological argument in this form must collapse. Can we then produce an adequate argument by appealing to the notion of cause without any intuitively accepted premise except the principle of causation itself?

The principle that everything has been caused is said to be vacuous, since it could be maintained to be true whatever the empirical facts by merely supposing that there was some unknown cause or causes which accounted for any irregularity that disclosed itself; but it is ridiculous to suggest that it does not make any difference whether there is causation or not, since without assuming its occurrence we could not predict what is likely or take any practical means to further our ends or avert disasters. But, though we must assume that there are some causes at work, the general principle that everything is caused is no longer generally considered self-evident, has no agreed demonstration and is thought by many deserving of downright rejection because it conflicts with human free will. But it may be replied that, even if a being once in existence may act in a way not completely determined by antecedent causes, surely even the staunchest indeterminist would find it hard to believe that the whole world came into being simply from nothing without any cause. But the assumption even of universal causality does not necessarily exclude

---

[1] Unless the question is begged in the definition of 'contingent'.

the possibility of the world having always existed in some form, if 'world' is used sufficiently widely to cover the whole spatio-temporal process so that this means that there always have been objects in space and time to which events occurred. That would indeed still be logically compatible with the world being dependent on God, but does not as yet provide a starting point for an argument for the existence of God. One way of providing such an argument would be indeed to contend that the world must have had a beginning on the ground that there would otherwise have been a vicious infinite regress of past events, and that, since a first event can have no cause in the natural order, its cause must be found in a being outside the natural order. But it would be risky to stake very much on this argument, I think. The notion that the world, i.e. the whole temporo-spatial series of changing things, had no beginning seems to me a very difficult one; but I must admit that the philosophers most skilled in investigating the antinomies of infinity usually do not now feel this difficulty and that Kant's attempt in the first antinomy to show that it is on a realist view insuperable failed.

But the real argument is this. We came to the conclusion in an earlier chapter that explanatory efficiency is the one fundamental criterion when we get beyond observation and logical necessity, and if this is so for science and ordinary life it is reasonable in the absence of a positive objection to apply this criterion also in metaphysics. Now, if one explains A by B, B by C, C by D and so on ad infinitum, nothing is ultimately explained at all. To find a real explanation one would have to go back to something that was evident in its own right, and so the explanation could not be satisfactory ultimately without the introduction of some being the existence of which could be held not to need a reason beyond itself. Such an explanation will be needed even if the world had no beginning but had always existed. For we should still need an ultimate explanation of the particular characteristics which things have. And this still would be the case even if it were true, as has been contended – I cannot make myself clear why – that it is logically inconceivable that nothing might have been in existence at all. It is not only the existence of the world that has to be explained but its qualities. Nor would it be an explanation in any ultimate sense if the existence of the 'first cause' were merely a fact without any reason for it. Yet the reason could not lie in something else; it would have to lie in the ultimate cause itself. Otherwise nothing is really explained at all for the same reason as that which makes it impossible to justify any statement unless I can come back to some premise which has to be accepted in its own right.

The notion of explanation to which I am referring is allied with a view of causation which was practically universal before Hume but is now not very widely held. A more common view is that 'causal laws' are simply statements of regular sequence or concomitance and do not either imply any sort of necessary connection or give any explanation why things happen. I think, however, that such a view of causation is liable to severe criticism on its own ground[1] without any reference to the problem of theism.

But quite apart from the question of the correct analysis of the concept of causation, the problem still forces itself on me – what is the reason why things are as they are? After all, it does seem incredible that the physical universe should just have 'happened' to come into existence even if this be reduced to the juxtaposition of some trillions of electrons and other minute particles. Does it not cry out for a further explanation of some kind? Even if causal talk in science is regarded as simply talk about regular sequences, this question remains. It has often been said to be meaningless, but I cannot see any ground for thinking it so. The verification principle from which the meaninglessness of such enquiries was originally deduced has admittedly not been proved but is merely methodological, even according to most of those who assume it in their reasonings.

If the question is once asked, is there any possibility of its being answered, and must the answer be in terms of theism? This turns on the concept of a 'necessary being' or *causa sui*. It must be admitted that a second kind of 'causation' different from causation in the natural world, however we understand this causation, is here being alleged; but this is no serious objection if the second kind is needed to supplement the first and make it intelligible. God could not be cause of himself in the sense in which a physical thing or event could be cause of something happening in the world, but the contention is that ordinary causation could not give an adequate ultimate explanation

---

[1] See my *Idealism*, 4 sect. 3 and *Non-Linguistic Philosophy*, pp. 131 ff.; also G. F. Stout, *Proceedings of the Aristotelian Society*, vol. 14 (1935), pp. 46 ff.; B. Blanshard, *Reason and Analysis*, chapter 11.

unless it were supplemented by this other kind. No real explanation is given by an infinite regress of explanations, and what is needed to end the regress must be something that provides its own explanation. I should have no objection to the terminology being altered and 'cause' in the second sense being replaced by 'ground'.

So according to the 'first cause' argument no explanation of the world is possible unless there is a being that explains itself. But how could there possibly be such a being? A being would be 'necessary' in terms of this argument as usually understood if it were a true a priori proposition that the being existed. But there are grave difficulties about supposing that any proposition that something exists could be logically a priori. It is not merely that we do not see how such a proposition could be a priori; it seems as if we see that it could not be a priori.

I do not think it 'blasphemous' to worship a being who is not logically necessary, and I do not think that it derogates from the perfection of God if he does not possess perfections which it is logically impossible that he should possess; but I must admit that the concept of God for most philosophers who have reflected on it deeply does include necessity in some sense as an ingredient. The existence of God, it is felt, could not be merely a contingent fact; and, if it were, God could not be regarded as the completely supreme being but only as the being that *happened* to be strongest. But, I ask, need the necessity be logical necessity? Might not God be necessary in some sense other than that in which his necessity would mean that there was an internal contradiction in denying his existence? After all, it is not claimed by religious people that they see the internal logical necessity of God's existence unless they accept the ontological proof, and if they do that they are relying on a (bad) argument and not on religious intuition.

But before we discuss this topic further, let us consider another, even more vital point. Suppose that there exists as first cause a necessary being. How do we know that this being is to be identified with God as ordinarily conceived? How do we know or what reason have we even to surmise that this first cause and necessary being is a supremely good, wise, loving spirit possessed of all compatible and logically possible perfections in the fullest conceivable degree? The common line of argument which may be popularly expressed by saying that the cause must be at least as great as the effect could not establish more than that God is at least as good and wise as the best and wisest man, which, though comforting as far as it went, would certainly not be enough for most theologians, even apart from any doubts there may be about the axiom as to causation used in the argument. Descartes' attempt by reference to the idea of God to prove the existence of a perfect cause of this idea of a perfect being is rarely defended nowadays and invokes premises which do not seem self-evident.

As far as I can see, there is only one line of argument which could possibly establish the desired conclusion when combined with the 'first cause' argument. This would be the argument, if such an argument be possible, that for a being to be necessary that being would also have to be perfect. Such a proposition is not disproved by the fact that the ontological argument has failed to prove its converse, but I am not at all clear as to what I suppose is the orthodox argument for it, namely, that any being that was not perfect could not be a necessary existent because then its existence might be prevented by that of another being. We must not be misled by the metaphor of a number of unrealized essences trying to jostle their way into existence and the strongest prevailing in the struggle, a metaphor which is certainly suggested by the classical formulations of the argument with which I am familiar. But I find it difficult to understand the argument when we have eliminated metaphors like this. If there is a necessary being at all, it seems to me antecedently more plausible to suppose that the most perfect being conceivable should be necessary than that any imperfect being should have this position, but I should be very grateful to any philosopher who was able to state the argument that this was so in a more acceptable form than any I have encountered. But I myself feel more at ease in approaching the problem from a different angle.

So I shall now ask the question: if the universe as a whole is to be rationally explicable, as is claimed in the 'first cause' argument, what sort of explanation could it have? It is no ultimate explanation to refer it to God unless the existence of God is self-explanatory in a way in which the existence of no other being could be. Otherwise either the principle on which the cosmological argument depends, namely the principle that there must be an ultimate reason for the existence of anything, has to be abandoned, or another cause has to be posited beyond God. Without an answer on this point the child's question –

What is the cause of God? – is sufficient to make the argument collapse. And if we hold to the position, as I think we must, that an affirmative existential proposition cannot be logically necessary, an explanation in terms of logical argument is not possible. What ultimate explanation could there then be for the existence of the world? If we are to meet the demand of the human intellect that there should be a reason, we seem to need a reason of such a kind as will give an explanation of existence without making the non-existence of anything logically self-contradictory. There remains only one alternative, as far as can be seen, which might do this, namely an explanation in terms of values. In that case God's existence will be necessary not because there would be any internal self-contradiction in denying it but because it was supremely good that God should exist. It is not indeed evident to us a priori that the best possible being must exist, but a universe determined by values would certainly be rational in a very important sense in which a universe not determined by values would quite fail to be so, and the hypothesis that complete perfection does constitute an adequate ground for existence does seem to be the only one which could make the universe intelligible and give an ultimate explanation of anything, thus satisfying our very important third criterion of truth.

A contemporary philosopher who started on very different lines, J. N. Findlay, has said that 'such an argument seems to me to have force, and force of that ultimate, notional kind that deserves the name of "logical". Despite all that I have read about the emotive or prescriptive or non-natural character of ethical utterances or their content, I cannot call anything good or fitting in full seriousness, without thinking it likely, and intrinsically likely, that even *things* will show some tendency to conform to what I feel to be good and fitting rather than the opposite. I call the likelihood in question "intrinsic" because it is neither based on experience nor capable of being removed by experience, though experience may possibly increase it . . . I find in my deepest thought a persistent linkage between the "should" of likelihood and the "should" of value, so that I cannot conceive, except facilely and superficially, what either would mean without the other.'[1] I should not be nearly as sure as Findlay that we can see the connection positively and should not call it 'logical' but rather

[1] *Ascent to the Absolute*, pp. 98–9.

approach the conclusion less directly by reflecting that the universe needs explaining and value provides the only way of explaining it. To quote Archbishop Temple, 'the chain of causes is not self-explanatory . . . There is in fact only one principle which is self-explanatory; it is Purpose . . . If there is a principle which is accepted by the mind as self-explanatory it is justifiable to adopt it provisionally and see what happens. Now there is one such principle – Purpose. When in tracing any causal nexus we reach the activity of a will fulfilling a purpose with which we ourselves sympathize, we are in fact satisfied.'[1]

We thus seem to have come back after all to the conception of the ontological proof that the most perfect being must exist, except that I cannot accept any formal proof such as that argument offers, and should not call the necessity 'logical'.

If God's existence is determined by values, the existence of everything ultimately is. The problem of evil indeed starkly confronts us here, but so it does all theism. This problem I shall discuss in a later chapter. It should of course be noted that my suggestion is not that the universe is perfect but that God is.

The cosmological argument in the form proposed will, if valid, clearly establish the perfect goodness of the supreme being, which I do not see how any other form of the cosmological proof could do. If any being exists on account of its value, the most perfect possible being must. And like the ontological argument it is in accord with the widespread conviction that God's existence is not a contingent fact and that his existence is made necessary by his perfection.

While it has been common enough in the writings of theologians and philosophers of religion to derive the necessity of God's existence from his perfection, perfection in such arguments has commonly been conceived in a metaphysical way which seems to me to present great difficulties. It has been regarded as involving the inclusion in God's nature of all 'positive attributes', but in that case we can avoid assigning to God evil as well as good attributes only if we take the view that evil attributes are negative. I do not myself regard this view as a tolerable one. Perhaps evil is always the *consequence* either of the lack of something good or, as in moral evil, of the mal-arrangement of intrinsically good or at least indifferent elements in the nature of

---

[1] *Contemporary British Philosophy*, ed. J. H. Muirhead, First Series, p. 418.

certain finite beings, but this consequence is itself surely often something very evil in a very positive sense. Bereavement or blindness is just a lack of something that the subject has had or might have, but the misery caused may be very positive indeed. I do not see how all evil can be called negative in any reasonable sense unless pain can be regarded as just the absence of pleasure, which it obviously is not. And can malice be regarded as a desire in itself indifferent in respect of value but just out of place or excessive in its quantity in relation to other elements in a man's nature? I think not. But if God is the bearer of all positive attributes and we cannot maintain that the evil attributes are only negative, God will have to be conceived as hating men as well as loving them, as being unjust as well as just and that in an infinite degree, thus carrying in his being a logical contradiction of the most flagrant character.

This illustrates a possibility which, even if my objection against the notion of evil attributes as negative should rest on a misunderstanding, cannot in any case be eliminated. How can one in any case possibly know that some positive attributes might not be incompatible with each other unless we knew the nature of all possible positive attributes? If any were, this would make the notion of a being with all positive attributes one that was internally self-contradictory in character. Qualities which present themselves to us in experience as positive, e.g. different shapes and colours, certainly can conflict. Of course shapes and colours would never be admitted by the theologians to be attributes of God, but our experience does seem to make it quite clear that on principle attributes can conflict in respect of their positive nature since one can exclude another of the same kind, and if so how do we know that this might not apply to attributes that otherwise could be applied to God? Indeed, going further, is it even thinkable that a being could have some positive attribute without excluding another except as regards attributes so abstract and general as to apply to everything? Further, it is not at all clear in what sense God could be said to have all the positive attributes there are, if God is not, for example, coloured and triangular, as of course nobody would say he was. Triangularity and even colour are surely given in experience as the attributes of something, if only of sense-data, and they are surely positive qualities and not the mere absence of some quality. Perhaps I have missed here the precise sense in which the philosophers I have been criticizing used the terms, positive and negative attributes, but at any rate they need to make it a great deal clearer than, as far as I know, they have yet done if they are to escape these objections.

It looks therefore as if the traditional definition of God as the sum of all perfections ought to be revised. 'God' might be defined as the most perfect logically possible being, and then if all perfections are not compatible God would not possess them all. This may sound very shocking, but if we take seriously the notion that God includes in his nature all perfections there are, are we not really committed to pantheism, which also is very shocking to the orthodox? The traditional metaphysical conception of God in terms of perfections has always seemed to me highly obscure. I suppose the usual answer to the objections about for example, colour would be that God somehow includes all that is of positive value in beautiful colours without himself being coloured, but the beauty of a rose seems to me quite inseparable from its colour and spatial form so that, if you took these away you would have destroyed the particular beauty of the rose, even if you had substituted a better, 'spiritual' beauty. If we mean by the phrase 'all perfections' every positive quality there is, then what is left outside God is simply a collection of negatives, i.e. really nothing; even if we mean only that God possesses in the supreme degree every kind of value possessed by anything, the difficulty arises that a non-physical beauty must be different in kind from a physical. But, even if no single being could include all perfections, there might still be a most perfect possible being. There may be some values, for example physical beauty, moral struggle, religious faith (as opposed to knowledge) which could not from the nature of the case be realized in God but only in imperfect beings, and that might even be the reason for our creation, because the more kinds of values there are realized the better, though our values are far inferior to God's. The religious attach great importance to the value of worship, yet God could not worship himself, at any rate in anything like the sense in which he may be worshipped by men. Unless we identify God with the whole, we must admit, shocking as it may seem, that God is finite in the sense of not including in his being everything that is and therefore being limited, if ultimately only self-limited, by the beings other than himself which he has brought into existence.

Another reason is that we cannot know, and I doubt whether there is any reason to suppose, that there is a maximum degree to all positive qualities, and with any which do not possess such a necessary limit we seem to have no alternative but to conceive God's perfection as consisting in the further and further development of qualities in an unending time[1] (or the correlate of time in God's experience, whatever that may be).

In traditional philosophical arguments about God too much stress, I think, has been laid on the metaphysical and too little on the ethical attributes of God. The thing that matters in religion and makes it worth having is that it tells us that the being on whom everything depends is absolutely and supremely good. The doctrine of the omnipotence of God is of great importance because it matters very much whether we can regard the supremely good being as in control of everything or as fighting a war in which he might well be defeated, but I do not see how any quality could give a title to worship except supreme goodness. The power and awesome mystery of God have often assumed the centre of the stage, but while a fully satisfying religious view does require the omnipotence of God, and a being so much above us as God is must be deeply mysterious to us, the worship of power as such is not good but evil and to worship mystery as such is to worship something simply because we do not know what it is like. I sound rather Kantian in this, but I do not like Kant wish to make religion of value only as a means to morality. If God exists, the experience of communion with God must have value in its own right and not only because it makes those who enjoy it better morally. But it can only have this value because of the supreme goodness of God.

I may still be blamed for having after all admitted an a priori affirmative existential proposition when I suggested that it might be the case that God's existence depended on his supreme goodness. Such a proposition would plainly not be empirical, and it would plainly also be affirmative existential. But it escapes what seems to me the main objection to the admission of logically necessary affirmative existential propositions in that it is not claimed there would be any contradiction in denying it. It remains the case, I think, that we cannot actually see it to be true – perhaps to see that, as St Thomas held, we must wait for the 'beatific vision' in 'heaven' – and all I can say in its

---

[1] Cf. Hartshorne, *Man's Vision of God*, pp. 98 ff., 271 ff.

F

defence is that it is the view which comes nearest to providing a rational explanation of things. I do not think this is by any means a negligible argument in its favour, although a great host of theologians who have attempted to tie religion to irrationalism will look upon it as a positive objection. As I have said earlier, one of our chief criteria of truth in science and elsewhere is explanatory ability.

There remains the question which not only Barthian theologians but positivistically inclined philosophers will press – have we a right to demand a reason for things? Have we a right to assume that the view which seems to come nearest to providing us with a rational explanation of the universe is likely to be any nearer the ultimate truth than a view which does not? The most plausible alternative to theism is not any rival metaphysic but agnosticism. But if explanatory ability is a criterion of very major importance in science and in ordinary life, as is indeed the case, I do not see how, unless the possibility of metaphysics is denied on principle, as I have tried to show in chapter 2 it cannot be, we can deny that the same criterion is also relevant in that sphere. And the use of this criterion seems to lead straight here to the explanation of the universe by values, since there is no other way we can conceive as even possible of explaining it.

It is objected that the 'first cause' argument depends on an illegitimate extension of the concepts of cause and explanation from the part to the whole. It does not necessarily follow, it is said, that because science must ask for the explanation of elements in the whole by other factors within the universe, therefore the universe as a whole could be explained. But it seems to me on the contrary harder to conceive that the world as a whole and so everything in it should have originally come into existence out of the blue without any explanation than that particular events in it should not have been caused.

It has further been objected that, while to explain anything you have to presuppose something as ultimate relatively to it, it does not follow that there must be some being absolutely ultimate by which everything is to be explained, any more than it follows that, because in a dictionary no word can be explained except in terms of other words, there is one and only one set of ultimate words in terms of which all other words must be explained, or that because an object can be spatially located only by reference to other spatial objects therefore there are particular objects which must be the ultimate landmarks by reference to which everything else has to be located.[1] But this objection overlooks the differences between the logic of explaining in the sense of giving reasons and the logic of defining in dictionaries or locating in space. With both the latter operations it is necessary and sufficient that a start should be made with something given in experience as a brute fact. To use a dictionary it is enough to have first an ostensive definition of some words by reference to what is directly given in experience in some way, and in order to locate objects in space it is enough to know empirically the spatial position of some other objects already known to us by reference to which we can locate them. But an explanation why something is true by reference to something else which is itself unexplained is not a satisfying explanation, though it might be the best we can have, any more than it would be a proof of anything to show that it followed from a proposition which was neither self-evident nor proved.

But, it is retorted, to ask for the cause of E is to ask for something outside E which explains E, and there is nothing outside the whole, so the category of cause cannot be applied to the whole universe. But there is an ambiguity here: the objection can apply only if by 'the whole universe' is meant everything whatever that there is, and this will include God if God is. Theists however do not ask for a cause outside God to account for God, but at the most say that God is 'his own cause'. And since it is far from obvious that the physical universe is or could be its own cause, there is no absurdity in asking for a cause beyond itself to account for it. Neither is the explanation given one which puts God inside the natural order. He is conceived as the ground of that order as a whole, and therefore could not be put inside it.

It may be objected that in invoking the value principle to give the ultimate explanation I have contradicted the principle that the existent can only be explained by the existent, a principle on which advocates of the cosmological proof, like St Thomas, usually insist. But, if so, this principle is really by implication already denied when a philosopher says that God is a necessary being, for this implies saying that there is a necessary a priori proposition from which God's existence follows, whether he claims to know it directly a priori or not himself.

A specially strong objection is felt today against making 'essence

---

[1] V. Bambrough, *Reason, Truth and God*, pp. 94 ff.

prior to existence', and it will be objected that my view falls into this error. But precisely the reverse is true in the orthodox sense of 'prior'. If p entails q, it is q that is prior to p and not p that is prior to q. So if the principle that the most perfect being must exist be true a priori – let us call it the value principle for short – since it entails that God exists, this would exclude and not imply the priority to God of the value principle. If essence entails existence, it will be because essence cannot subsist without being realized in existence. Somebody who argued, as many have done, that there must be a God because the laws of logic and ethics could not have being except in a mind is saying that these laws entail God, but he certainly would not be accused of therefore making them prior to God. On the contrary he would be saying, rightly or wrongly, not that God could not exist without their being true but that they could not be true without God existing. In fact it seems to me that essence cannot be prior to existence in the sense under discussion, because the mere existence of something could never imply the truth of an a priori proposition.

However there is another sense of 'prior' in which p is prior to q where p is the reason of q in the sense of *ratio essendi*. The applicability of this sense of 'prior' to anything is often ignored today and might be denied by some (except in some cases of causal connection), but hardly by anybody who regarded it as a legitimate question to ask what is the reason of the universe, and if the legitimacy of such a question is granted at all we must hold that what is the reason of q is in some sense prior to q, whether we are talking of propositions or existences. Almost all theists will hold that God is prior to the world in this sense.[1] 'Prior' must of course be distinguished from 'temporally prior'; this could be the case even for a theist who thought that there was no creation in time and the world was eternal. But my view will give offence as seeming to make in this sense something else, a principle, prior to God. However this objection, if it is an objection, will apply equally to any view which regards God as a necessary being, for if he is so a principle holding a priori that characteristics we attribute to God must be exemplified in existence will be a reason for God's existence and therefore prior to the latter in one

---

[1] The great majority will hold that he is also prior to the world in the other sense because they will think that, while God need not necessarily have created a world or at least such a world as exists in fact, the world could not have existed without God.

sense. But this is very different from saying that there is something outside God which makes him exist. A principle is not a foreign existent outside God, and to assert the principle is simply to say that God's nature is such that he is completely self-sufficient and must exist. It is further equally true that the principle could not be realized in existence and therefore could not be a true principle if God did not exist.

Let us now turn to the third argument of 'natural theology', usually called *the argument from design*. We must grant at once, as Kant insisted, that this argument cannot establish an omnipotent, omniscient, or perfectly good God, or even a creator as opposed to an 'architect' who made the world out of given material, or for that matter a single God as opposed to a plurality of gods (provided at least the latter were, unlike some gods of polytheists, sufficiently in agreement to produce a unified plan). But to have good grounds for thinking that mind was at the basis of the material world, even without a proof of these additional doctrines of normal theism, would be something of value in itself and would give additional confirmatory support to other arguments or claims to intuition which themselves went further. It is significant that Kant, and even Hume,[1] were greatly impressed with the force of the argument, though according to either of their epistemological doctrines it ought as metaphysical to have had no force at all.

It must be fully grasped from the beginning that what the argument of design will support, if anything, for a modern thinker is not the rejection of the evolution theory, but the view that the processes of natural selection are somehow controlled by a superior mind either through arranging the initial conditions from which the rest of the process (till the rise of free will at or near the human level) follows inevitably, or in some other way which it is beyond our capacity to understand. Evolution should be regarded by the theist as the way in which God has worked, and he need not suppose himself necessarily committed to postulating extra divine interpositions in the process by way of miracles in order to save himself from naturalism, though in some sense of 'miracle' the whole process will be for him a miracle.

---

[1] See Hume's *Dialogues concerning Natural Religion*, pt. iii. We should note that Philo is said to be 'embarrassed and confounded' by Cleanthes' argument here and that Demea is made to intervene irrelevantly in order to save him from having to reply.

There is a generally prevailing misapprehension of the argument from design which must be corrected before its force can be properly assessed. It is commonly regarded as an argument from analogy, and I must agree with critics like Hume that, regarded as such, it is distinctly weak. It would then take the form: living organisms are like machines, in our experience machines are always designed by an intelligence with an end in view, therefore living organisms are probably designed by a mind. But it is objected that the two likenesses on which the argument depends are neither of them at all marked. Organisms are not very like machines, and the mind posited must be admittedly conceived as very different indeed from human minds. This criticism of the analogy argument must be regarded as serious (even though the first analogy has been strengthened by the recent comparison of the brain to computers). As C. D. Broad has pointed out, there is the further objection that in the realm of our experience all machines have been made not only by a mind but by an embodied mind, and therefore if the analogy is to be used to establish a mind that created the world it will lead equally to the conclusion that that mind is attached to a body, and then by the same analogy another embodied mind will have to be supposed to create that body and so on *ad infinitum*.

But I think the force of the argument from design depends mainly on its being an argument from inverse probability rather than an argument from analogy. No doubt analogy enters into it since we cannot think of God at all without using an imperfect analogy with the human mind, but to this extent it would enter into any conceivable argument for the existence of God. This is not enough to make the argument itself one from analogy. The sense in which it has been said to be an argument from analogy is that it is of the type: A is like B, B is related by r to C, so A is related by r or, it would be better to say by some relation like r, to something like C. But this is a mistake because the argument in the sense in which it mainly appeals to people depends not on the concept of likeness but on the concept of probability. This is not altered by the fact that, when you have reached the conclusion, you have to use analogy in thinking of it, any more than the cosmological argument of St Thomas was rendered an argument by analogy because it was admitted that you could only think of God by using analogies. As I understand it, the argument from design is an argument that to posit a purpose in our account of the universe is the only way of explaining certain phenomena which will remove the stupendously unlikely coincidence that they should show all the characteristic features of being apparent results of purpose without there being any purpose behind their production. Whatever the defects of Paley's work, this is at least brought out well by his illustration of the watch. It does seem fantastically improbable that living bodies should show such extraordinarily detailed adjustments to ends as they do unless some explanation of this can be given, and it cannot be explained by ascribing the adjustments to the purposes of minds inhabiting the living bodies in question. Human beings, let alone animals, have no idea as to how they, for example, do their digesting, or whatever idea they have of it is derived from scientific researches which were only initiated hundreds of thousands of years after they had started digesting. If we hold that the empirical facts adduced by the argument from design have no need for any special explanation, shall we not be acting like someone who on finding a number of fallen leaves in autumn arranged in such a way as to make an intelligible discourse was quite content to say that they had been blown into their positions by the wind and did not accept the phenomenon as any ground for supposing that an intelligent being had arranged them thus? Since they must fall in some order or other, it is logically and scientifically possible that the wind might have blown them all into the positions they occupied, but still no one would for a moment accept this suggestion as reasonable.

A number of criticisms have been directed against this argument, of which the most serious in my opinion is that the establishment of the theory of evolution has now provided an alternative explanation of the appearance of purposiveness in nature, thus cutting away the ground for the postulation of a designer. This objection I shall discuss last. A more general argument has, however, been used to the effect that any particular arrangement of matter whatever is bound to be immensely improbable, as with any particular distribution of properly shuffled cards. But the improbability on which the argument from design is based is not the improbability of the existing arrangement of matter in itself, but the improbability of a chance arrangement which fitted in so well with certain purposes. It would be irrational to accuse a man of cheating at cards merely because the odds were many millions

to one against his getting just the cards he did get, since this would
apply to any distribution of cards whatever, but the accusation would
take a very different guise if the distribution involved all the trumps
being in his hand several times running. Yet the odds against this
happening by chance, fantastically high as they are, can be shown to
be less than the odds against the existence of such a vast number of
bodies apparently purposive in such intricate detail being due to mere
chance. If an observed distribution fits in with what a mind could have
contrived in order to fulfil a certain purpose and the odds are immensely against this having occurred by chance, surely it would in
any other context make it extremely probable that the distribution
was the result of purpose unless there were some conclusive objection
to this. The monstrous unlikelihood of what otherwise would be a
fantastically improbable coincidence can be removed by the simple
assumption that the apparently purposive arrangements are really
brought about for a purpose.

It is objected, however, that while we can use an argument from
inverse probability in favour of a particular hypothesis about something in the world, it does not follow that we can use it about the world
as a whole. But to say that the circumstances are different from those in
which an argument is generally used does not vitiate the argument
unless it can be quite specifically shown that the circumstances are
different in a way *relevant* to the logic of the argument. As far as I
know, in the present case the only argument used to show this has
been that the notion of probability cannot be applied where the class
of thing concerned has only one member. But it seems to me that the
fact that there is (by definition) only one universe is quite irrelevant
to the argument, based as this is, not on the universe regarded as a
whole, but on certain things in the whole, namely living organisms.
The universe as a whole is involved only because the explanation of
the purposive features of these things suggests a metaphysical hypothesis about the whole universe, since the organic depends closely on
its inorganic environment, and it has never seemed plausible if you
admit God at all to think of him as having made only part of the
universe and not the whole. The fact that there is only one universe
would certainly be no objection to our admitting that it is very
improbable that, however long people went on playing bridge, they
would without manipulation of the cards in any considerable pro-

portion of cases get all the spades in one hand, and I do not see how the fact that there is only one universe would make it any less improbable that molecules should have come together to form such complex organs as our brain.

Further, it has been objected that in an infinite time (and space, if space should turn out infinite after all) there is room for an infinite number of possible combinations, and that therefore it is not, even apart from a designing mind, improbable that there should be worlds or stages in the development of a world which display great apparent purposiveness. Given enough time an army of monkeys strumming on typewriters at random would according to the laws of probability be likely to produce all the books in the British Museum. There is, I think, no scientific evidence that matter has been changing for an infinite time or extends infinitely in space, but if anything the contrary, and I doubt very much whether even the generous time allowance given by the 'big bang theory' of current astronomy would be anything like sufficient to remove the improbability of there being so many purposively organized bodies in the world, at least if we do not appeal to natural selection to lessen this improbability, a point which I shall discuss later in the chapter. But if we were satisfied that matter had existed and gone on changing for ever, would we conclude that the presence of leaves on the ground in such positions as to make an intelligible book no longer provided evidence in favour of the supposition that somebody had deliberately arranged them there? If not, why should this assumption overthrow the argument from design? Granted the world as it is today, it is still a much less improbable hypothesis that it should really have been designed than that it should constitute one of the infinitely rare stages which showed design in an infinite series of chance universes. Similarly about space. It may be replied that we could not have lived at all except at such a stage, but the point just is that it is antecedently extremely unlikely that there should be conditions now under which we or any beings, similar to us could live. The objection shows that it *might* be so, but leaves it most unlikely. A person who uses any of the objections mentioned against the argument from design should be asked whether he would still regard the argument as having no force if this were a world in which all things most obviously went splendidly well, if everything without exception seemed designed for the benefit of high-quality life, if we were so adapted that we never fell ill and that some mechanism always came into force to save us when we were threatened by an accident. For the objections he has so far given would apply, if at all, whatever the amount of apparent design there was in the world.

I do not think we can do justice to the empirical facts adduced by talking of 'unconscious purpose'. This notion seems to me unintelligible or outright self-contradictory unless it means either simply that things go on as if there were a conscious purpose without there really being one or refers to the presence in a conscious mind of a purpose which that mind has not introspectively discriminated though it was present as an element in his total experience (or perhaps one which for reasons such as those on which psychoanalysts dwell he could not discriminate). In the former sense it does not solve but merely restates the problem, in the latter it would already presuppose a conscious mind. To explain by natural selection is not to explain by unconscious purpose but to explain without purpose at all. If the coincidence between the mode of structure of animal bodies and the interests of the animals is to be explained by purpose, the purpose would have to involve foresight into the effects of a certain structure and a decision accordingly to develop this structure, and that certainly implies a conscious mind and one far above the animal level or the level of intelligence of a baby (or embryo) when the lines of structure of its body are being laid down in its growth. Indeed the complication of the human body (or any animal body) is such that this would be beyond the level of intelligence of even the cleverest human engineer. To talk of a purpose which is not present in any mind seems to me as unintelligible as it would be to talk of triangles which had no extension. Spinoza sought to explain the appearance of design by reference to necessary laws without presupposing a designing mind, but even if we supposed, as Spinoza seems to have done, that the laws could be deduced by some kind of superhuman logic, it would still be a most incredible coincidence if they just happened to fit in with results that might have been expected if purpose had been at work. There is nothing I can see in the nature of logic as such that makes it any more likely to lead to results which fulfil purposes than would the mechanical alogical laws posited by the modern physicist (other than the purpose to reason logically). If on the other hand we suppose mind in thinking of the origin of things, mind by its own intrinsic nature is teleological and there is no question of coincidence.

It is objected against the philosophical use of arguments from inverse probability that the probability of a hypothesis based on such an argument is always some multiple of its probability antecedent to the argument and that the argument is therefore invalid unless we can first show that the antecedent probability of its conclusion is not zero or infinitesimal. For a finite result can never be reached by the multiplication of zero or of one divided by infinity. It might be retorted, however, that, even apart from any other arguments for God, the widespread and deep intuitive conviction in his existence at least gives a finite probability antecedent to any argument from design. This only amounts to saying that this is some point, however slight the value you may give to it, in favour of theism. Even if this antecedent probability were held to be very small indeed, it would very quickly, if other objections to the argument from design can be overthrown, be multiplied into an overwhelming probability in favour of its conclusion by the odds against such a purposive world as we know resulting from a chance conglomeration of atoms. This would directly follow from accepted formulae in probability theory. So to reply in this way it is not necessary to argue, even if it is true, that the belief in a mind behind the world is made very probable by other considerations, all that is needed is that its probability prior to the argument from design should not be zero or quite negligible, i.e. of the order of one in thousands of millions, a minimum degree of probability which would be granted even by most atheists. It might be thought that this argument would require the fulfilment of the impossible task of measuring the probabilities involved strictly in numerical terms, but even though an exact numerical probability or improbability cannot here be specified, it is clear that in the absence of some explanation or counter-argument the occurrence of such a degree of purposiveness as we observe in nature would be more improbable than phenomena, such as the throwing of a die with the six uppermost a hundred times in succession, to the probability of which a definite numerical value had to be assigned so low as to disprove the theory of coincidence decisively for any reasonable man.

This is really sufficient, but I also think that the objection about antecedent probability can be met in a more radical way, namely by denying its fundamental assumption. It is true that before evaluating the probability of the conclusion supported by a particular argument we ought to consider its antecedent probability in the sense that we ought to take account not only of any probability given to it by the argument before us but of the probability it would have prior to this argument. But this antecedent probability should mean the probability or improbability given to it by other arguments which have been or could have been brought, and it does not follow that we should take into account the probability that the hypothesis under consideration would have prior to any argument whatever. This would be absurd, I should say, because probability is essentially relative to some data, and in that case it is no more reasonable to say that a proposition could be probable prior to any argument for it than to say something was inferior if there were nothing to which to compare it that could be called superior. So inability to establish such absolute antecedent probability is no ground for rejecting an argument. We cannot reject it just because it does not fulfil a self-contradiction condition. And, if applied thoroughly in practice, the argument would lead to the conclusion that nothing that was not directly observed could ever be made probable because any argument establishing its probability would have to be supplemented by another argument showing that it was probable prior to the first argument and so on ad infinitum.[1]

We have now considered a number of objections to the argument from design, but two of the most difficult problems remain, that raised by the occurrence of dysteleology and the question whether the acceptance of the theory of evolution does not largely destroy the force of the argument from design. The former is part of the general problem of evil of which I shall speak in a later chapter, and which must, whether the argument from design be accepted or not, in any case be a problem for the theist. I shall just make a remark which may seem unfair but which I think is highly apposite, namely that apparent design is a much stronger argument for the presence of a superhuman mind than is apparent absence of design or even apparent presence of poor design an argument against it. For it is extremely probable that, if there is a God, a large proportion of his doings will

[1] Cf. my *Non-Linguistic Philosophy* (pp. 134–9) for a more detailed account of my argument.

be quite incomprehensible to us and so appear without purpose or even appear to have a bad purpose. What view should we take of the logic of a dog who should argue that I was a being with no intelligence because he could not see any purpose in my writing this book? Yet the wisdom of God presumably exceeds ours in a much greater degree than our intelligence exceeds the intelligence of a dog. We may add that, supposing a dog could think far enough, he could still find sufficient ground for an argument for design at the human level in the small proportion of the actions of a good master which were directed to the dog specifically and concerned things such as his food, shelter and exercise which could be appreciated by a dog.

I thus am convinced that at least prior to the adoption of the theory of evolution by natural selection the argument from design was an extremely powerful one as evidence for a mind controlling nature, though it did not in itself provide any ground for thinking of God as perfectly good or omnipotent. In some respects indeed the evolution theory helps us in dealing with the appearance of dys-teleology just noted as an objection to the design argument since it explains imperfections in animal organs and the existence of vestigial organs like the appendix which are apparently useless and may do harm, whereas the hypothesis of special creation by God of each species seems quite incompatible with these. However it has diminished the force of the argument from design by providing an alternative explanation of the purposiveness we empirically find in nature, but it may be questioned whether the explanation is adequate. To the view that there is no ground now for postulating a designing mind because the appearance of design is explained by natural selection, various objections have been made, though I must repeat that there can be no question of rejecting the theory of evolution in favour of one of creation but at the most of supplementing the former by the latter. It has been said that for the evolutionary process of natural selection to get started at all there must be organisms capable of reproduction but the simplest such are more complex than a motor-car, and it would be ridiculous to suppose inorganic matter coming to-gether of itself fortuitously to make a motor-car.

Such a strict critic as C. D. Broad admitted that the argument from design was 'extremely strong' if we assumed that otherwise organisms must have arisen from inorganic matter and their char-

acteristic behaviour was explicable wholly 'from the peculiar arrangement of their parts and the laws and properties of inorganic matter'.[1]
But the opponent of the argument could, it seems to me, hardly avoid
these objections without making one of three very implausible
suppositions. One would be that organisms always existed on earth,
which contradicts the view of science that the world was originally
either terrifically hot or gaseous or both; another that the properties
in organisms indicating purposiveness arose from inorganic matter
without any cause at all; the third, less intolerable indeed but pretty
fantastic, that the first organisms were transferred from some other
planet, which is unlikely in view of what we now know to have
belonged to our solar system and thus must have involved their
transit through the incredible void which separates them from even
the nearest star that might have planets, besides only putting the
solution of the problem further back.

It has also been urged against the probability of the explanation
of the appearance of design simply by the theory of natural selection
that, since you may go wrong in a vast number of ways for any one in
which you may go right, the probability of a random variation being
unfavourable to survival or reproduction is much greater than that
of its being favourable; that in order to produce the required effect a
variation would have to be large, but if it were large it would usually
decrease rather than increase the chances of survival unless balanced
by other variations the occurrence of which simultaneously with the
first would be much more improbable still; that it can be calculated
that the odds are very great against either a large number of individuals
in a species having the variations together by chance or their spreading
from a single animal through the species by natural selection. It has
further been contended that, since any organic life depends on extremely complex inorganic conditions, the necessity for supposing
design reappears in the inorganic world, where evolution by natural
selection cannot be adduced as a possible explanation. I am afraid I have
not the biological knowledge required to discuss these arguments
adequately; but at any rate when we reflect that the human brain
contains as many as ten thousand million cells organized in a working
system and that each of these cells is immensely more complex than
the workshop of any human engineer or the laboratory of any human

[1] *Religion, Philosophy and Psychical Research*, p. 171.

physicists, it should surely appear very far from clear that it is not
wiser to suppose that this is ultimately the result of design than to
suppose even with the help of natural selection that a world in which
such systems are so common resulted ultimately from a fortuitous
concourse of atoms. The argument from design I hope I have shown
by no means deserves the contempt which in so many quarters is
poured on it. It may be viewed as another application of the criterion
of explanatory efficacy to some features in the universe, the
apparently purposive ones.

But apart from the specific argument from design I am still more
impressed by the fact that, when I consider the physical world its
order, its system, its beauty strongly suggest that it is a product of
mind, or at any rate that the least inadequate category for interpreting
it is mind.

It has been objected that the appearance of the world as orderly
may be due to our own minds because we can only perceive what is
orderly, whether the order be thought of as imposed by the mind or
whether the relation between mind and the physical world be regarded
as analogous to that between a sieve and what passes through it. We
can conclude a priori that whatever passes through a sieve must be
less than a certain size, but this does not imply that the stuff present
before sieving did not contain any objects larger than that size, and
similarly it has been suggested that it might be the case that most of
the real was in a state of disorder but we could only perceive the parts
which were ordered. But if this were so, we should expect to perceive
order everywhere in the high degree in which it appears when we
consider certain aspects of things. Further, only a small fraction of
the order was apparent to perception prior to the development of
scientific investigation. If it were to be explained as a condition of
perception, all things would have to appear even at first sight well
ordered, as much as do some aspects of things. But this is by no means
the case. Most of the regularities we do find emerge not when we first
perceive the objects concerned but only as the fruit of scientific
research. We must therefore suppose that order where it appears
cannot be due to the necessary conditions of perception alone. Still
less could this suggestion be used as an objection to the argument
from design, for we can perceive things which do not appear teleological in the least.

As regards the argument from beauty it may be retorted that beauty is not objective but only in the mind of the beholder. To this we can reply that at any rate the qualities which produce the experience of beauty for an apprehending mind are objectively there independent of the mind, and we have still got to explain how it is that we quite unconsciously produce visions of such wonderful beauty in our experience when we apprehend certain physical objects. We after all belong to the order of nature as well as do the physical things which we apprehend as beautiful. The grounds of beauty are found in the world order, and beauty strikes one as the expression of something still more wonderful behind the beauty. The 'argument from beauty' is not indeed an argument logically entailing its conclusion but rather owes its force to an intuitive insight which at least many minds have when experiencing beauty, not indeed into the truth of an a priori axiom but of something at once richer and more vague. As such it links with the approach to theism in the preceding chapter.

These arguments for theism would seem still more plausible if we adopted a phenomenalist instead of a realist view of matter, a step which I myself however am by no means prepared to take.

While the cosmological argument, at least in the form in which I have stated it, would give us not only a supreme mind but a supremely good mind, the goodness of the creative mind would not necessarily follow from the argument from design or from any general argument based on the order in the natural world; but it would seem only reasonable to suppose that a being who was so much above us in intelligence as the creator of the whole universe would have to be was far above us in goodness as well. Such a being would surely discern the nature of good and evil much more clearly than we do and so could hardly find advantage in doing wrong. Further, the wonderful beauty present in the world by itself strongly suggests to me goodness behind it as well as intelligence. But to go beyond goodness and assert perfection is plainly not warranted by anything I have said after ending my discussion of the cosmological argument proper, and I think that the chief ground for a conviction of the perfect goodness of God still more than of his existence must lie in an intuition present in the experience of religious people.

There is a further argument that has occurred to me which it is perhaps most suitable to insert at this stage. It may be regarded as in some sense Descartes' well known argument in reverse. As is well known, Descartes started by asking what reply could be given to the sceptic and gave one by proving to his satisfaction the existence of a perfectly good God and then concluded that such a being could never deceive us, so that we could always trust our 'clear and distinct' ideas. Like most philosophers I do not accept Descartes' arguments for God as valid, but the question can still be asked why we are entitled to trust our faculties, what guarantee there is that our brain is not constructed in such a way that it totally misleads us and yields quite wrong results when we have taken every precaution against error possible to us and are most certain that we are right. Earlier in criticizing the epiphenomenalist theory of the relation between body and mind I argued that, if epiphenomenalism were true, nobody could ever be justified in believing either it or anything else to be true since their belief would not be due to any good reasons or the apprehension of such, as on the epiphenomenalist view what causes a man to form a belief is always a change in the state of his brain and never an apprehension of a reason for holding the belief to be true. It could only be a matter of luck whether a belief thus caused was true or not and the chances against its just happening to conform with the truth would be immense so that, if such a line of argument is accepted, we may go further still indeed and say that it would follow from the epiphenomenalist view that it was practically certain that all our affirmative beliefs were radically false. Now in criticizing epiphenomenalism I used this sceptical argument only against the view that all mental states of belief were directly caused entirely by merely physical states. But why should it make any difference to the force of the argument if they are so caused indirectly? Suppose once mental states have been brought into existence they can act as causes themselves, though they were originally caused by the brain processes, it must still remain true that our beliefs, ultimately at least, were all determined by purely physical causes and never by good reasons, so that my argument would still hold. Similarly with the notion of purpose. Purposive action would be always futile, except by accident, unless there were sometimes good reasons for it, but it would never be determined by good reasons if it were always determined simply by the brain, and whether it was directly or only ultimately so determined should make no difference to the argument.

Now the view that the mind is simply produced by material conditions and that every mental event is ultimately determined by material
causes is not the only alternative to theism. But I think my argument
would apply to the beliefs of most opponents of religion. It is generally
enough held, even by theists, that thinking is dependent on our
brain so that the processes in the latter decide for us what seems right
and reasonable; and even if we are allowed free will to choose between
alternative beliefs and alternative acts, this is not very much help if it
is merely a physical accident whether a belief appears to us right or
reasonable or not. We absolutely need some guarantee that our brain
can be relied on to give us reasonable beliefs on the whole if we try
to think carefully, and not merely results that are seemingly reasonable,
and I do not see how we can possibly have this guarantee unless we
may regard it as ultimately teleologically constructed with a view
to giving us these results. It may be said that the sceptical argument I
gave is self-refuting because it is itself an argument; but granted its
premises it could only refute itself by refuting all other arguments too,
and this leaves its correctness and so its premises incredible. It entails
that no arguments have any validity if it is correct, but it is itself an
argument, therefore it has no validity if it is correct and a fortiori it
has no validity if it is incorrect. If it is retorted that we could not have
succeeded in the struggle for existence if our brains had not been
capable of yielding knowledge or reasonable belief and that this is a
sufficient ground for trusting in the validity of our reasoning processes,
the reply may still be made that this is itself an argument. We are
assuming a faith in our capacities if we accept any argument at all.
Descartes argued that God exists and so we cannot be sceptics; I have
argued that we cannot be absolute sceptics and so we must assume
that our capacities are constituted as if God exists. This of course need
not commit us to Descartes' view that every soul was specially created
at birth by God. All it requires is the assumption that the natural
processes involved as a whole are ultimately determined by purpose.

It will be noted that my arguments admittedly do not give certainty
but only probability, and it has been held that there was no place for
probability in metaphysics. This view was taken by no less an authority
than Kant, though he virtually abandoned it later by admitting that
you can have a rational belief in God justified by his moral argument
and by giving at least some weight to the argument from design. It

has been put forward recently by Hartshorne,[1] who thought the existence of God could be proved a priori, and John Hick,[2] who denied that it could but took an intuitive view. It seems to me, with Hick at least, this attitude is due to the limitation of the concept of probability to cases where the latter could be measured numerically, which would not by any means cover even all the probable arguments that occur in science. It is only in exceptional and artificially simplified cases that we can give a numerical measurement of probability in terms of frequency. Even with dice the probability measurements depend on an assumption to which no numerical probability can be assigned, i.e. that the dice are not loaded. Yet it is perfectly plain that in a given empirical context we can often quite plainly see without numerical calculation that one alternative is more probable than another. If we could not do this we should be completely at a loss in handling most scientific research and most practical problems. We no doubt handle these questions on the basis of past experience, but we can do so without counting the number of instances in which the relevant experience had occurred, and if we did this we still should not have usually had anything like an adequate numerical measurement of the probability of the anticipated event since the relative degree of their varying relevance to our present problem could usually even in science hardly be numerically assessed.

But with the exception of the argument from design arguments for God do not deal in probabilities in the sense of the term in which they appear in scientific induction, and there is therefore a temptation to conclude that being a priori they must either prove with certainty or be mere fallacies which do not give any support to their alleged conclusions. But while it is true that in itself an a priori argument, granted the truth of its premises, must either strictly prove its conclusion or be a mere fallacy, it does not follow at all that we must either accept it as certain or reject it as a mere fallacy. It would be different if we could, as in pure arithmetic or those simple syllogisms which leave no room for ambiguity, be sure that we had committed no error which rendered the argument invalid, but whatever philosophical view we take on disputed questions we shall have to admit that it is hardly ever possible to be certain of this in philosophy, be-

[1] *Creative Synthesis and Philosophic Method*, e.g. chapter XIV.
[2] *Arguments for the Existence of God*, pp. 28 ff.

cause whatever arguments we produce we shall almost always find competent philosophers who oppose us and both parties can not be right. But the fact that I may have committed an error even when I feel certain myself, or even the fact that I am myself without the subjective feeling of complete certainty that I have got the argument quite right does not force me to disclaim all probability for an argument. If I adopted such a line I should cut myself off completely from most interesting topics of discussion anywhere and from all in philosophy. The uncertainty I have mentioned does, as I have already insisted, apply also to philosophical intuitions, with few if any exceptions. Many think that liberalism is dependent on an empirical epistemology and on an ethics which does not admit objective values or laws, but this is by no means the case. Provided he allows for human fallibility any philosopher, however much he deals in a priori principles, and any holder of objective views in ethics may escape the vice of intolerance without committing himself to any particular theory of knowledge or of philosophical ethics.

However, while there must be no doubt a deductive element in most arguments for God, as there is in the process by which most scientific theories are established, it will be noted that the arguments I have defended here, and I think any in the next chapter, will partake rather of the nature of the postulation of explanatory hypotheses than of straightforward deductive argument. Such metaphysical hypotheses have indeed one important advantage over those of natural science. The difficulty about vindicating an explanatory hypothesis is that it is very hard to be sure that all tenable alternative hypotheses have been excluded, but in the field with which I am concerned the number of explanatory hypotheses that could be suggested is far more drastically limited. For example, turning to the cosmological argument, it is impossible to see what other modes of explanation there could be of the world except that by logic, that by ordinary causal explanation, and that by values, and there are reasons of an a priori kind which exclude the first two, thus driving us, if we believe there must be an explanation, to accept that in terms of values. To set against this, however, are the facts that verification in the ordinary sense of scientific verification seems to be excluded, though we have seen that there are other senses of verification in which at least partial verification might be obtained, and that there is a greater risk of errors through conceptual confusion. But where, as we find in the case of theism, a hypothesis does seem the best explanation, or the only possible explanation not merely of one kind but of a number of different kinds of fact about the universe and our knowledge of it, the different arguments for it as an explanatory hypothesis mutually strengthen each other by converging on the same result. Suppose it were a case of numerical probability and there were four independent arguments each by itself giving a probability of $\frac{1}{3}$ to a conclusion, the probability of its being false in view of all four arguments together would would be only $\frac{2}{3} \times \frac{2}{3} \times \frac{2}{3} \times \frac{2}{3}$, i.e. about one in five, and we must suppose a roughly corresponding escalation in arguments to which no numerical evaluation but only vague adjectives expressions such as; very strong; strong; favourable; in some degree supporting; can be applied.

There is one type of argument for the existence of God of a deductive rather than an explanatory character which I have not discussed here, partly because I am not convinced of its validity, partly because it is rarely used today, at least in the English-speaking world, and partly because I have already dealt with it extensively in an earlier work, *Idealism*.[1] There is little of that book which I should wish to retract except that I now think I gave a too fundamental place to coherence. The Berkeleian argument for God still seems more plausible to me than it does to most philosophers today, but I am not convinced of its fundamental premise that the *esse* of physical things is *percipi*. As I said in *Idealism*, it is my view that the arguments given for the premise fail and that it becomes a question of intuitive insight as to whether we do or do not see that the particular properties we attribute to matter are necessarily connected with the property of being experienced. I did think I saw this at one time but had changed my mind long before I completed *Idealism*.

But one point I should like to add. It seems to me that Berkeley's argument would have been much more plausible if he had based it on the notion of time.[2] There is this peculiarity about time. If time is real at all we must admit that in the primary sense of 'real' the present alone is real; but if we mean by 'the present' only the strictly instantaneous present, it becomes a mere point without any duration at all. We cannot say that anything is present in this sense because by the

---

[1] See chapters 2 and 8.
[2] I rather think I owe this suggestion to a former pupil at Cambridge, Pyman.

time we have said it it has gone. We are therefore driven back on the notion of the specious present as the primary reality, but this notion seems to imply a consciousness which holds the strictly present together with what is just past and therefore not strictly an object of actual present perception but of memory. Yet the notion of the specious present itself seems subjective. It is thought to vary for different minds so that what is present for one mind may not be present for another at the same time. Further, if we are talking of simply inanimate matter, it is senseless to speak of the specious present here except in so far as we are speaking of a mind's experience of the matter. So what exists at present in the inanimate world, realistically conceived, is an infinitesimal moment, a mere nothing in other words, a very strange thing to have to admit. To make it anything more we have to introduce a mind to which it is relative. If it is only the individual mind, this is subjective idealism and we have to grant that everybody has a different time, and that the unperceived parts of the body are not in time in the same sense as my mind. I have defended a dualistic view of the mind–body relation at a time when most philosophers seem to regard it with hostility, but to carry dualism so far as that would imply is too much even for me. Yet if the physical world is to be objectively in time, what alternative is there but to suppose that the whole of it is present to a superhuman mind. This seems to me the most plausible argument of the idealist type for a deity, whose specious present would presumably include the whole temporal process.

8

MORAL ARGUMENTS FOR GOD

If the essential concept of religion is that of the dominance of the world by good, one would expect there to be a quite particularly close connection between ethics and religion. That there is such a close connection is indeed assumed by all the major religions, and it is therefore surprising that there have not been still more attempts than there have at a moral proof of God. The best-known one in Western philosophy, that of Kant, has been very severely and, one must admit, not undeservedly, criticized by many thinkers and, as far as I know, would not nowadays be regarded as sufficient in any quarter. We should indeed distinguish between defects which could be removed by amending Kant's particular kind of ethical theory and defects which are necessarily inherent in that general type of argument. Kant contends that the moral law commands the pursuit of an ideal which we cannot attain in this life in any case, nor at all unless external conditions are arranged with a view to its being attainable, which we can only conceive to be the case if we think of the world as created by a perfectly good, omnipotent and omniscient being, since such a being alone could and would effect the adjustment required, and that therefore we are justified in positing both another life and the existence of God. He limits very much the kinds of things to be conceived as intrinsically good and therefore constituting part of the ideal good to be attained. They are in fact reduced by him to two only, the good will, which is described as the only thing unconditionally good, and in a subordinate degree happiness, if and only if the happiness of a man is in proportion to his goodness. Since the good will is regarded as entirely in the agent's own power and not producible by anyone else acting on him, it does not figure in the proof of God, though it does in the proof of immortality, but Kant does argue that, if men are to attain happiness in proportion to their deserts, since their happiness is dependent not only on themselves, nature must be ordered in such a way as to make this possible at least in a future life, since it is plainly not so in this. The adequacy of Kant's conception of the good may be challenged on two main grounds. (1) Surely what matters *very much more* than that sinners should be punished in proportion to their deserts (even if one were, like Kant, to accept the retributive theory so far as to hold that it is an end in itself that they should be) is that they should become good instead of bad, and surely the summum bonum could not be fully attained unless every being in the universe were or became both happy and good. It is not enough to say that it is in each man's power to show the good will as far as he himself is concerned and he will then be rewarded with happiness in proportion to his own deserts, for if somebody he loved neglected to exercise the good will and were in consequence eternally damned the first man could also never attain the summum bonum himself. (2) It is very widely indeed and, I think, rightly held that there are other intrinsic goods besides the moral will (which is what Kant means by the 'good will') and happiness. It is thought that knowledge and understanding, aesthetic good and above all love have an intrinsic value of their own which is not reducible just to the value of the pleasure they give as pleasure and that the will to do one's duty for duty's sake is not the only intrinsically good quality of mind.

But these amendments to his view need not destroy the general principle of Kant's argument, but might even be used to strengthen it further. For the other things pronounced intrinsically good are more obviously dependent partly on external circumstances than is the good will. (Actually the good will is so dependent also, since if I had the brain of a complete idiot I certainly could not form any idea of moral duty and so could not display the good will.)

But there remains a defect in Kant's argument which prevents it from having any decisive weight. It is certainly true that if we ought to attain the supreme good we can attain it, but do we know that we ought to attain it or only that we ought to strive after it? Plainly the latter. To know that we ought to attain it we should first have to know that we can attain it and so we cannot argue in the reverse direction. What is then left of Kant's argument? Only the presumption that the fact that we have in our mind goals which go far beyond anything that is possible in this life suggests a future life in which we may attain them and suggests also in view of the centrality for moral action of these goals that the world is so constituted that they are attainable by us. Kant's view is that the fact that we are bound to regard it as our duty to pursue certain ends as if they were attainable is not indeed a logically certain proof but a quite adequate justification for believing that they are attainable. But I have not encountered any contemporary philosopher who was convinced by this argument. The most I can concede is that it in a slight degree increases the presumption in favour of a belief in God, although I should admit that the presence of ideas in the human mind which so outrun its biological purpose is a stronger argument for our survival of bodily death. (I should however be far from calling it, as Kant does,[1] an incontrovertible proof of this.) As has frequently been pointed out, it is perfectly possible and by no means irrational to devote much effort to getting as near as possible to a goal which we shall never attain or even nearly approach. What would be fatal to the validity of the whole conception of duty would be if we could not make any difference at all by moral striving, but of course we can make some difference, though not as much as we should like.

Let us consider then what other moral arguments might be used to establish the existence of God. I think that, if any such arguments are to be accepted, we must assume an objective view of ethics and one that does not analyse all ethical concepts naturalistically, but it seems to me that such a view must be adopted in any case if we are to do justice to ethics, let alone theology.[2]

There are, further, various pitfalls which an argument for God based on ethics must avoid. Some arguments that have been put forward would, if really taken seriously, actually have the effect of destroying all that is of value in ethics and in religion. If we argued, as some have done, that theology was a necessary presupposition of ethics because we should have no motive or ground for acting morally unless we were to be rewarded or punished by God in proportion to our deserts, we should be denying that the fact that something was our duty could ever be any ground or motive for doing it and thus be denying morality altogether. All motives would on the view

[1] *Critique of Pure Reason*, B426. The argument is here reinforced by an appeal to the teleology in nature.
[2] See above, chapter 7.

suggested be selfish; and there would be no moral value even in what is called moral action, since it would consist simply in accepting bribes or yielding to threats.

Kant later uses another argument in lieu of the one just discussed.[1] It is that a moral law implies a law giver and a judge, and this argument has very commonly been employed. But while a 'law' implies a lawgiver in the political context and a judge to determine whether the law has been broken and by whom and to fix a penalty, we cannot argue straightaway that 'law' in the moral sense does so. It may be urged that the argument depends on a confusion between different senses of 'law'. Further, this argument would again, if accepted in any at all literal sense, have very damaging repercussions both for ethics and for religion. If the sole ground for the moral law were that it was the command of God, God's commands and therefore the moral law itself would be completely arbitrary because God could have no ground for issuing his commands. He could not issue them because they were right or did good, since they would only be right because they were his commands. *A fortiori* 'right' or 'duty' must be analysed as meaning sanctioned or commanded by God.

The reply has been made that God is perfectly good by definition and that therefore there is no heteronomy in making ethics dependent on the commands of God. But the inclusion of the notion of goodness makes no significant difference to the definition of God unless 'goodness' means something more than just doing as God wills. If that was all it meant, belief in God's goodness would be no security against God acting like a devil and damning everybody, since everything God did would be by definition good, whatever it was; and the same result would follow even if goodness or rightness were not defined in such a way, provided God determined what was right or wrong simply by commanding or forbidding it. If on the other hand 'goodness' as figuring in the definition of God means something other than this, we are not entitled to say that God exists unless we have satisfied ourselves that the supreme being has this quality, and cannot just say that he must have it because this is part of what we mean by 'God', and its meaning must be derived for us from our understanding of ethics, which we do not derive from a prior knowledge of God.

There are other pitfalls which those who advance a moral argument

[1] See Abbott, *Kant's Theory of Ethics*, p. 322, and posthumous work.

for the existence of God must be careful to avoid. They must not commit the vicious circle of deducing God from ethics and also ethics from theology. There is no chance of the first argument being valid unless we start by assuming the validity of ethical knowledge in its own right prior to a consideration of theology, even if it does turn out later that it implies theology. If ethical beliefs can be justified only by theological considerations, we cannot begin an ethical argument for God till we have already established God's existence. Such an argument must not depend on the analysis of ethical concepts without remainder in terms of theology; and it must not contradict experience by implying that a person who does not know God, an atheist or agnostic, cannot be a morally good man. Any person who insists on a primarily religious ethics must realize that, apart from revelation, which does not fall within my subject, we are not in a position to find out what the will of God is except by using our ordinary ethical standards to determine what is right and assuming that God being good will do what is right.

The above remarks do not by any means exclude the possibility that the acceptance of belief in God may provide a rational ground for the acceptance of new moral obligations which we should otherwise not have had. To put it at the lowest, if we believe in God we are under an obligation sometimes to think of God and to think of him in a way which would not be appropriate if we did not believe in God. But likewise duties in relation to other men depend on the existence of these men. Obviously I could be rendered subject to fresh duties if my father were missing and believed dead and then I discovered him to be alive. Nor do I mean to exclude the possibility that moral and immoral action in general should take on a somewhat different character for a theist to what they have for a person who does not believe in God; indeed I could consistently with what I have said go further and admit that much and possibly all of what a man did out of a sense of duty before he was converted to the belief in God he might now do from love of God, and that this would be a real change and not necessarily a change for the worse by any means. Nor should the autonomy of ethics be pressed so far as to exclude the possibility of its having metaphysical implications. Anything may have metaphysical implications, and the philosopher should feel himself impelled to ask the question how his moral judgements are to be fitted in with the rest of his knowledge and rational beliefs.

Whether we think there to be any specific moral argument for the existence of God or not, we must admit that ethics is extremely important for theology simply because it is quite essential to think of God as good and it is only in terms of our ethical standards that we can conceive what it is like to be good. It is only by using these that it is possible to infer from God's goodness even that he will not delight in torturing human beings (as some older theologians seem to have thought) or that if he does communicate a revelation he will not deliberately deceive us, an assumption which must be made before the revelation can be accepted as such. Consequently, even if the existence and goodness of God can be established by other arguments, these must be supplemented by considerations from straightforward ordinary ethics to form an idea of what the admission of God's goodness involves. It follows that ethics is of great importance for theology even if it should turn out that no specific argument for God's existence based on ethics can be approved. It is an essential part of religion that God should be conceived as good, and it is the province of ethics to tell us the kind of things a good being will do. Further, even if there are no independent ethical arguments for God, we might be able to use an ethical argument to show that if we on other grounds postulate a mind that rules the universe this being should be conceived as good.

There can further be no doubt as to the close connection between the moral and the religious life, at least in the religions we regard as more advanced. We can hardly imagine a man being in a sincerely religious state of mind and yet at the same time deliberately deciding to do what he believes to be morally wrong, though such a man might indeed be in grave error as to what was right or wrong, as were the inquisitors, and also might well be conceived as sometimes failing to resist temptation despite his sincere prayers. In so far as religion is a matter of intuition, characteristically religious intuition is very closely linked to intuition of values, being indeed a finding of value in or behind the cosmic order as a whole. In view of the connection between ethics and religion it seems antecedently very probable that there should be some powerful argument from ethics to the existence of God, although it does not follow necessarily that this will turn out actually to be the case. Let us now consider whether we can find subtler arguments which will escape the objections I have mentioned. There are certainly various circumstances about ethical experience which seem, at first sight at least, to support a religious view.

(1) The attitude of the good man to the moral law is very like the attitude of the religious man to God. To both is ascribed an absolute and unconditional authority and a sanctity which transcends any other values. Since two different values could not both occupy this supreme position, it follows that the moral law must be realized in God if both these two attitudes are right. Hence if once the existence of God is accepted on the strength of religious experience we have a strong argument for his complete goodness even apart from the fact that a sense of goodness is itself normally part of the actual content which seems to be presented in religious experience. This is not to say that our ethical experience by itself establishes the existence of God, but it is useful enough to have additional confirmation of the proposition that, if there is a supreme being, that being is supremely good. But further, it may be argued that, if we do not worship God, we must worship the moral law, and this is a mere abstraction and so not a possible object of worship. The validity of the experience to which I have appealed might indeed be challenged. It might be said that to suppose that any existent being at all is a suitable object of worship is only to be a vicitim of an illusion, but this is to contradict the core of religious experience.

Are there any ethical arguments for God which do not presuppose the validity of religious intuition?

(2) It might be argued that even if, as I have insisted, ethical concepts cannot be reduced without residuum to theological, there is an element in our ordinary ethical thinking which must be interpreted in terms of such a reference and that without this the moral ought would be reduced to the ought of mere rationality or that of aesthetic or quasi-aesthetic fittingness. In my *Definition of Good* I suggested, without adopting the suggestion, that moral wrongness might be analysed in terms of fittingness to be blamed and that this was the distinction between it and mere imprudence. But 'fitting to be blamed' does not express an ultimate fact. We are driven to ask why an act is fitting to be blamed (blameworthy), and the answer must be

that the man has done not merely what is unfitting (inappropriate or mistaken) but what he morally ought not to have done. To talk about the moral ought is not merely to express a relation between the circumstances and certain possible acts, but to demand that one should act in a certain way. There is something authoritative about it which the analysis of moral wrongness proposed fails to express adequately. And, it may then be said, authoritativeness implies an authority. Such an argument would certainly not reduce ethical concepts without residuum to theological. All that it would claim is that we should admit an element in the 'ought' of morality which could not be explained without a reference to God since 'demanded' implies somebody who demands. The argument assumes, I think very rightly, that moral judgements are not merely demands made by the person who utters them but express an objective claim. Nor can we say that they just mean that the conduct is demanded of us by any finite human beings. Mere human beings have no authority to demand of us that we act in a certain way except the authority of the state and society, and such human organizations are fallible and may rightly be disobeyed under some circumstances. A person who uses this argument need not say that 'morally obligatory' *means* 'commanded by God'. All he need maintain is that the concept cannot be thought out fully without reference to God. He does not need necessarily to say the same about 'good' or any other value concepts except the distinctively moral one. 'Ought' itself is not always used in a distinctively moral sense, and in no other sense do the people who use this argument need to conceive it as requiring for its full intelligibility a reference to God. On this view what actions are obligatory would be settled by their empirical circumstances and likely effects, but it would be the relation to God on which the characteristic of moral obligatoriness in its fullness depended if it was to qualify anything at all, although what it qualified in particular would depend on the circumstances of the action in each case and would therefore, even if God is the ultimate creator, not depend in the same direct way on God. As the relation to God is held by theologians to give wrongdoing a specific character which differentiates it from wrongdoing for the secularist, making it 'sin', so in addition to being what we ought to do, say, in being liable to produce better effects than its alternatives or fulfilling an explicit or implicit undertaking to other human beings, or even in having an indefinable non-natural property of rightness, the right action would be obligatory in the full sense only because of its relation to God. Even if we regarded this relation as depending directly on God's will, our view would not be open to the objections to which a view is liable that conceives God as deciding by an act of will, which would have to be arbitrary, what particular acts are right. God would be conceived as commanding that we should not do wrong, and this, even if it did not make wrong what was not already otherwise wrong in a sense of morally wrong which can consistently figure in the teaching of a secularist,[1] would to all the acts that were thus wrong add the further characteristic of sinfulness; and to the abstention from those acts, besides the characteristic of rightness in whatever sense it had it on a secularist view, the further characteristic of obligatoriness. This moral argument for the existence of God would depend for its validity on its being possible to see that ethical concepts involved the notion of God. As the man who said 'I am of course not talking morally, but I should be a swine if I let down that girl' was really using and implying a belief in moral concepts though he disavowed it, so the moral secularist would be really without knowing it using concepts which could not be made intelligible without a reference to God. The use of the argument would therefore by no means commit one to implying that atheists and agnostics cannot be moral. What it would imply is that, if they believe in moral obligation as distinct from mere prudence or a sort of aesthetic fittingness, their view is ultimately inconsistent because moral obligation implies a deity. I am not fully convinced by this argument, but I do not see any other way of supplying the missing element in the moral 'ought'.

(3) The following argument has been used frequently. In what does the moral law reside, it is asked. It cannot reside in the material world. Matter is not moral or immoral. Such a law could only reside in a mind; yet it is objective. In forming moral beliefs and even where we have moral knowledge we are aiming at discovering what holds quite independently of our minds. The whole moral law is not known by any human beings even if we conceive the moral knowledge of all different people as added together into one whole, and all men may

---

[1] Except violations of specifically religious duties involving the cultivation of a certain attitude to God.

be mistaken as to what is right or wrong. Therefore we cannot hold that it resides only in human minds. The objective moral law then resides in a mind, but no human mind. Therefore it must reside in a superhuman mind. In order to be thus aware of the whole law the mind must be conceived as supremely intelligent. Further, although it does not follow logically that this mind must have will as well as intelligence, it would be gratuitous and unreasonable to suppose that it made no use of its perfect knowledge. If so, it would either be completely impotent and so not really a mind or grossly and gravely immoral. It is hardly credible that a being who had such a supremely perfect moral knowledge would not act on it, and this argument is reinforced if we think of moral judgements as primarily expressing practical attitudes, though combined with a cognitive claim to objectivity. Nor could we reasonably think of a being that occupied such a unique position in relation to the moral law as just one finite being among others, so this can be regarded as a genuine independent argument for God. Still more is it reasonable if we already believe in God on other grounds to identify the being thus postulated with God. This moral argument could then be regarded as an additional confirmation of the existence of God and especially of his supreme goodness.

We cannot bring against this argument the objection that we may perfectly well make rational ethical decisions without presupposing any knowledge of or even belief in God. The proposition that God exists is introduced not as a premise of our moral judgements but as a conclusion inferred from them. It would indeed be no more justifiable to reject the argument on this ground than it would be to reject the cosmological or design argument on the ground that one can be a good physicist or biologist without introducing premises about God or even believing in God. Just as these arguments are brought forward to account for a world of which we obtain knowledge by sense-perception and science without needing to make any assumptions about God, so the moral argument I have just stated is brought forward to explain the objectivity of the moral law which we know without making religious assumptions but the status in reality of which requires explanation. This applies in whichever of the two possible ways that occur to me the argument is taken. It may be taken like the preceding argument as showing that an intuitive conviction which even non-religious people can hardly help assuming in practice already includes an implicit religious belief, i.e. they could not think of the moral law as objectively binding without at least some confused and unanalysed notion of a mind in which the law resided. The argument would then be a means of disclosing to people an intuition of God which they really had all along. If to intuit moral obligations is already to intuit God, it follows that a man cannot be moral without some implicit awareness of God, but he need not consciously recognize it for what it is. If, on the other hand, and I think myself this is preferable, we view the moral argument just given not as an analysis of moral concepts but rather as an inference from them or an explanation of their objectivity, there is a fortiori no reason why the atheist or agnostic should not be good. You can believe something and act accordingly without being aware of its implications. The moral argument in question assumes that we can at the ethical level see the moral law to be objective and then asks how it can be so, as the argument from design assumes that at the scientific level we have found out that organisms are adapted to maintain life in all sorts of intricate ways and then asks how this phenomenon can be explained. I am not implying that the moral argument is similar to the argument from design in other respects, e.g. that it shares the quasi-inductive character of the latter.

It may be objected that this argument presupposes a naïve form of the correspondence theory of truth. If we are to assert true affirmative propositions about a monster in Loch Ness, there must be such a monster actually existing, but need it be the case likewise that, if we are to assert true affirmative propositions about the moral law, there must be a moral law existing somewhere in the totality of being? I myself used to hold that, since our moral judgements are sometimes true and I thought (as I still think) that there are fatal objections to a naturalist theory of ethics, we must hold that there is a non-natural relation of obligation existing in the real world beween certain actions and their empirical circumstances; but in a later book, *Second Thoughts in Moral Philosophy*, I suggested that this view was due to a too literal interpretation of the correspondence theory of truth. Even if all true judgements must correspond to reality in the very wide sense in which this means simply that their truth depends somehow on a relation to what really exists, we cannot reasonably hold that there is an exact correlation between each true judgement and a fact or element in

G

reality to which it corresponds.[1] Hypothetical judgements can be true even in cases where their antecedent is never realized in actual fact, but we are not bound therefore to suppose that corresponding to each contrafactual conditional there is somehow subsisting in reality a hypothetical fact. Yet even these hypothetical judgements correspond to reality in the sense of depending for their truth on the nature of the existing world including the causal laws which govern it. I never wanted to suggest that the relation between propositions of ethics and actual reality is very like that between contrafactual conditionals and reality, but these propositions do seem to resemble hypotheticals in depending for their truth or falsity on the factual nature of something in the existent world without being ordinary descriptive judgements. I am inclined to accept the view that they are primarily the expression of practical attitudes and thus primarily do something other than make a truth-claim, but whatever we do can be done rightly or wrongly, justifiably or unjustifiably, and they claim also that the mental attitudes they express are justified and this can be true.[2] Now if a descriptive judgement categorically assigning to something an actual property, definable not only in dispositional terms, is true, it follows that that property must be present as an actual existent in that object, and misled, as I now think, by this analogy I formerly supposed that, as there was no natural property of obligatoriness, moral judgements must describe a 'non-natural' one, whereas I should have concluded that obligatoriness was not a property at all except in a verbal sense, i.e. that moral and evaluative judgements have a function quite distinct from that of ascribing qualities to anything. They do not say that there is anything in reality beyond the natural qualities but evaluates attitudes towards what has these qualities.

It may seem to follow from this account that we do not need to say the moral law is 'in anything' and therefore cannot conclude that it is in a mind. But I do not now think that this change of view really does remove the foundations of the argument. We are still saying something at any rate about our attitudes. We are still saying that they must conform to or are discrepant with some law or standard, and it may be argued that if the judgements are true this law or standard must have some place in reality. The view to which I was opposing

[1] See *Second Thoughts in Moral Philosophy*, pp. 43 ff.   [2] See pp. 96 ff.

myself was the one formerly held by me according to which obligation though itself 'non-natural', was a relation existing in the natural
world as much as, say, spatial relations and when we made moral
judgements we asserted just that this relation was present or absent
in a given case. It does not seem to me now that this is the right way
to think of moral judgements, but my new account made it more
clear what we were not saying than what we were saying when we
made such judgements. And it does seem that, if we are not ascribing
any non-natural properties to the acts or attitudes evaluated themselves, we must at least be saying something about their relation to a
law, thus suggesting the question what the status in reality of that
law is. I have said elsewhere that the truth of true moral judgements
followed from the empirical facts, but what are we saying when we
say that they are true? What is it exactly that does follow? That 'I
ought' to act in a certain way or adopt a certain attitude. To say this is
not to describe anything, but it must be to assert something. It does
assert that there is an objective law binding us, and it may be argued
that this still leaves the question what is the metaphysical status, the
being of this law. We need not invoke the argument rejected above
as fallacious that a law implies a lawgiver, but surely in any case a
law, even a moral law, is not a thing which could have being by
itself. And, if it has being only for something else, for what could it
have being but a mind? I have said that what we ought to do in a given
situation follows from the empirical nature of the situation directly
without our having to perceive or postulate any non-natural qualities
or relations in the latter, but what about the laws which fix what
obligations follow from different situations, telling us, for example,
that we ought to try to relieve pain? If our moral judgements are true,
there are such laws, and they follow from the nature of pain, or again,
for instance, happiness and intelligence, which makes them objects
worth pursuing, or in the case of pain, avoiding, on their own account.
But in what does the being of a moral law consist? It has not the
status of a causal law, for it is not a law as to what actually happens,
therefore it cannot be said to be immanent in the natural world as
such. How then can it have being except for a mind? I cannot therefore
eliminate even this Berkeleian type of argument.

It may be objected that the argument confuses existence and
subsistence, since such a law need only be conceived as subsisting and

not as existing; but what the argument really presupposes is not that the subsistence of the law is a form of existence, but that it can be understood only in relation to an existent, the divine mind. 'Subsistence' is not a term which can be understood as having a clear meaning by itself, but is merely a technical way of expressing the point that moral judgements have some kind of objectivity, we know not what without the addition of some further explanation, the explanation being given by reference to an existent. To quote from Dawes Hicks, 'I do not say that the moral ideal must exist in the mind of God, because as an ideal it does not seem to be an existent, either in a mind or elsewhere. I would, however, submit that only on the assumption of the existence of a Mind by whom it is known in its entirety and on whom its reality is dependent can we rationally think of this ideal as subsisting at all.'[1] As will appear later, I shall retain the argument only in a form in which the words 'on whom its reality is dependent' do not figure, since these words deny the autonomy of ethics.

When I abandoned my former view in ethics which made 'ought' express a 'non-natural relation' between an act and its conditions, I thought this destroyed or at least weakened the argument in question for God, but I now think the contrary is the case. For on my old view I thought of moral judgements as true because they bore a relation of correspondence to non-natural properties in the objective world of ordinary life, i.e. just as the statement that A is north of B is true because it describes correctly an objective spatial relation, so the statement that A's act was right would be true because it described correctly an objective moral relation between the act and something in the circumstances, for example a promise by A. There was no reason in this, so far as it went, to bring in a deity or make any further supposition about the nature of reality in general except that it must be such as to admit of the occurrence of these relations between some (perhaps relatively only very few)[2] of the particulars contained in it. This account of moral objectivity I have now abandoned, but another is needed. In my *Second Thoughts* I maintained that moral judgements and value judgements in general could still be said to correspond to

---

[1] See M. Dawes Hicks, *Philosophical Bases of Theism*, p. 238.
[2] I say 'perhaps relatively very few' because obligations can only apply to personal beings.

reality in the very wide sense of following from objective empirical qualities in the existent world, since it was the empirical nature of something which made it intrinsically good (or bad), though its goodness must not be identified with its 'natural' properties, and similarly empirical (natural) circumstances in its context which made an act right or wrong. I there instanced contrafactual conditionals as judgements which, though they did not describe anything that actually existed or happened, and so could not correspond to reality in an ordinary sense, were true simply because they corresponded in a wider sense – i.e. followed from the nature of existing things. I hope I shall never jump from the top of a skyscraper, but this will not prevent the judgement that if I did I should be killed being true, because its truth follows from true categorical judgements about the real. But this does not solve the problem of moral judgements because (*a*) I did not make clear what the status was of what did follow. It still must be a law of some kind about the attitudes one ought to have or the things one ought to do, and therefore the argument could still be used that the being of such a law can only be being for a mind. (*b*) The analogy of hypothetical propositions is somewhat misleading here because a contrafactual conditional does not assert anything actual and we cannot be obliged by what is not actual.

This gives rise to a fresh argument (4) for the view that there are inescapable metaphysical implications involved in ethics. When I am under an obligation to do something, what I ought to do is always something that is not yet a fact. If it were a fact, I should have already done it and no longer be under an obligation to do it. Further, any reason that I can give why I ought to perform a particular action itself refers to what is not already a fact and may indeed, if I neglect my duty, never become one at all, for example that if I do *A* I shall keep a promise or save somebody pain. The basis of obligation in any particular case would therefore seem to be something hypothetical, not yet real. But if we take obligation seriously, it is hard to see how it can be based on a merely hypothetical proposition, and the difficulty is increased when we consider that the obligation remains an obligation even if it was not fulfilled, so that its alleged basis is never real at all. If the obligation depended simply on some condition which was never fulfilled we could not blame a man for violating it since its violation would remove the very condition which gave it validity. What *would* happen if a man did *A* might be a reason why he chose to do it and why it would be wise of him to do it, but it is hard to see how the power to oblige us could be possessed by something not yet real and which will perhaps never be real. Here we again have an argument for the view that the existence of obligation as such presupposes something over and above the particular empirical facts which will decide what is obligatory in particular cases. The position is quite different with other hypotheticals, for with them what is asserted does not *oblige*. We could therefore use the argument that ethical principles require a mind for their objective realization without using a similar argument about all hypotheticals. In *Second Thoughts* I may have sometimes spoken misleadingly as if one's duty were based entirely on the actual empirical situation immediately prior to the action to be done, but it is after all my duty to do something in a particular situation only because I shall then be obeying a moral law including the laws to pursue certain kinds of things as ends in themselves, though it depends on this situation what law I am to apply and what results I am likely to be able to achieve. The difficulty is not removed by denying that obligatoriness is a property of actions and maintaining that the same fact we express by saying an act is obligatory is better expressed by saying that some person is obliged to act in this way, as Prichard[1] and Ross[2] do, but only recurs in face of the question what put him under an obligation to do so and so, for this is always some property which the act would have had if done and would not therefore exist until and unless the act were done.

(5) When we talk about the moral law and consider its implications, we clearly should consider it not as it actually is for us but as it ought to be for us. And if we view it as it ought to be for us, its authority cannot from the nature of the case possibly be overestimated; it ought absolutely to control our whole life.[3] Now this already by itself at least strongly suggests that it is bound up with the essential structure, the fundamental groundwork of the real. If it is to have this absolute authority, it cannot be based, one would think, simply on some subsidiary element or elements in the real, as it would be if the whole

---

[1] *Moral Obligation*, pp. 36–7. [2] *Foundations of Ethics*, p. 56.

[3] I mean only that a moral obligation always has priority where it clashes with any other reason for action and not that an action must always be either morally obligatory or morally wrong. I do not mean to leave no place for permissible but non-obligatory acts.

ground for the moral law lay in some particular natural or non-natural properties of certain things, for example pleasantness or Moore's indefinable goodness conceived as one quality among others. It is not fair to reply to this argument that the proposition that the moral law ought to control our whole life is merely analytic, amounting to the assertion that we ought always to do what we ought, for it is not an analytic proposition that there is such a thing as obligation at all. It comes on the contrary with the force of a revelation. 'It is impossible to express the peculiar quality of the specifically *moral* ought in the conclusion of a conditional proposition concerning one's wants. For the specifically moral ought imposes itself, immediately it is apprehended, directly, finally, unconditionally, on the will, whatever one's wants.'[1] It seems to have the absoluteness which we can attribute only to God.

Suppose these arguments or any of them are accepted. What kind of supreme being do they imply? The being in question must be conceived as supremely good, otherwise the moral law is not realized in this being. But to be ethically good a being must have intelligence and will, and these are the essentials of personality, however much the way in which they are realized in the being will differ from the way in which they are realized in finite beings. The arguments are therefore arguments for a personal God.

This is supported by a further consideration. How can we conceive the ethical ideal as objectively realized? Not merely in the shape of a set of universal laws. For it to be conceivable adequately it would have to be objectified in a concrete life. Hence the being in whom it was objectified would have not merely to think certain laws but to live in the supremely good, the perfect way. God must not merely lay down good laws or think what is good but be himself good. If he is not fully and perfectly good, the ideal is not objectified in God. So my argument supports not mere pantheism but the belief in a transcendent, personal, ethically perfect God. In fact no moral argument could lead to pantheism since not everything is good. Nor could the objectivity of the moral law be regarded as consisting in a moral order without God such as was conceived by the non-theistic forms of Buddhism in Kharma. For that would make the moral law simply a system of natural laws which brought it about that we gained happiness

[1] H. H. Farmer, *Towards Belief in God*, p. 192.

for what we had done right and suffered for what we did wrong. A law that, for example, if a man were cruel, he should be reincarnated as a beast of prey or be exposed to the cruelty of others in a subsequent life would not be a moral law making cruelty wrong as opposed to imprudent, still less would it be identical with the law that cruelty is wrong. It would only be on a par with the law of gravitation which makes us suffer if we allow ourselves to fall.

But there remains an antinomy with which we must deal. As I pointed out earlier, it is inadmissible to *explain* the moral law by saying it is the command of God. I am not saying that, if God exists, he does not command us to act morally, although I do not know how far the analogy with human commands is to be pushed. What I am saying is that his command must not be made the sole basis of ethics. None of the arguments which I have endorsed requires us to suppose this. Nor do any of them require us to suppose that God created the moral law as God is supposed to have created the existent world. But can we on principle have moral arguments for God which do not imply that the moral law is somehow dependent on God. Even if we do not say that God made the moral law by willing it or commanding us to obey it, still if we are to explain ethics by reference to God, must we not suppose at least that he made the moral law in some way by thinking it? And if so, either he has grounds for thinking like that or he has not. If he has not, the moral law is arbitrary; if he has, he must be dependent in his thought on something other than himself. It may be objected that it is not possible to distinguish God's thought and God's will, but if so the reply to the objection that moral law cannot be explained as the act of God collapses because we cannot then make the distinction used to save moral arguments for God. Even if we just say that the moral law is dependent on God's nature, the same antinomy arises. If God produced it somehow without knowing that it was right or without that knowing influencing its production he is not fully good because he is only unconsciously or at least not voluntarily so; if he did so because he thought it good, he was dependent on knowledge of what was not dependent on himself. In any case it seems to me logically absurd to suppose that the moral law could be created or brought into being, but the reply might be made to this part of the objection that it could be conceived as eternal but depending eternally on the eternal God for its being. The main difficulty however remains, whether the dependence is conceived as causal or as non-temporal: God would be making things right and wrong without any reason why he should make them right or wrong. He might therefore just as well have made cruelty a duty and benevolence a vice and been equally good, because he himself made the law by which his goodness is to be judged. Yet theists have almost universally objected to there being supposed to be something outside God independent of him and still more something outside God on which God is dependent.

What are we to say about this antinomy? It may be put in a more general form. To explain the moral by reference to God is after all to derive ethics from what exists and indeed, at least in the way in which this explanation has usually been effected, to reduce ethical statements to factual statements about God's will or mind. This is to commit the same type of error as is committed by naturalist ethics. It is to reduce the ethical to the factual, or at least explain the ethical wholly by the purely factual and so destroy the autonomy of ethics. It will be replied that the position escapes the objections to naturalism and does not really reduce the ethical to the merely factual because the reduction is in terms of God and God is already conceived as supremely good, but if the view I am criticizing be accepted, to say that God is good could only mean that God thinks or acts like God, since this is held to be what makes anything good. If on the other hand, as I suggested earlier, the relation to God is invoked only to explain why acts rightly approved by secular ethics have the additional characteristic of obligatoriness, this will have in the eyes of theologians the contrary fault of making the moral law that decides which acts will have this quality (while it is God's doing that any should have it at all) independent of God and will indeed make God dependent on the law since the law will decide the attitude of God.

These difficulties seem to call for a radically new method of approach, and I have one to suggest. Hitherto those who have argued from the moral law to the existence of God have usually in effect based what ought to be on what is,[1] but since this breaks down why not try the reverse order? Suppose what is is ultimately based on what ought to be? No doubt we must admit that particular acts are rendered obligatory or the reverse by the presence of certain characteristics in existent

---

[1] Kant and Urban (*The Intelligible World*, chapter 4), are exceptions.

beings, as for example the capacity of human beings to feel pain and the law of gravitation together make it normally wrong to throw a man out of a window 10 feet high. But might not principles of ethics still be prior to reality in the sense that the ultimate ground of existence lay in what was good or what ought to be? Our consideration of the cosmological argument has already suggested that such a supposition alone could supply a rational explanation of what is; and it might also be the key to the solution of the problem of the status of ethics in the universe. Such a solution would, unlike the ordinary type of theological solution, not threaten the autonomy of ethics. Yet it would agree with orthodox theism in making the moral law fundamental to the universe, and this might explain its peculiarly authoritative character. Not that the suggested solution would provide a substitute for God. On the contrary it would of itself entail the existence of God. For, if values are the ground of being, the most perfect conceivable being at least must exist, whatever other beings do so. But, while the notion of obligation either implies or at least strongly suggests that values are in some way themselves central to reality, it does not imply but rather contradicts the view that they are themselves dependent on some other being, God, who is. The possibility of reversing the argument in a way such as that I have suggested should, I think, be carefully considered by all who are attracted by the idea of a moral argument for the existence of God.

I think that only one of the five moral arguments for God which I have put forward, namely, (3), might seem to depend for its validity on the supposition that God actually made the moral law by thinking it, but I do not believe that even this argument does so really, since it contends only that God exists because the moral law must be completely realized in some being, which makes God's existence depend on principles in the realm of value and not vice versa.

At first sight my suggestion may horrify most theologians. They commonly altogether repudiate the idea that there can be anything independent of God, even a law of some kind, and one would expect them to feel a still stronger objection to the suggestion that God himself is dependent on the law, owing his very existence to it. But I do not see that I am saying anything worse than what every theologian who holds God to be a 'necessary being' must admit. For, if God is a necessary being it can only be because he owes his existence

to some a priori principle to the effect that a being that has the attribute
of complete perfection must exist.[1] Otherwise the supposition that
God is a necessary being cannot be held to fulfil the purpose of the
first cause argument and put an end to the potentially infinite regress
of causal explanation. I am therefore not really more liable to the
charge brought forward than most metaphysical theologians. To say
that God was created by another being would indeed be incompatible
with his complete perfection, but to say what I have said is only
another way of saying that God is *causa sui*, a well-recognized
theological doctrine by no means unorthodox in character. To the
objection that I am really suggesting that God is dependent on something other than himself, if only a principle, I reply that to say that
God depends on a principle for his existence is radically different
from saying that God depends for his existence on some other existent
being. The principle is not conceived as existing before God and
creating him. If the value principle is true a priori, then it must always
have been exemplified in the existence of God. It would be as true to
say that the principle could not be true without God existing as to say
that God could not exist without the principle being true. But God's
nature could not depend on the value principle alone as the abstract
principle that what is best must exist, for this by itself would carry
with it no consequences as to the specific nature of the being that did
exist. God's nature would have to depend on the principle together
with specific principles determining what is best or what qualities
ought to be exemplified in existence; i.e. on the value principle plus
the principles determining the nature of a good life which appear to
us so far as we do not make moral mistakes in the guise of the supreme
moral law. This would give the moral law the objective fundamental
status which our arguments call for as basis through God of the entire
universe and also as actualized in the mind of God. These principles
and God would be inseparably linked, though in some respect or sense
one might regard God as prior and in another sense the principles.
The latter would be prior in the sense that they gave the reason why
God existed, and God in that the principles could only be realized in
being, have objectivity through God. It is in any case no limitation

---

[1] 'Perfection' thus applied has indeed ordinarily been conceived as meaning something more than just the possession of absolutely supreme value, for example it includes
omnipotence, but this does not make any difference to the point I have made.

of God's power that he cannot create either the value principle or the moral law. His omnipotence cannot without logical absurdity be supposed to enable him to do what is logically impossible.

The arguments I have formulated on my own behalf are not put forward as proofs. There is no logical absurdity that I can see in accepting an objective ethics and yet denying the 'value principle' and the existence of God. I cannot even claim that my theory completely explains the authoritativeness of the moral law. I have asked how the mere fact, if it be a fact, that it is the command of an omnipotent being could make it morally obligatory, and it is no more my contention that the fact, if it be a fact, that it is a general principle on which the whole of reality depends or an offshoot of such could make it obligatory. I should not hold that, if the basic law of reality were that the worst possible being should exist, this would make it our duty to produce evil. All I mean to say is that the unconditionally compelling character of the moral law as it presents itself to us in so far as we are good men suggests as an explanatory hypothesis the view that the law is in some way bound up with the fundamental nature of reality, and that the easiest way of conceiving the objectivity of the moral law is to think of it as realized in the mind of a deity.

This lack of rigorous conclusiveness in the argument has indeed some advantages. It is a danger in moral arguments for God that somebody who found God's existence incredible might think he must then reverse the argument and repudiate any objective ethics. There is in my view nothing to justify this. My position is that it is certainly evident that we have moral obligations and that these cannot be interpreted as merely subjective or the commands of society. People are apt to overlook this because they concentrate their attention on disputable propositions which, just because they are disputable, naturally occupy the centre of the stage, and do not waste their time thinking about those propositions which would be universally regarded as truisms, for instance the proposition that one ought not to eat one's mother in order to experiment with a new kind of meat. If it would not be too boring, I could easily produce hundreds or thousands of ethical propositions about what I ought not to do now (even if not general rules about what I ought under no circumstances to do) which would be accepted without question by anybody except perhaps a few odd lunatics, and some such might deny even that

$2 + 2 = 4$. Now if *any* ethical propositions are, properly speaking, true, the objectivity of ethics is a fact, and some account of it is needed in philosophy. But while it is certainly evident that some ethical propositions are objectively true, this clear evidence does not necessarily extend to any particular account of their objectivity. That the moral law has being in God and that the moral law is bound up with the basic principle on which the whole of reality depends are not certain entailments of ethical propositions but hypotheses supported by the objectivity and authority of the moral law and intended to help towards solving the problem of its connection with existent reality. It is important to remember that, where we have believed q on the strength of p and decide that we must reject q, there are two alternatives open and not just one. We may have been mistaken in supposing p to be true or we may be mistaken in supposing that q does follow from p, and if we are fixed in our conviction that q at any rate is false we must not then automatically reject p but consider first which of the two alternatives mentioned seems less open to objection. Even where it is a case of apparent a priori entailment we must remember how many mistakes must have been made about entailments, at least in philosophy, in view of the extent of disagreement between philosophers, and so it may well be more reasonable in some cases to retain p and reject the view that p entails q. In the case before us it is not however even a question of entailment but only of a metaphysical hypothesis. That some theory like this is needed in view of the objective authority of ethics seems to me indeed a reasonable suggestion, which should be accepted as a weighty argument for God in the absence of preponderating arguments to the contrary, but not anything which has the same certainty as is possessed by many propositions in the field of ethics.

It might be contended that an ethical argument for the existence of God shared the objectionable character of the ontological argument in passing from a non-existential premise to an existential conclusion. But this is not the case, for the premise is that we, existent beings, are under obligations. I have not however accepted the view that there cannot be affirmative existential necessary propositions but only the view that it could not be logically self-contradictory to deny such a proposition.

There is no objection on principle to an ethical argument as such leading to a metaphysical conclusion, especially where the conclusion is put forward simply as a hypothesis required to explain the facts of ethics. Practice is at least as large a part of our life as knowledge, and it is therefore no more justifiable to use as an argument in favour of a metaphysical theory that it makes our factual and logical knowledge intelligible than that it makes intelligible the truth of the ethical principles on which our practice should depend.

I have never suggested that the actual content of duties is to be derived from the supposition that the value principle is the basis of reality or deduced in any metaphysical way. What I have been considering is the nature of duty in general and not why we have some duties rather than others. What acts we ought to perform is to be determined on the whole by our ethical and not by our metaphysical thinking. However, there are exceptions to this. A person who believes that there is a God will at least have the additional duty of cultivating certain mental attitudes towards God which an unbeliever will not have. But while I have rejected the view that God was creator of the moral law, there is no difficulty about admitting that his existence makes men subject to certain duties to which they would not be subject if he did not exist, any more than there is a difficulty about admitting that a man whose father is alive has certain duties which he would not have if his father were dead. Further, belief in God's existence should give a man a new motive for doing right which he would not otherwise have had, namely love of God. A man may also find an additional motive to do right in the love of a human being whom he wishes to please, but with a really religious man love of God will no doubt influence ethical attitude in a more subtle and potent way than that. As regards ordinary secular duties there is no metaphysical explanation required why an act is obligatory or wrong. We do not need the belief in God to see that it is wrong to cheat or torture other men.

It is sometimes said that God might be good and yet not act according to our ethical standards, so that to establish his goodness would still not give us any justifiable comfort or any indication as to how the universe is run or even that acts we count most evil would not be approved by the deity. But there are only two alternatives – either our ethical propositions are false, or a good being in so far as he is good will act in accord with them, though he may also act in accord

with others which we do not know. No doubt some ethical propositions commonly believed by men to be true are really false or
partly false, but *in so far as* they are true, to say that a perfectly good
God might still act against them is like saying that an omniscient God
might not know that $5 + 7 = 12$.[1] If anything is evident in ethics,
it is that love and benevolence are better than hate and indifference,
and therefore we may be quite confident that a good God will concern
himself closely with our real welfare. The badness of inflicting unnecessary evil on a human being depends on the degree of the evil
and not on the fact that human beings are infinitely less important
than God, and one would think than many other beings existing
somewhere in the universe, so that for God to cause it would be as
much a crime as for a man to do so, or rather much worse since God
would not have our excuses, and God does not commit crimes. We
need not heed the anthropomorphic argument that God has more
important things than our welfare with which to deal, as if he were
short of time; and after all he presumably thought it worth while
bringing us into existence. The argument attributed to Jesus Christ
that, if we know how to give good gifts to our children, so much the
more will our Father in Heaven do so is a good one.

It is not true, as theologians are fond of saying, that we are
dependent on a special supernatural revelation for the doctrine of
God's love. If God includes all possible perfections, a doctrine not
usually held to be dependent on this revelation and which I certainly
would not make so depend, his nature must include the highest value
we know, love in its best sense, even if it includes also other values
still higher of which we can have no conception, at least at present.
Further, the consciousness or conviction of God's love has played
and still plays a fundamental role in the religious experience of countless numbers.

There is however an element of truth in the view that God's
goodness must be generically different from man's simply because
God is such a different kind of being. What this must not be taken as
implying is that God could do things which in a man who, *per im-*

---

[1] I am not talking about propositions as to what ought to be done in so far as they
depend on knowledge as to means to a given end. If physical conditions were different
many of these could be falsified, and means adopted by God would not necessarily be
means it was legitimate for us to adopt, because we cannot know adequately their effects.

possible, had God's knowledge of the consequences would be objectively wrong. (This reservation is needed since an act might have effects which a man could not foresee but which made what would otherwise have been wrong right.) But I am prepared to admit that we cannot appropriately apply to God all the ethical categories suitably applied to good men. Thus we do not speak of God as 'doing his duty' since the concept of 'duty' is understood as implying that the person concerned might conceivably not do his duty and will sometimes be at least tempted not to do it. There is a point in Kant's distinction between the good (moral) will and the holy will. For this reason also we usually do not find theologians applying the term 'moral' to God, though of course they think of God as a moral being in the sense that he applies moral distinctions and acts accordingly.

What ground have we for saying that God is good apart from the specifically ethical arguments, on which many would cast great doubt, or if the proposition that God is good is regarded as analytic, what ground have we for saying that this part of the definition of God applies to any being even if the other part does? This is a question of great importance, for it would be of no religious value to believe in an omnipotent creator if the latter were indifferent to good and evil. It is however hardly conceivable that one who had the other attributes ascribed to God could be other than good. A being who was omnipotent could have no temptation to do wrong unless he were attracted to it for its own sake, and an omniscient being could not fail to realize the nature of evil and therefore would not be attracted to it for its own sake. Nor could he do it by mistake. And since he would not need us as means, what motive could God have for creating us except love or the welfare of the created beings?[1] Further, in so far as belief in God is based on the intuitive conviction present in religious experience it is inseparable from the notion of supreme goodness.

[1] C. Hartshorne in *Faith and the Philosophy*, ed. J. Hick, p. 27.

9

THE PROBLEM OF EVIL

The most obvious and probably the greatest obstacle to religious belief is the problem of evil. It does not indeed at the worst exclude the hypothesis of a limited God, and this is a view we shall have to discuss; but let us first consider whether it can possibly be reconciled with the view held by the vast majority of religious thinkers that God is omnipotent creator and sustainer of all that is. On the face of it does it not seem quite incredible that a perfectly good God capable of creating any world he chose should have created one like this? Unlike most metaphysical arguments this one seems to need no amplification or explanation for its plausibility to be obvious to anyone capable of the least thought. I need not dwell on the multitude and gravity of human evils to bring the argument home.

In defiance of common sense it has however recently been objected that there can be no intellectual problem here because that God exists, if true at all, is necessarily true a priori, and therefore no empirical evidence can be relevant to its truth.[1] Yet it is also a priori true that a perfectly good being will not produce evil unnecessarily, and it is by no means easy to see why it should be necessary for an omnipotent being to do so. Even if we were as certain a priori of the existence of God as we are that $2 + 2$ is equal to 4, it would still be a puzzle why there should be evil and such great evils, though in that case we should have to assume that the problem was somehow soluble, even if we had no notion how. But the position is different from this. Even if there are a priori arguments for the existence of God, they have not the clear inexpugnable certainty of mathematical calculations, nor have the ostensible intuitions of God the clear indisputable self-evidence of the law of contradiction. However convinced we may be of God's existence, we cannot, if only because of the difference of

[1] Hartshorne, e.g. *Creative Synthesis and Philosophic Method*, p. 258.

opinion on the matter between people fully competent to discuss philosophy intelligently, be entitled to regard the belief as established with such certainty that no possible argument on the other side could overthrow it, and unless something can be said to mitigate its force the argument from evil is a very potent one. This is still more the case with most theistic philosophers today, who have no a priori argument for God which strikes even themselves as completely conclusive. Where we cannot, presumably because the subject is too difficult for human beings completely to master it, be sure as to the connection of concepts involved, it may be quite right to reject an a priori argument on empirical grounds. If some calculation which seemed to me perfectly correct as I performed it led from indisputable empirical premises to the conclusion that I owned £500,000, it would be perfectly reasonable for me to conclude with complete confidence that I had made some mistake in the process of a priori calculation though I might not know at the time what the mistake was. In this case I could no doubt eventually detect the mistake, but in philosophical topics it is so hard to be clear about the concepts involved that even great thinkers seem to be in a similar position here to elementary students of arithmetic who cannot be certain that they have even done simple sums right. So it is not true that an a priori proposition cannot be refuted by empirical facts. With the proposition that $2 + 2 = 4$ we are so certain as to its truth that we could have no doubt that any apparent discrepancy with empirical facts could be explained. But with the proposition that God exists we are not entitled to be so certain logically and therefore a serious counter-argument may well be based on discrepant empirical facts. This is all the more so if we think that arguments for God are rather explanatory metaphysical hypotheses than deductive proofs.

It has also been denied that there can be a 'problem of evil' on the ground that the Christian God is by definition the highest standard of the good, and therefore nothing that he does or produces can be incompatible with his being good. But the problem cannot possibly be shelved in any simple way like that. The Christian God is also defined as omnipotent creator and ruler of the universe, and one would not be guilty of any contradiction if one doubted whether the complex definition 'perfectly good omnipotent creator of the world' applied to anything because there was so much evil in the world.

As the word 'God' is commonly used today it would be self-contradictory to say 'God is wicked' but not to say 'The Creator of a world like this would be wicked, therefore God, as the term is understood by Christians, cannot exist'.[1] However, whether the evils of the world do refute Christian theism is a question for a priori argument and not only empirical observation.

'The problem of evil' is how the evil in the world can be reconciled with the belief that the world was created and is controlled by a being who is both omnipotent and perfectly good. It would however be generally admitted that 'omnipotent' should not be understood as implying ability to do what is logically impossible. This at any rate leaves open the theoretical possibility that evil can be justified as a necessary condition of good or at least certain goods. Whether this idea can be applied here with plausibility can be discussed later. It certainly seems to me that the problem, if soluble at all, must be soluble in some such way. To say that evil is unreal simply will not do. It may mean either of two things: (1) that, for example, I only seem to feel pain but never really do so. This contradicts my most certain judgements of introspection. Or (2) it may mean that, though I feel severe pain, it is not really an evil, and that contradicts my surest judgements of value. Nor can we escape the problem by saying that evil is really 'negative'. To say this is not without point, since it is meant to bring out the fact that evil depends on the objective side either on a deficiency, i.e. the privation of something good as with bereavement or blindness or on a mal-arrangement of elements which are not themselves intrinsically evil but either indifferent or actually needful for life. But when we turn to the actual experience constituting lives – and few would say that anything outside experiences and mental states can be either intrinsically good or intrinsically bad – there can surely be no doubt that the experience of severe pain or misery, as opposed to its physical conditions, does not constitute merely the absence of a good but the presence of a positive evil. If it were merely the former, anaesthetics would be pointless and the worst form of torture would be to put one to sleep. And as regards moral evil, while it may be argued that it always arises through seeking what appears *sub facie boni*, this does not alter the fact that to seek consciously a lesser good at the expense of one much greater or of a

[1] See Patterson Brown, *Mind*, no. 72 (1963), pp. 235 ff.

positive evil to another man may involve a state of mind which is not only not good but intrinsically evil. It would be much worse that I should spend the next hour delightedly plotting to murder or torture somebody for my supposed gain than that I should spend it asleep, and this would be the case even if the plot completely failed and produced none of the evil effects contemplated by me. And unless there is some overriding reason for producing or permitting it, what is intrinsically evil ought not to be produced, either directly or indirectly, or even permitted.

Theists have usually dealt with the problem by having recourse to the notion of human free will. Moral evil and a very large part of human suffering is ascribed to this, and it is said that this evil is reconcilable with the goodness of God because, if free will is a necessary condition of moral evil, it is also a necessary condition of the greatest goods. Even if it is itself not intrinsically good, the good exercise of it is intrinsically good. This solution has the great advantage of enabling one to say that moral evil, at any rate, is not even indirectly caused by God but is due to the abuse of human free will which need not have occurred and for which man and not God is to be blamed. But at the best this solution by itself only removes part of the problem and not all. No doubt a great deal of suffering, as well as all moral evil in this world, could on an indeterminist view be ascribed to the abuse of human free will, but what about the rest? I suppose almost all the suffering due to disease could have been averted if human beings had not been ignorant, but ignorance is not in itself a morally culpable fault, and even if it is maintained that by now we should have discovered all the remedies medically possible if human free will had been directed towards that end on a sufficiently large scale and not instead wasted on less worthwhile ends and on the evil end of war with all the suffering it produces, there would still, even if all human beings had lived up to their lights, have been a vast quantity of suffering during the long interim period in which they learnt how to deal with illness and pain by scientific research. However it cannot be denied that it is at least less hard to deal with the problem of evil on indeterminist than on purely determinist lines. It may perhaps even be argued, as has been suggested, that on the former view we could explain the evils I have mentioned by the supposition that the indeterminism necessary if we are to have moral goodness would be metaphysically impossible if there were not an element of indeterminism present from the start of the world. I do not know what independent ground we could have for supposing this, but if it were true it would enable us to deal with the problems of disease and animal suffering by extending indeterminism to the animal world and even to disease germs and the physical conditions which produce earthquakes and similar disasters, but I cannot help feeling suspicious of this as too fanciful a speculation. I shall however discuss the question of human indeterminism in the next chapter and not assume it here at any rate.

We should note that if the indeterminist view is adopted it will not come under the heading of a solution which makes evil a necessary condition of certain goods, since it is not necessary that free will should be abused if it exists. But it would make the *possibility* of evil a necessary condition of certain goods, and so could fairly be called at least 'a solution of this type'. That is why I said earlier that if the problem of evil is soluble at all it 'must be soluble in some such way'.[1] However the mere possibility of evil could itself be called an evil in a very important sense.

Turning now to other solutions or parts of a solution, we must consider whether it is possible – not indeed to solve the problem in detail by showing each evil to be conducive to good, an end which must in any case be completely beyond human capacity to attain, and beyond any conceivable capacity if some of the evil is due to unnecessary abuses of human free will – but to suggest ways in which evil could be deemed capable of justification as a necessary condition of the attainment of good. One is suggested by the idea that everything other than God must be finite, and finiteness entails imperfection. Imperfection need not entail positive evil for anything we can see, but I think it might well be the case that it really did so. This however is only a speculation, and it is hardly possible to apply it to moral evil. Surely moral evil at least is a blot on the universe which cannot possibly be made good by the presence somewhere of some other patch of evil, like a picture which was as a whole a beautiful work of art though the parts taken by themselves had each some aesthetic defect of a positive kind, which I suppose would be possible. Even the retributive theory of punishment understood as implying that the

---

[1] See p. 211.

sin punished and the pain of the punishment taken together are less of an evil than the sin taken alone does not maintain that (except possibly in some rare cases for the subsequent effects) it would have been better if a man had sinned and been punished than if he had not sinned at all, and still less could sin or pain in another man make up for my sinning so that the man's sin or pain and my sin fitted together to constitute an intrinsically good whole. Whatever is the truth about the 'atonement theory', it was surely not the pain Christ suffered as such but the goodness of his unselfish love which provided a remedy for the sins of man. And it would be unreasonable to expect one to worship a God who included as part of himself beings such as Hitler or Caligula supplementing each other as imperfect parts of a perfect whole, or even who deliberately created them as they were so that they might by their wickedness supplement somebody else's wickedness and thus make up a good whole. But if the evil in these men could not be compensated for by some evil, could it be compensated for by some good? It is clear that the mere existence of good (even a vastly preponderant amount of good over evil) in the cosmic process could not compensate for whatever evil there is in the sense of justifying the infliction or permission of the evil merely by the fact that it followed it. A father could not be excused for hitting his child merely because he was able to point out that he had given him a long holiday at the seaside afterwards for a treat the pleasure of which greatly outweighed the pain of the blow. What is needed to justify evil by means of subsequent good is to show that the evil was either a necessary condition of the good or a consequence of something else which was a necessary condition of the good. Even this may not be a sufficient justification; it is not always right for a man to do evil that good may come, but in many cases, for instance with surgical operations and their attendant pain, the justification may be adequate. We shall now ask in what way evil could be a necessary condition of good not only for men but even for an omnipotent God.

Here we may seem brought to a standstill. We can easily understand how a human being might be justified in bringing about evil in the shape of suffering in medical treatment, for example, but then the surgeon did not create the conditions under which he has to operate. He did not create the germs which led to the blood poisoning which made it necessary for him to amputate a limb in order to save life. But

God is supposed to have ultimately created everything. However, there is another way in which the problem of evil may be alleviated.

The point is this, and it is an extremely important one. When we consider our values it does appear quite clear that some goods, and these by no means the lowest but among the highest, are such that they necessarily involve some evil as the condition of their attainment. Courage, unselfishness and the highest forms of love are of very great intrinsic and not only instrumental value but one could hardly have them if there were no such thing as suffering. And this, I think, is not a case of causal necessity but an amended form of Moore's principle of organic unities. Moore pointed out that it is not necessarily true that the value of a whole is equal to the sum of the values of its parts taken separately.[1] This is not arithmetically absurd or even, when looked at rightly as a general principle, at all paradoxical. It only amounts to saying that the total value of something for good or for ill may be affected not only by the nature of its parts by themselves but by the way in which they are related. Why should the value of something depend only on the items which make it up apart from their relations with each other? It would be very odd if such an important feature in reality as relation did not make any difference to value. And the principle could enable one to take a very important step towards the solution of our problem. For according to it the addition to a whole of a part which was bad in itself might conceivably actually increase the value of the whole to which it belonged, and if so the production of the evil part might be justified provided it added to the whole a value which outweighed the disvalue of this part.

It would be best, I think, to state the principle of organic unities as the principle 'that the value of a, b and c together is not always dependent only on the value of a, b and c as they would be taken apart'. This avoids committing oneself to saying whether the difference, when it occurs, is due to the parts, as Moore thought, producing an additional value or disvalue in the whole when combined in certain ways while remaining the same in value themselves or to the value of the parts being itself modified by their relation to each other. One alternative may be realized in some and the other in other cases. It also avoids the notion of summing with its arithmetical suggestions.

[1] *Principia Ethica*, chapter 1. For the application of this principle to the problem of evil see J. Wisdom in *Mind*, vol. 44 (January 1935).

Now this principle of organic unities can be applied in considering the problem of evil, although it was not so applied by Moore. For it to be applicable there must be cases where the existence of something in itself evil is a necessary condition of there being something intrinsically good. Can evil be thus considered as a necessary condition of the attainment of good? Now I think it is clear that this cannot be said in relation to all goods. I do not think that the good of intelligent understanding need imply the existence of anything intrinsically bad except where what is to be understood already includes evil elements itself. In finite beings the knowledge process itself necessarily implies partial ignorance and I think error but I do not consider ignorance and error to be evil in themselves, though they often have effects and causes which are thus evil. And I certainly cannot see how the intrinsic value of the experience of contemplating a beautiful landscape taken as an experience by itself can be regarded as necessarily implying the presence of any evil whatever. The only thing that could be said here is that, if we seek anything as good, we shall be liable sometimes to fail and that will give us the pain of frustration and disappointment. If we care about beautiful landscapes we shall sometimes feel in some degree frustrated if we are unable to see them or to see them to advantage for some reason, for example preoccupations of various sorts or mist and rain, and similarly with knowledge and understanding. But I should class this under the heading earlier mentioned of finitude implying imperfection and not under the principle of organic unities applied to values; and in any case it would hardly be adequate by itself to justify all the major evils of human life, though it might justify more in the way of evils than strikes one at first sight. It could hardly be best to make this present physical life everlasting, and this involves, if we are to have the great value of love between different human beings, the grave suffering of bereavement.

But there are certain kinds of good which we can clearly see in a more direct way to imply evils if they are to be realized at all; and this might be sufficient to explain the existence of evil even if some other goods can be realized without evil. For the more different kinds of good there are the better the world, provided they are not purchased at too high a price in evil. For example, if there were no evil, what would become of the virtues of courage and unselfishness? The word 'love' has sometimes been used for mental attitudes which involved no sympathy and no readiness to make the smallest sacrifice for the sake of the person loved, but certainly such forms of 'love' would be evil rather than 'good', yet how could sympathy or self-sacrifice as they occur in all the higher forms of love we know be possible without the least evil? In order to conquer evil we must have real evil to conquer, and conquering evil is a great good. It seems to me we should distinguish three kinds of case here.

(1) An intrinsically good whole may contain some parts which are bad per se and yet necessary for the goodness of the whole. Examples of this are provided by the pain present in loving sympathy for the sufferings of others or in a state of mind which exemplifies courage[1] or even in the aesthetic experience provided by a tragedy or a sorrowful tale or poem. Some aesthetic experiences, though happy as a whole, must include an element of pain and would lose most of their value without this. Another kind of example is provided by the fact that moral virtue in any form known by us implies the overcoming of real temptation and that real temptation must involve both an element of pain and I think an element of ethical deficiency which in itself is undesirable. (I call it 'ethical' not 'moral deficiency' because temptation is compatible with sinlessness but not with perfection. If our will were absolutely and completely impervious to the influence of desire except in so far as this coincided with what is right there would, I think, be no temptation and certainly no moral struggle.) Yet there is something of very great intrinsic value in a successful moral struggle.

The connection I am referring to in these cases between the evil part and the good whole is not a causal one. It is not that pain is a precedent causal condition of a display of love or courage, but that it is part of the experience or state of mind which has the value. Nor is what I am asserting an analytic proposition – for example that, if there were no pain involved, by definition it would not be courage. It would not indeed, but besides the analytic proposition that the state of mind which accompanies brave action includes pain there is the synthetic one that the whole state which includes the pain is good on the whole and that its full value depends on the pain being present.

(2) Something intrinsically good may be dependent for its value on

---

[1] Courage may be shown not only by bearing pain but by facing danger, but in that case there must still be a painful element, greater or smaller, if the danger is apprehended as such, and if it were not so apprehended I should not call it courage.

something not actually contained in it that is itself bad. For example what would become of the goodness of sympathy or benevolence if there were no evils which made these appropriate? It might be replied that what matters is a benevolent and sympathetic disposition and that this might exist even if there were no evil to call for its active exercise. But what is a mere disposition apart from its realization in acts or at least states of mind? A totally unrealized disposition would be a merely hypothetical possibility, and such a non-entity could have no intrinsic value whatever. Our opponent might then urge that the intrinsic value of benevolence or sympathy lies solely in the state of mind and not in any outward circumstances which accompany it, and therefore all that is needed for it is not actual evil but a belief that the evil has occurred or will occur. But such cases of false belief surely presuppose that there are some real cases of suffering, as lies presuppose that some statements made are true. It is again not a causal connection but something different that is involved. No doubt the evil which calls for relief is a part cause of the act of benevolence which relieves it, but what makes it relevant to the goodness of the benevolence is not the relation of causality but the relation of appropriateness to it which alone gives the self-sacrifice point and makes it right and not senseless or wrong.

(3) The principle of organic unities can be applied (though Moore himself does not actually apply it) to temporal sequences of events. The intrinsic value or disvalue of an action or emotional state will depend partly on its appropriateness or the reverse relation to a situation which may be past and the cognition of which at any rate must be. My emotional attitude of gratefulness to somebody will gain in intrinsic value if it is proportionate to his services (sufficient and yet not unreasonably and sentimentally excessive) and it will be intrinsically more valuable if it is really proportionate than if I merely mistakenly think it so. Another example is provided by the case of a poem or play, the value of which certainly cannot be regarded as just the sum of the value of the successive lines or scenes. It may be retorted that there is no value in the poem or play except as read or acted and in order to arrive at the total value of the experience of reading it or seeing the play performed we need only take into account the value of the successive experiences of reading or seeing the parts. No doubt the value of an earlier scene or line may reasonably be

said to be enhanced by a later one, but if so it might be said that this only means that the later experience is altered in felt quality in a way which improves its value by the remembrance of the experience earlier, so that this is not a case of the principle of organic unities, which implies even in the form in which I stated it that the same experiences qualitatively, *a* and *b*, when combined can have a different value because of the way in which they are related and not merely that the factual qualities of one can be altered by its relations to another. But we may answer that the value of the experiences does not depend merely on the reader's consciousness, but on whether the poem or play is really in 'good or bad taste'. If the reader or spectator thinks something in good taste when it really is not, however we analyse 'good taste', the value of his experience will be lessened and this lessening of value will depend on a real relation between the parts and not on the factual quality of the experiences, which is *ex hypothesi* the same. A case of greater importance for our purpose is this. A life the earlier part of which was morally inferior and the later part morally superior would be intrinsically much more valuable than a life the earlier part of which was superior in the same degree and the later part equally inferior. It is not merely that if the relatively good part has come earlier and the relatively bad part later the man in question will feel the badness of the latter more acutely by contrast; if the defect is moral he may even feel it less because he has become less sensitive to it through having got worse and does not realize his deterioration. On the other hand the great good in the opposite process of gradual 'self-conquest' and moral improvement presupposes earlier evil, and the goodness is not taken away by the man being too modest to realize and delight in his advance.

There are thus certain goods (we may call them 'mixed goods') which we could not have without corresponding evils. May this serve as a justification of 'the ways of God to man'? It might at first sight be thought not, because it cannot be claimed that this is the case with all goods. (I do not think it true as a universal proposition that we could only appreciate good by contrast with evil, though of course the appreciation may be very much enhanced thereby.) But the best universe would not be confined to any one kind of good but should presumably include all sorts unless a particular sort were unattainable without a degree of evil that outweighed the good gained. The need

for a variety of goods is shown by the extent to which we feel the
eternal recurrence theory pointless and depressing, and not here
because lack of variety is boring since each recurrent period would be
exactly the same and therefore would be no more boring than when it
occurred on the first occasion. Now whether the value of these mixed
goods as attained by the human race is great enough to outweigh
the evil not only of the pain but of the moral badness displayed in the
historical process is not a question which we can possibly settle by
summing up the good and evil on either side, but I do not see how
we can be in a position to give a dogmatic negative. If some goods
cannot be produced without evil, would it not still be the part of a
good God to see that they were produced provided the good of their
production outweighed the evil? But, it may be asked, why not
produce more pure goods which involve no evil rather than mixed
ones which do? If that had been done, would not the universe be still
better? However, the objection assumes that God had to choose
between producing so many mixed goods and so many pure goods,
but if conscious beings will always be in existence there is room for an
infinite amount of goods in any case. Further, we must not assume
that pure goods are necessarily better than mixed. They are certainly
not always so. The pleasure of eating sweets is a good which can
occur without involving any evil and is thus a pure good in my sense,
but it does not follow that it is a greater good than the moral virtues
the realization of which is impossible except in a struggle against
evil. There may indeed be pure goods higher than any of the mixed
goods I have mentioned, but if so we do not know of them in our
experience, or at least most of us do not. I add this clause because
some forms of religious experience may fall in this class, though I
think most include some element of pain or sadness if only in the
form of a sense of unworthiness, and in a world with so much evil
it may be questioned whether a religious experience which contains
no element of sympathetic sorrow for the suffering in the world is
one that ought to be cultivated, though, if God exists, happiness
should be predominant on the whole in the experience. Perhaps, if
God created us, the reason may have been because there was something even God could not do by himself, that is, produce the kind
of goods which involve pain and moral struggle and so evil. I suggest
elsewhere that God himself may through his love for us experience

something of the nature of suffering, as seems indeed assumed in the Christian tradition, though not very consistently since God is also spoken of as destitute of passions. But this element could be present in a perfect God only because finite beings he loved were suffering and partly evil. And the distinctive good of successful moral struggle and moral progress as opposed to the different, though higher, good of moral perfection could not be present in God. Would we or ought we to want to be transferred to a morally higher state of being without having done anything to earn it?

It would not follow from what I have said that evil must necessarily always exist. For even if it is desirable that the goods of which evil is a necessary condition should be realized as well as other, pure goods, it does not follow that these mixed goods must be realized at every stage of the time process. It is conceivable that there will once come a time, as portrayed in the Christian heaven, after which none but pure goods will be realized, and these might take forms of goodness far, far beyond any we know now or can even faintly imagine. This world would not have been created by a good God if there were not in it some goods as well as in 'heaven', but though it is good that there should be these goods, they need not last for ever. It is not necessary to suppose that evil must always be kept in existence so that there may always be those goods which depend on conquering evil, provided there are other goods which do not involve evil. The more different kinds of good realized the better, but they need not all be realized simultaneously.

The kind of solution I have suggested does not deny the reality of evil; on the contrary it presupposes it. For the good organic unities of which I have been speaking arise through the overcoming of evil, and if so there must be real evil to overcome. Nor should it discourage us from fighting against evil, for evil can only be part of a good organic unity if fought against and conquered. By a 'good organic unity' I mean a combination of elements which taken together are intrinsically good in a way which depends on but outweighs so as to more than compensate for an element of evil. Evils are there to be fought against. Certainly the evils are very great, but we cannot prove that they are greater than necessary for the production of the good (granted that human beings abuse their free will as much as they do till they are eventually redeemed). Little evils would in any

case not be sufficient, for it is great and not small evils that have called
out what is best in man.

My view is that the principle of organic unities is necessary but not
sufficient for a solution of the problem of evil. There is much that
inclines – in view of the following chapter I shall speak more strongly
and say 'drives' – one to be an indeterminist, and indeterminists are
in a strong position because, as it is logically impossible to guarantee
completely that an undetermined being will always do what is best,
much of the evil there is may be regarded as independent of God's
will. But I do not hold that indeterminism of itself is sufficient to
solve the problem. All evil cannot be traced to abuse of free will.

③   Apart from the supposition of indeterminism and organic unities
there are two other considerations, both surprisingly neglected by
theologians, which can help with the problem. Firstly, if something
A is related by a relation r to something else B, it is logically necessary
that B should stand in the converse relation to A, this covering both
the cases where the converse of a relation is the same as the relation
and the cases where it is different. Yet it may well be that, while it
would be best for A to be related to B by r, it would be by no means
best but even very bad for B to be related by the converse relation
to A. To take examples, it might well be best for A to be monogamously married to B but much better for B that she should be
monogamously married to C, so that A and B cannot both be satisfied,
and at least one of them has to bear the evil, generally esteemed a by
no means small one, of frustrated love. It might well be best for the
happiness and even the real good of each of several competitors to
have a certain post. Since what is best for one will sometimes clash
logically with what is best for another, it would be impossible to
satisfy everyone always even in the best possible world.

④   A further circumstance which might account for some of the evil
in the world by limiting what is logically possible is the existence of
causal laws. Most theologians, perhaps almost all, think that causal,
as opposed to logical laws, cannot be independent of God's will,
but there are considerable difficulties about holding this position.
Few would accept the 'occasionalist' view that God is the direct
cause of everything which happens in the physical world; and if this
were held, it would certainly not make the problem of evil less difficult.
When a man was tortured, we should then have to suppose that God

THE PROBLEM OF EVIL

obliged the torturer by directly causing fearful pain in his victim, i.e. that God was the real torturer and not, for example, Hitler's minion. But what can be meant by intermediate causes, the laws governing which depend on God? If we regard causation as simply regular sequence, what distinction is there between saying that God caused, for example, the pain of cancer, by producing a universe in which according to its causal laws pain-producing cancers developed and that God caused the pain directly whenever the cancer in a developed form was present. On this view causal laws all depend on God's will, and to will that *A* caused *B* would simply amount to willing that *B* should regularly follow *A*. To make the distinction we should have to think of the natural, secondary causes as of their own nature necessitating the effects, and I find it hard to see what could be understood by this if it does not mean that there is something in the nature of the cause which necessarily involves the effect. The 'entailment' theory of causation usually taken for granted before Hume has fallen on evil days, but it seems to me the only intelligible alternative to the untenable regularity view,[1] and if it is true some at any rate of what we call 'causal laws' (not all, because what appears to us as a causal law might still in some cases be a regularity fixed by God) will have to be regarded like other a priori laws as independent of God's will, since it is not part of God's omnipotence to do the logically impossible. This will have the advantage of making the problem of evil less acute and helping to explain why God seems to have to produce effects by elaborate physical means. I think otherwise this presents a serious difficulty to the theist. It is usually met by saying that it is better for the mental and moral education and development of man that there should be regular laws, but why should one course be better than another for the development of man if there are not causal laws of psychology which make it so? Even on an indeterminist view, if one course of training is to be better than another as a general rule, it must be because there are causal laws which make it at any rate more likely that it will be followed by right acts of human free will. The best possible effects that did not violate freedom but give opportunities and encouragement for its right exercise could be produced without any sort of training if there were no psychological causal laws making this impossible. The following might serve as an

[1] See p. 154.

example. It does seem to me a causal law which we ourselves can see to be necessary that failure to gain what we desire will in so far tend in the direction of unhappiness, yet since desire is necessary for action or for any life of the type we live, and men being finite could not possibly always get what they desire, and moral progress depends on a disciplining of desires, we have an entailment which renders some evil in the pursuit of good inevitable.

But we cannot see a priori necessity in all psychological, or, I think, any physical causal laws. No doubt a necessity may be present even where we cannot see it, so with those laws into which we have no insight, and many would deny we ever had such insight, there is no means of knowing which elements in what appears to us as a causal law are the result of God's choice and which are due to entailments independent of his will, and it would only be the latter and not the former which could help us as regards the problem of evil. However, since we do not know what they are, it remains an open possibility that the causal entailments independent of God's will are sufficient to explain the existence of much of the evil in the world.

It is thus not impossible to work out a tolerable outline for the solution of the problem of evil in general terms. But when we consider the actual world before us with the depths of misery and evil it contains any such solution may seem intolerably smug and artificial. It is all very well, it is said, working out schemes for the solution of the problem in the background of a sheltered, comfortable, pleasant life, but could this stand up for a moment to real overwhelming suffering and disaster such as is the lot of so many, probably of most men at some time or other in their lives, and such as has been so prominent during the period of the two world wars? If this is intended as a personal question – would I be able to hold to such a solution if I had to face the intenser forms of suffering? – I can only say that such an *argumentum ad hominem* is quite irrelevant. If I as a result of the suffering became so embittered as to cease to hold such a belief, that would not prove the belief wrong any more than the fact that somebody was led only by his desire for a comfortable belief to accept theism would prove atheism mistaken. The point hits me more when I reflect that it would seem like a cruel mockery to talk in the way in which I have just been talking to somebody who was watching her child die in agony from illness or who was being tortured in a

Nazi concentration camp. But it is undeniable that many people who
have had to face terrible suffering have in the midst of it still held
to their faith in God and believed that somehow the evil would prove
a stepping-stone for others and, if they believed in another life, even
for themselves to a good which far outweighed the miseries they had
endured.

But this brings us to a point I must now emphasize, namely, that
no answer to the problem of evil that is in the least plausible can be
given if this life is all. In the abstract we may be clear that evil can
on occasion be explained as a condition without which certain goods
could not have been attained, but when we think of the actual nature
and distribution of the evil in the world difficulties thicken. I do
indeed think that the apparent difficulty which has perhaps worried
religious people most about the distribution of evil is not to be taken
as a very serious one. It is that so much suffering falls on the innocent.
The term 'suffering of the innocent' has indeed judicial associations
which are here very misleading. It suggests a court deliberately
condemning to imprisonment persons who have not committed any
crime, a thing which would of course be gravely wrong, but this is very
different from misfortune falling on them in the ordinary course of
nature, which carries with it no unjust stigma of guilt except in the
mind of somebody who has a preconceived theological prejudice.
The misfortunes are often no doubt the result of someone else's
guilt, but if God always intervened to stop a man wrongly injuring
another there would be no possibility of doing wrong and so no
intrinsic value in doing right. I do not wish to deny that the intensity
and frequency of apparently useless suffering is a great difficulty for
theism especially if immortality is denied – I have just said so – but
I doubt whether the difficulty is much increased by the addition of this
word 'innocent', and I certainly could not agree with C. A. Campbell
when he says that deserved suffering constitutes no problem for the
theist.[1] It seems to me that the idea that the main problem lies in the
distribution of unhappiness in a way not proportionate to men's
deserts presupposes various unjustified assumptions. (1) It assumes a
retributive theory of punishment, and not only in the milder sense in
which many philosophers hold what they call a retributive view
today, according to which it only asserts that it is intrinsically wrong,

[1] *Selfhood and Godhood*, p. 287.

H

and not merely wrong on account of its consequences, to punish the innocent, but in the older and extremer form which held it to be positively good that the wicked should suffer for their wickedness, at least good in a sufficient degree to cancel out the intrinsic badness of their pain. But (2) it goes further than this and implies not merely that it is good in itself that happiness and unhappiness should be distributed in proportion to desert but that it is a good so important that every other good ought to be subordinated to it. For the course which involves a distribution of happiness or unhappiness in proportion to goodness or badness (if there is indeed any meaning in such a proportion), will hardly always coincide with the course which would otherwise be best for the persons concerned. It is plainly less important that the sinner should get his exact deserts than that he should become a good man in the fullest sense of the word, and therefore if the two clash the former end ought to be sacrificed to the latter. We cannot therefore conclude that even in the best possible universe happiness and unhappiness would always be in proportion to desert. (3) Those who assume that it is even desirable that there should be this proportion forget that such a system of exact payments and penalties would destroy disinterestedness. Campbell admits that for reasons of this sort the occurrence of some undeserved suffering is only to be expected even in the best of worlds, but says that what does constitute a problem is the occurrence of those forms of suffering which are so prolonged and acute as to reduce the sufferer 'by slow torture to a state of mind in which he is no longer a rational being at all, but just one vast feeling-centre for devastating and all-enveloping pain.'[1] I agree that this does constitute a difficult problem, but I should think that it does even if the man who suffers it is wicked. I do not imagine that the introduction of 'slow torture' into our penal system would meet with Campbell's approval.

But when I consider the vast amount of evil in human life and its apparent complete failure in so many, many cases to produce a benefit worth the cost I cannot believe that reality is such as to satisfy in any degree the religious aspirations of man if this life is all. Such aspirations require for their satisfaction at least that good is preponderant in a very high degree, and that plainly does not seem to be the case with this world of ours taken by itself. Even if sin is ascribed

[1] Op. cit., p. 288.

to human free will, it is still very puzzling why God should give so much scope for free will if it produces all this evil and why he did not make the dispositions of the weaker brethren such that they were less inclined to sin. If the struggle required to overcome temptation had been less severe or hardly needed at all, there would have been less credit in their virtue, but it is better that a man have little credit for his virtue than that he should ruin himself and others by vice. I should feel very different about this if it were admitted that failures in this life were not final but more like the early mistakes and mis-behaviour of school-children beginning a process of education that will eventually take them to heights far beyond any of which they could now dream. In that case all for anything we know might well be worth while. But if we consider only this world we have to admit that at least a very large part of the evil is sheer waste. It is all very well to say that a man can greatly improve in character as a result of bearing his misfortunes well, but men certainly do not always bear them well but often deteriorate rather than improve, sometimes very seriously; and even when they do improve, the good so painfully gained is, if there is no other life than this, very soon thrown away by death. When one thinks of the miserable conditions of poverty under which till quite recently the vast majority of the human race have lived and at least half still live, the absence of opportunity for most of them to have a reasonably satisfying life, the appalling suffering from disease, especially prior to proper medical care due mostly to ignorance inevitable, at least for the individuals suffering, the horrors of war, oppression and cruelty from the grossest to the most subtle forms, it must be conceded that this world looks and, as far as we know, always has looked most unlike a world created and governed by an ethically perfect and omnipotent deity. In view of what I have said we must admit that there is no outright logical contradiction in the supposition, so that we should still have to accept it if the existence of such a God had been strictly proved, and if it had also been proved that there could not be a future life, but neither condition is fulfilled. It is not a case of impeccable logical proofs but of balancing arguments and ostensible intuitions, and if I were con-vinced that there could be no survival of bodily death, I should consider myself that, despite what I have said, the problem of evil made the belief in an omnipotent God so plausible that it should be abandoned. But in my chapter on Mind and Body I found despite all the modern philosophical tendencies to the contrary that there was no strong philosophical objection to survival. The physiological facts give it a certain antecedent improbability, but against this must be set the evidence of 'physical research', and while I should not venture to say that this proved survival it does, since it can vouch for phenomena of which survival is at any rate the simplest and least unplausible explanation, give the hypothesis a certain probability which balances the antecedent improbability I have mentioned. The upshot of this is that we need not scruple to accept this hypothesis if we think both that we are justified in believing in God and that such a belief would be incredible if this life were all. Hume argues that since our premises are derived from the distribution of happiness and suffering in this world, we have no right to go beyond them in the conclusion to another life in which we suppose them to be distributed better; and he is right if and only if we accept his assumptions: namely (1) that happiness is the only good and suffering the only evil, (2) that the belief in God is a purely empirical induction. I do not make either of these assumptions and am therefore not refuted by his argument. It is obvious that a mere empirical survey of the amount of good and evil we encounter in the world would not justify an inference to a perfect creator (which is by no means the same as saying that it is necessarily incompatible with its being the work of one); but I have never tried to base the case for theism on this. It also seems obvious to me that the problem is on principle quite insoluble if hedonism be true, but I have elsewhere discussed and rejected hedonism considered on its own merits as a theory of ethics.[1] One cannot believe that this world is the best possible device for the production of the greatest balance of pleasure over pain, but if we introduce other goods and suppose that the character developed by trial and error in this life can be made the basis of a further development including the reversal of its unfavourable traits the situation is altered considerably. Many defects in the universe from a hedonistic point of view are advantages from the point of view of character training and even those features which do not seem so we can hope will turn out to be advantages in a long enough run (subject at least to the abuses

---

[1] *Ethics*, pp. 42 ff.

of human free will) if the perspective is not limited to this life, but extended to include immortality.

But to be consistent the theist should go further than postulating a life beyond the present. He should realize that the logical course is to suppose ultimate universal salvation for every man, meaning by 'salvation' at least the attainment of a life which is worth living as a whole. It is an extraordinary and lamentable fact that this view was not taken by the Christian Church, for nothing is clearer than that it is the logical corollary of the Christian conception of God. It raises me to white-hot indignation to think of all the cruel misery that must have been inflicted on many millions by what, if it had not strangely been accepted by so many saintly men, I should have called the *criminal stupidity* that grafted on the religion of a loving God the belief that this loving being was going to have the majority of the human race tortured for ever as a punishment for their sins, and it is one of the most puzzling phenomena of history that such a belief could have been held and taught for many centuries by so many good and even otherwise mostly wise men. The belief in hell has by now been toned down and at least in educated quarters the fire and brimstone have disappeared, but nothing less will suffice than the outright denial of the occurrence of such an event in God's universe as the eternal damnation of a single human being, meaning by that not torture for ever but the ultimate failure of his life so that it would be better that he had never come into existence at all. The improbability of the texts in the Bible which seemed to support the doctrine of eternal damnation not being authentic revelations as thus interpreted should on any sensible view at least be very much less than the improbability of such an occurrence. For if I were eternally damned I should be defeating God and that is surely not a thing any human being could be conceived as doing. The doctrine was made even more open to objection if that be possible by the totally gratuitous assumption that our behaviour (or faith) in this life settled our destiny for all eternity without any hope of recovery.

People have been afraid of admitting the doctrine of universal salvation, to use an old-fashioned word, because they thought that, if a man believes that he will be saved in the end whatever he does, he will not be encouraged to make an effort to do right or be deterred from doing wrong, but the fact, if indeed it be a fact, that the belief in hell is useful for frightening people into a good behaviour – and it seems to have been more effective at frightening people who were already good than people who were bad, except perhaps when it was too late to stop their crimes – does not go any way to show it right. Besides, to say that we shall all be saved in the end is not to say that it will be all the same whatever we do. My view is not that a man will be saved whatever he does, for there are some kinds of action which are such that nobody could be saved as long as he persisted in them, but that all will ultimately do the things required for salvation. Further, the end to be attained may be a very long way off, and it may be enormously retarded with great suffering to ourselves if we act sufficiently badly. This should provide quite sufficient scope for anybody who wishes to help to deter people from wrongdoing by reference to a future life. We cannot even say that, though we may delay the good day, it will be the same even in the end whatever we have done before that day arrives. Even if we are ultimately saved in the sense of our life as a whole being worthwhile there are degrees of worthwhileness. Even if Hitler is saved in the end, it may very well be not only that his progress is retarded and that he will have to endure prolonged and acute mental suffering which he would have avoided if he had led a decent life on earth, but also that when he finally attains salvation his state, though good, will be vastly less good than it would have been if he had not so abominably misused his opportunities. In this sense there may be a very serious danger for us of eternal loss (or if you like punishment), namely that a person might through his own fault miss for ever the opportunity of much good which he would otherwise have attained. Even though he will, if there is a God in the Christian sense, finally attain a good which makes his life as a whole worth while, the total value of it may be very much less than it would otherwise have been.

It is said in defence of eternal hell that God must allow men freedom even at the risk of ultimate failure, but, even on an indeterminist view, freedom only excludes compulsion. It does not exclude a vast diversity of forms of beneficial influence by one mind on another; and we may be sure that a good God would arrange that all these were brought to bear to avoid final catastrophe. A great deal has always been said by religious people about the duty of faith in God, but surely they should have had sufficient faith to believe that God, who according to their faith loved all human beings with an unimaginable intensity and had all logically possible resources at his command, would succeed in averting such a horrible and irretrievable disaster. Even humanly speaking it is now generally recognized that most criminals could have been saved from criminal tendencies if they had had suitable treatment when young, and how can we deny that it would be possible for an omnipotent God to see that the hard core too were, if necessary after a long series of lives each of which gave them a fresh start, eventually persuaded voluntarily to take the steps necessary to end the wretched state in which they were? If children turn out very badly, it is thought that in almost all cases the parents are partly to blame, and God has far more power over environment, good will, wisdom and foresight than any human parent. Even if he were to fail, though the suggestion that he might ultimately fail seems to me blasphemous, he surely would see as a last resort either that their freedom was overruled and they were brought to a tolerable state of mind even against their will, since an eternal and complete abuse of freedom would be worse than having no freedom at all or that they were annihilated rather than continued to blacken the cosmos by their survival in eternal 'hell'. To reply that for all we know annihilation may be impossible would be to suggest – in complete opposition both to Christianity as almost always taught and the general attitude of most believers in God anywhere – that human selves were capable of existence independent of and even against the will of the deity. We may add that if, as Christians commonly suppose, God is omniscient, he would foresee the damnation of any being who was going to be eternally damned, in which case a good God would certainly see that the being did not come into existence, even if the foreseen damnation was going to be the result of a wicked abuse of the latter's own freedom.

We must bear in mind that to say that all people will ultimately be saved is not to deny that the process may take an immensely long time. If 'universalism' meant that everybody will go to heaven as soon as they die it would be a most unreasonable, not to say demoralizing doctrine. Not one in ten thousand is at death yet fit for heaven, if this means a state of sinless bliss, of complete and unbroken harmony with other finite beings and with God. It seems to me that the Hindu and Buddhist view that it will for most of us take thousands of years is likely to be nearer the truth than the old-fashioned Christian view that everything is settled at the conclusion of this life, though I do not see why the progress from this life to heaven should as in the Catholic view of purgatory be regarded as predominantly painful. There is no need to suppose that it will not like the present life be mixed in character. (If spiritualist evidence does turn out reliable, happiness will generally preponderate, at least for people who have not been exceptionally bad.) But how long and how painful the process was would depend mainly upon ourselves. Nor do I see any reason to exclude but rather some reason to expect that the process will include, as eastern religions commonly hold, a series of reincarnations in physical form. Of how many men could it be said that by the time of their death they had already learnt all the lessons that can be taught by life in the body where such things as birth, marriage, death, illness occur, where you can learn to face physical difficulties and take the right attitude to physical possessions? How these things are arranged if they occur is to us unimaginable, whatever our view of the future life, but so would this life have been if we had had the intelligence to discuss it in our mother's womb or, before scientific development, what we now know of the constitution of matter.

I have dwelt at length on a subject of which philosophers as such are usually loath to speak, though the tendency to do so has notably increased in the last few years, but the importance of the subject cannot be denied since the whole prospect for our future destiny depends on the answer to such questions as I have raised, and I think it most desirable for the intellectual, moral and religious credit of Christianity that the doctrine of eternal hell as a real possibility for anyone, now widely discredited and commonly tacitly ignored even where it is not repudiated, should be completely and conclusively ruled out as inconsistent with any belief in an omnipotent perfectly good God such as Christians profess. It is a doctrine about which no good man who realized a fraction of what it meant could be happy even if he felt constrained to accept it on authority. It is only reasonable to believe that people will on the whole in any future life be liable to suffer for their sins, though I do not think an exact proportion between happiness or unhappiness and desert a useful or intelligible conception, but this does not mean that the suffering should go on for ever (or timelessly). I should add that, while I have used the word 'punishment', this should be regarded rather as the natural effect of our misdoing than as an imposition from outside by God.

We must not indeed think of God as directly creating the beings who work evil rather than as having let them evolve, but this of itself does not do much to alleviate the problem except in so far as it brings in human free will. A being is just as responsible for the evil he knowingly produces if he produces it through an instrument. He is indeed almost as responsible if he does not cause it even indirectly himself but merely puts free agents in a position in which it is practically certain that some of them will commit crimes, so that we can in any case only suppose the problem of evil soluble if we suppose that for a being who knew everything that could be known it was worth doing even this for the sake of a greater good eventually to be achieved. But at any rate we need not think of God as having devised the production of each specific evil to produce a specific good or goods, but rather as having produced a natural system which would make for the greatest good as a whole, but which, unless he were to make countless miraculous interventions, a course which would destroy much of the value of the system of natural laws for the education of humanity, must from the nature of the case have incidental bad effects. In the absence of gravitation we could not keep our foothold on the earth and yet the existence of gravitation strong enough to secure this makes falls dangerous; perhaps a body as complex as ours could not have been developed without all sorts of things sometimes going wrong, thus making us liable to many diseases; it would be perhaps intrinsically impossible to have a universe in which the living species developed by a process of evolution without their preying on each other directly or indirectly by interfering with each other's food supply.

Take a human life, of which there must have been an overwhelming number, very possibly the majority yet lived on earth, in which evil exceeded good. The evil in such lives could, if there is no survival, be justified only as means to another's good. But this would be itself immoral; it would be making a man a mere means and not an end in himself. It can only be redeemed if it eventually is to form part of a good organic unity, but for this to happen it seems to me essential that the good organic unity should occur in the same being who endures the suffering or commits the evil acts in question.[1] That even the worst suffering can be made an integral part of something which is good as a whole and that this may happen even with sin I think to be one of the most important lessons taught by Christianity, though the idea has far too often been blended with superstition in magical conceptions of the atonement and the forgiveness of sins. But there is a difference here between suffering and moral evil. Suffering may be thus transcended at the very time of its occurrence; moral evil only subsequently. If it were transcended at the time, the man's state would not be morally evil. Further, the transcendence of the worst sufferings at the time they occur is also impossible for most human beings, but suffering and sin might still form part of a good organic unity, i.e. of a life good on the whole not merely in the sense that it contains more good than evil but in the sense that the particular form its goodness takes is bound up with the conquest of an element of evil, and even the worst parts can be regarded as contributory elements to such a life or at least to learning by trial and error how to live it. The same may be said, I hope, even of sin. This view does not excuse sin, for sin can only serve the good by being overcome, and nobody sins for the sake of overcoming his sins. It has been objected that pain cannot be redeemed by the way men take it because the better a man takes it the more indignant we should be at his sufferings; but (a) this is by no means the attitude of saintly men to their own sufferings, (b) we hardly take this attitude if the suffering is voluntarily incurred for the sake of others, though we may be indignant at the abuse of free will by other people which has sometimes alone rendered this sacrifice necessary, (c) even if the suffering is not voluntarily incurred it may be accepted in the spirit of a man who makes a voluntary sacrifice since under the circumstances, whether other human beings are to blame for them or not, he can regard it for himself as a necessary incident in the process of contributing to the ultimate conquest of evil.

But suppose I had not sinned as much as I have, could I not still attain salvation, and if so how can we say that the evil is a necessary condition of the good? And similarly with suffering? The answer is that it would have been a different, though perhaps greater good.

---

[1] G. F. Stout, *God and Nature*, p. 322.

To satisfy the religious consciousness it is not necessary that the universe should be the best logically possible (at least if indeterminism is true), but it is required that every evil should in some way be redeemed. It will then be necessary for just this good, though if I had not done so much evil I might attain a greater good. But nobody can really atone for and conquer his sin except the sinner. In order to solve the problem the good must transcend and utilize the evil, not only occur after it. If it merely occurs after it, even if it much outweighs it, the evil is still an unredeemed blot on the universe. And it is only if the good and evil occur in the same person that it can thus transcend it. I think this applies to both pain and sin.

But what about the evil in the animal world in the form of suffering? The sufferings of animals on any view present peculiar difficulties. However, if we can form an idea of the solution of the problem of evil by its conquest in human life, we need not be too disturbed because we cannot have any idea as to how it is solved with animals. We after all cannot form much of an idea of what it is really like to be just an animal. And it may well be that the principle that the suffering of one being cannot be justified as a means to another's good only applies to beings who have attained or can attain the rank of personality, and not to animals. Also it is reasonable to think that with their much less developed nervous systems the sensibility of animals to pain is far less than that of human beings. What would be torture to us might hurt them little more than a severe human cold.

There remains another question to consider. Since the problem of evil at least raises considerable difficulties, why not cut the knot by postulating that God is himself limited not merely in the sense of being unable to do the logically impossible, which may be said to be no real limitation, but in the sense of being hindered by something existing independently of himself so that he could not produce as good a world as he wished? This view has sometimes been held, but it has not been much favoured by the religious.[1] There are three reasons for this.

(1) It is felt that this doctrine could not satisfy the religious consciousness because it does not guarantee the triumph of good. If

---

[1] The doctrine of the devil in Christianity is not an example of this because the devil was regarded as an angel fallen through abuse of his free will but ultimately created by God.

God is hindered by beings independent of himself what can guarantee that he will succeed? The sense of peace and security which gives serenity to the religious would be lost. This is probably the chief reason why the idea of a limited God has failed on the whole to appeal.

But here a dilemma may be posed: either the religious consciousness demands the ultimate triumph of good as a necessary condition of its validity or it does not. If it does not or it is essentially illusory, there is no argument; if it does and the religious consciousness is not illusory, then this is an independent ground for believing in the triumph of good whether God is omnipotent or not. It seems to me a necessary presupposition of the religious attitude being warranted that either reality or the being controlling reality or both should not be merely more good than evil but so good as to justify the full security and peace which ideally the religious man should feel about the ultimate course of the universe, and this can only be so if we are to have universal salvation. For this reason I contend that a similar view should be taken also by a mystic who apprehends the Whole as supremely good but does not believe in a personal God. For the Whole cannot have the attribute of supreme goodness (I do not say perfection because there is evil in it) unless all the evil is redeemed. Otherwise the world-order is not as a whole good, however much good there is in it.

(2) The second objection is that <u>a limited deity could not have some very important attributes which we ascribe to God</u>. This supplements the first objection and makes it more serious. The view of the religious man is not ordinarily that he is conscious of God and separately conscious that God's purpose will triumph but that his awareness in religious experience of God carries with it the conviction that God is all-powerful and therefore his purpose must triumph. The victory of good is bound up for him with the omnipotence of God and cannot be separated from it. If we regard religious experience as evidence for God it is also evidence for his being all-powerful.

(3) <u>If God is limited by beings not created ultimately by himself, there must be beings whose existence is not explained.</u> This objection is serious for anyone whose belief in the existence of God depends to a large extent on the cosmological argument or even merely holds that the existence of any being requires explanation, for the existence

of these independent beings would remain unexplained. The theistic hypothesis could no longer fulfil the function of rationalizing the world.

I am for these reasons inclined to reject this doctrine of a limited God, though not of a self-limited God.

THE PROBLEM OF FREEDOM

Most theists have held freedom in an indeterminist sense a necessary assumption if we are to hope for any solution of the problem of evil, and it has also been very widely held to be a necessary assumption of ethics. Neither view has however remained unchallenged, and the question certainly calls for further discussion. Many may think the problem in any acute form removed because philosophers are no longer confident of the truth of any metaphysical propositions, including the proposition that every event is caused, though I must certainly confess to a temptation to think this proposition self-evident, and also because physicists, if not physiologists and psychologists, themselves no longer regard universal causation as a necessary pre-supposition even of their own science. But to my mind the difficulty for indeterminism does not lie so much in its clash with the doctrine that every event must be causally explicable by what has happened in the past, as in the problem as to how indeterminism can itself be intelligibly thought in a form that is compatible with the very responsibility it is intended to save.

I had better say at the start of this chapter that I shall (*pace* Ryle) not shrink from talking of will as a psychological phenomenon.[1] I do not see how we can have freedom or morality if there is not such a thing as willing in the sense of exercising effective choices as to what we shall do, or if statements involving 'will' are to be translated entirely in terms of physical behaviour or dispositions to behave without any reference to consciousness. We must not indeed think of a psychological act of willing as accompanying every voluntary act, but a 'voluntary' act must, if not explicitly willed itself, be at least preventable by a contrary volition. And we throughout our social intercourse assume that certain kinds of behaviour are voluntary and

[1] See *Clarity Is Not Enough.*

also that if a man decides to do something he can in the absence of obstacles external to the mind do it except in rare cases of over-whelming contrary desire or where the act requires special skill, thus implying that mental decisions can have causal efficacy on action.

At the other extreme to the determinist there is a tendency now actually to deny altogether the application of the notion of 'cause' to human action. But this is extraordinarily misleading. In the first place there can surely be no doubt that even on the extremest form of the indeterminist view there must be many causes which affect my actions by limiting the alternatives between which I can choose or making one alternative more or less attractive to me than another. These causes are not only physical but psychological. The most that can be claimed is not that my free acts are totally unaffected by any causes but that these causes do not entirely settle what I do. A distinction is made between being influenced by physical or unconscious psychological factors, which is admitted to be a case of causation, and being in-fluenced by reasons, which is not called causation; but if the thought that an act has better consequences than its alternatives results in my doing it, this thought surely has the essential function of a cause. It may turn the scale and lead to my doing what I otherwise should not have done, though even on a determinist view it is far from being the whole cause. Very partial indetermination is the best that the in-determinist may claim, and we shall see that when we concentrate even on the central stronghold of freedom itself it is not so easy to exorcise the threatening demon of causal determination.

It has been made an objection to the application of the notion of cause to will, purpose, intention or motive that, whereas the causal relation is synthetic, in these cases the alleged cause is analytically connected with the effect on the ground that my will, purpose, in-tention, motive have to be defined in terms of the act purposed, willed, etc. But the analytic connection is not between the occurrence of the cause and that of the effect, for if so I should always do what I willed or purposed to do, but between the name of the cause and the name of the effect. A particular train might be specified as the 9.30 to Euston, but it would not follow that it would necessarily either start at 9.30 or get to Euston in the end. An opponent may reply that the different trains have other differentiating characteristics besides those mentioned, but the same would apply to the psychological states of purpose, etc., preceding different acts. My decision to do something is not just a thought of the thing intended but has other qualities which may vary compatibly with my doing the act. Just as the train may differ from other trains in various respects besides its destination, for instance in the number of carriages, so the experience in making a decision may vary in pleasantness or unpleasantness, reflectiveness or the reverse, ease or strain. It is only that the most convenient way of designating the states as of designating the train is in terms of their objectives. There is indeed a concept of will according to which it has been thought that every voluntary action requires a specific separate act of will, and 'will' in this sense may perhaps be a concept the whole notion of which is exhausted in the action to which it leads. But this view of will is now usually rightly rejected. However, decision or choice is a recognizable psychological occurrence even if it does not accompany every distinguishable act or even every act which can be called voluntary, though for the act to be voluntary it must be such that *if* the agent so decided he could prevent it. But in any case the question in the determinist controversy is not whether our intentions or decisions could be said to cause our actions but whether the intentions and decisions were not themselves determined by the past; and we cannot possibly deny that they are causally affected by the past, the question in doubt being only whether they are completely determined or not.

I am in fact very little impressed by any arguments for indeterminism except ethical ones (including under this heading the difficulty of reconciling determinism with a moral theology). It is argued that it could not be significantly said of all human acts that they are not free because there would then be no opposed class of free acts to give sense to the description of acts as unfree. It is however easy to see that there must be something radically wrong with this argument, for it is in any case easy enough to find a sense of 'free' in which it is indisputably true that no human acts are free. Such a sense is given by defining free as 'completely unaffected by any natural causes'. If there is even one sense of 'free' in which we can correctly say that no human acts are free, we cannot rule out a priori on the ground given the possibility of there still being another sense of 'free' in which we can correctly say that no human acts are free.

I shall not go in detail into Austin's well-known argument against determinism. I discussed and rejected it in an article in the *Proceedings of the Aristotelian Society*[1] which I had reprinted in my *Non-Linguistic Philosophy*[2] All I shall say now is that, even if his arguments were valid, which I do not admit, they could only show that our ordinary language and thought imply an indeterminist view. But this surely by no means needs the ingenuity of an Austin to establish but is in any case clear. It is by no means surprising because <u>determinism is one of those doctrines which, whether ultimately philosophically defensible or not, seems at first sight obviously false.</u> There are very plausible and obvious arguments against it which seem to rule it out at once, such as the argument that, if everything is determined beforehand, it is no good doing anything to produce what one wants. But at least some of the arguments, like this one, can be shown to be fallacies, and some important and highly respected philosophers have claimed that they all are. This takes away the point of appealing to common sense directly. If some of the arguments are valid, they refute determinism in any case without our having to call on common sense to back them; if they are not, their apparent plausibility is quite enough to account for the attitude of common sense. It might be replied that Austin has at least shown that a determinist analysis of 'could' is impossible and that, since we cannot escape talking about what human beings could or could not have done, this is a fatal objection to determinism. But even if I am not right in thinking that I refuted him in my article, it is plain that his arguments must be refutable somehow, because there must be some intelligible determinist meaning of 'could', however hard it may be to formulate it. For the word is often used perfectly intelligibly in contexts where free will is not implied, as in statements about inanimate objects. Further, even most indeterminists hold that only a small minority of human acts are free in their sense, and certainly many are not, yet there is always surely some sense in which a man could have acted differently unless he were physically compelled. All the indeterminist can claim is that there is another sense of 'can' and 'could', essential for talk about moral action, in which these words cannot be given an analysis that the determinist might consistently accept.

Nor am I much impressed by the argument that human acts could not on principle be predicted with certainty because it would always be possible for a man to falsify the predictions about his own acts. For there is no necessity to suppose that the predictions would be communicated to their subject, and if they were the predictor could allow for the falsification. I do not see what difficulty would arise unless this predicting and allowing for the predictions be supposed to be carried on ad infinitum, and if one prediction is certain it is that this will not go on ad infinitum.

I do not see how scientists could show that movements of sub-atomic particles are undetermined, but only that we are, at present at least, not in a position to form any idea of the way in which they could be determined. Further, for our acts to be free it is not sufficient that they should be partially undetermined, as I shall shortly insist. It is also necessary that we should positively bring them about, and this itself involves causation of a kind which science would hardly attribute to electrons. But there can be no doubt that the recent change in the atmosphere of science does lessen the plausibility of determinism by removing the suggestion that it is 'unscientific' to reject it, a suggestion which has had immense influence. Further, the determinist will find it harder to use the more definite argument that inductive arguments necessarily presuppose the assumption that everything is completely explicable by past causes, since science has discarded the assumption and yet gets on quite well without it. It might indeed be argued that, though scientists have discarded the assumption, they ought not to have done so since their scientific arguments really logically presuppose it, though scientists do not recognize this, but few philosophers of science would take such a view today. What may well be maintained is that causality should be accepted as a 'regulative' principle in the sense that we must always look for a cause without its being necessarily the case that there is always one to be found. I do not see how we can say that anything is scientifically explicable unless its causes could be given, but we may doubt whether everything in the world is completely explicable by science.

Gödel's theorem has been invoked in order to show that human actions could not possibly ever be predicted in all detail.[1] This argument I must admit I am mathematically not competent to follow,

---

[1] See J. R. Lucas in *Philosophy*, vol. 36 (1961), pp. 112 ff., reprinted in *Minds and Machines*, ed. A. Ross Anderson.

and if valid it would no doubt show complete determinism impossible; but to my mind it would not remove the main difficulty, that of combining causation by the self with indeterminism.

For to speak even of free acts as uncaused seems to me most misleading. We can thus arbitrarily limit the use of 'cause' if we like, but surely when I do something I determine what I do, fix what the act is to be, bring it about. If this is not causation I do not know what it is. Further, it is absolutely essential to the notion of responsibility that I should fix my acts like this. Even if determinism is incompatible with responsibility, it is still clearer that an indeterminism which denied that I so caused them would be so. I can only be responsible for conduct which is in some way an expression of myself. If my fist struck somebody I should not be responsible for this any more than for a blow dealt by somebody else unless the blow was in this sense caused by my mind. It will now be objected that, though this applies to physical acts, the mental decisions, or 'acts of will', which cause them, are undetermined. But the same difficulty arises about these. It is not I at all who decide if my mental decision is not determined by myself. A completely undetermined mental act or decision would not be anybody's act or decision. It may then be retorted that my acts are in some respects determined and in others undetermined, and that it is only in so far as they are undetermined that I can be responsible for them; but I should reply that, if 'undetermined' is taken literally it excludes determination by myself, and therefore in so far as they are undetermined I cannot be responsible. So my chief difficulty is not that freedom and responsibility require an absence of causation but that they require a kind of causation which it is hard to understand. It is not enough to say that it cannot be shown that everything is completely determined causally and therefore freedom is safe and we need not trouble any more, for whether everything else is caused or not, the free volitions for which we are responsible must be caused since otherwise we are not responsible for them and they are not even our volitions. It is plain indeed that, whatever the indeterminist says, he can hardly mean that our free acts are not caused. What he really means is that they are caused but caused in a peculiar way, i.e. in such a way that their occurrence is not completely determined by anything in the past, whether of the order of events or of qualities pre-existing either in the agent or in somebody or something else.

The main questions to settle now are whether (*a*) we need such an account or whether ordinary determinism would do, (*b*) whether an intelligible account can be given of free acts if determinism will not do. In using the term 'intelligible' here I do not mean to ask how they can be explained. That would be begging the question because, as indeterminists rightly say, if their view is true, free acts just cannot be completely explained. To explain them would be to say what earlier events and previous qualities of things fixed their character, and if the indeterminist is right their character was not in its entirety fixed by anything in the past. No doubt they could be explained up to a point by specifying the motives which gave rise to them and the beliefs which led the agent to think they would satisfy the desires which constituted his motives, and certainly we can never acquiesce in an account which gives no motive at all for a free action, but if there are undetermined actions they occur in cases of conflict where it is not possible to give a complete explanation why the agent chose to perform the action impelled by one and not by the other motive. But it is reasonable to expect of the indeterminist an intelligible account of his view in the sense of an account which is philosophically defensible and compatible with the responsibility in order to defend which it is devised. Responsibility is not secured by a mere negative, the fact, if it be a fact, that the volition in question is not determined by the past. The volition must also be positively brought about by the self; and by 'determinism' I shall mean, as indeed people generally do, not merely the view that what we call free acts are caused by the self but the view that there are causal laws such that the nature of the acts is completely fixed by what had already happened before they occurred,[1] and by 'indeterminism' simply the view which denies this. On the indeterminist view, though whether I yield to a particular temptation is determined by me, it is not determined by the circumstances together with my previous character (or not always so). It should be noted that I have spoken of my previous and not of my present or total character since the latter would include my response to this particular temptation so that to say my response could not have been different without my character being so would be a tautology, and not a causal

---

[1] This includes both those determinists who say that the acts are still sometimes free and those who do not.

proposition connecting the present with the past, and so should incur no objection from the indeterminist.

The attempt to give an intelligible account of freedom must not be dismissed by anyone, even a positivist, as metaphysics and so as an attempt to achieve what must be beyond human power. Whatever may be the case with other metaphysical questions this one concerns human experience and action, subjects which even positivists admit can be intelligibly discussed by us in philosophy. Yet indeterminists have too often contented themselves with refuting determinism without doing much in the way of giving a positive account of the indeterminism they put in its place. Such an account is essential if only because mere indeterminism, mere absence of causal determination is not in the least sufficient. So far from saving responsibility or freedom in any sense which matters ethically, a view which merely asserted the absence of causation would be as incompatible with responsiblity as is the most rigid materialist determinism. I cannot be responsible for what I did not bring about or at least help to bring about, and to bring something about requires causation. To try to save ethics from determinism by adopting this purely negative line would be to jump from the frying-pan into the fire.

But let us first see if ordinary determinism is a defensible doctrine or not and how far it can be reconciled with ethics. I am not here referring to the materialistic determinism according to which all our mental states are completely determined by our brain-states and not at all by psychological causes. This form of determinism would certainly be quite incompatible with ethics. If all our acts are completely determined by our brain-states they are never determined by moral motives, and there is no place for ethics. To act on ethical precepts except by a physical accident is then causally impossible. As I remarked earlier,[1] such a determinism is also incompatible with our ever believing anything for good reasons or deciding deliberately to make experiments in order to discover facts about causation. And I cannot see any case for this kind of determinism. But let us consider the determinism which admits mental as well as physical causation. Even of such determinism there seems to be no proof available, but responsibility itself, as we have seen, requires causation, and it seems that the *onus probandi* is on anyone who introduces such an odd kind

[1] See pp. 77 ff.

of causation as that supported by the indeterminist. It would thus seem reasonable to accept determinism as regards human action unless there are adequate arguments against it.

And they must be *arguments*, I think. I am not prepared to lay stress on an immediate consciousness that our acts are not determined by the past. What our immediate awareness does clearly seem to tell us is that we determine our acts and not that they are undetermined by the past, including our own past. We are certainly not aware of any past causes as determining them completely, but that is different from saying we know directly that there are not any. This strikes me as a very odd thing to say we could know directly, though there may be other knowledge from which it is an inference and a justified one.

But a theory must be consistent with all our knowledge, and this includes ethical knowledge. Such knowledge exists. Though there are many dubious points in ethics, there are thousands of acts which I could enumerate that I know it would be wrong for me to do at the present moment as well as I know anything. It is therefore a most serious objection to a view if it should be found to entail that the word 'ought' cannot be applied in the moral sense to anything, for example that it is not the case that I ought not to shoot the next person I meet. Such a view would contradict what we really know to be true. Now it cannot be claimed that determinism makes a complete mess of ethics. A determinist can consistently hold that some states of mind and actions are better than others both as means and even as ends in themselves, and he can even make some sense of the concepts of blame and punishment. Whether determinism is true or not, it is certain that some acts have very undesirable results, and there is there-fore plenty of point in discouraging people from doing such things. To discourage this is the function of blame and punishment, and it is a useful function even for the determinist. He need not indeed take a purely utilitarian view, though he has usually done so. He may still hold that there are certain states of mind which are intrinsically evil and that not merely in the sense of painful. This is not necessarily incompatible with the states of mind being produced by causes. Pain is by general admission an intrinsic evil, yet it is produced by causes in a thoroughly determinist way. Similarly a state of mind might be held to be intrinsically good and yet determined by causes. There are intellectual and aesthetic goods and even qualities of character which are generally treated as in this position. The only quality of character that even indeterminists ordinarily think necessarily implies free will is readiness or unreadiness to do what one thinks one's duty, and a determinist too might hold without contradicting himself that this was intrinsically good or bad.

But there is one major difficulty at least that a determinist ethics cannot overcome, namely, that ought in its primary moral sense implies can. Determinism is comparable with some acts being better than others, but to say that *A* would be the best act to perform in my situation is not to say that I ought to do *A*, and to say that I ought not to have done *B* is not just to say that I should have been a better person if I had not done *B*. The determinist has to say that what obligation presupposes is simply that the act depended on the agent's choice or will, and this must make it a merely hypothetical 'could', i.e. if the man had been different in a certain way (in respect of his choice or will) he would have acted differently. But that I ought to do something surely cannot follow merely from the fact that I should have done it if I had been in some way different. When I tentatively defended determinism on those lines in earlier works I did not lay sufficient stress on the point that if determinism is true a man's present choice is fixed inevitably by what happened before he was born. I admitted that determinism would affect the concept of responsibility in some degree, but I did not realize that given determinism the notion of moral obligation would have no application at all. But among the things which we know are that we morally ought to do certain things and not do others. This therefore is a definite disproof of determinism, and we must reject determinism unless indeed it should be possible to produce an argument of equal force on the other side, in which case we should be confronted with an insoluble antinomy. It is true, the determinist can still say that an action depends on the agent's choice and the agent's choice depends on his nature; but he did not originally make his nature. I surely cannot alter the qualities of my dead ancestors, and from these my nature or character, except in so far as it is affected by an environment equally independent of me till I have altered it in a way which was equally fixed for me by my ancestors, must inevitably follow, if determinism be true. We cannot get away from the fact that a man cannot be said to have been under a moral obligation in its proper sense to do anything whatever if what he did was always settled from the beginning of the universe or indeed from any time before he was first born. Indeed, as Kant insisted, even in so far as my action is determined by my own past, I am not free now because I cannot alter the past. It has been said that this objection to determinism is due to a wrong view of causation as involving not merely regularity but an anthropomorphically conceived coercion by the cause. But one thing at least is clear, namely, that if it is true that all I have done could be predicted on principle from what has happened before, then it was inevitable at the time it happened; and if it was inevitable, though the past does not compel me, in the sense in which a dictator might, it plainly compels me to do what I have done in the sense that it left no other alternative open. I have said above that a determinist can make some sense of blame, but he cannot give the full sense of moral blame. It is generally agreed that a man could not be blamed morally for a deterioration of character simply due to illness, but if determinism is true all of us are morally in the same position as such a man, for we are certainly no more responsible for what are purely the effects of heredity than he was for his illness, whether these effects are for good or evil. We can indeed still blame if this means that we can assert the inferiority of a man's character, but in that strained sense we can blame even the man whose deterioration of character is due wholly to illness. Again, if the whole course of our life were determined by hypnotic suggestions made a long time ago from which all our conduct inevitably though indirectly followed, it would be generally agreed that we were not morally free or responsible, yet if determinism is true our moral position does not differ from that of such a person. If a man is not to be accounted free because his actions are determined ultimately by physical disease or by the action of another person in hypnotizing him, he is equally not free if his actions are determined by his physical constitution at birth or by the psychology of his parents.

Determinists have often contended that, so far from determinism being incompatible with responsibility, it is indeterminism that is thus incompatible, for to blame a man is to say that his action issues from and is so caused by bad traits in his character.[1] Why should I blame a man if his act does not display any defect of character? Do

[1] See Rashdall, *Theory of Good and Evil*, vol. II, p. 336; Hobart in *Mind*, vol. 43 (1934), p. 5.

not we praise or blame him for the sort of man he is? Now of course we are not blaming a man simply for his physical acts. In that sense we certainly go behind a man's actions to his character, but so far this only means that in assessing his moral merits or demerits we should think of his state of mind in so far as we can gather what that was and not of the external effects of his acts, which he may not have intended in the least or brought about from motives which make his conduct very much better or worse than what it appears on the surface to be. But in order to assess the morality of his action need we go further back still to a character behind his actual mental state and motives in acting? The difficulty now arises that, unless we fall back on the much criticised faculty psychology, we have no such thing as a character over and above the acts and states of mind in which the character is manifested. The indeterminist can retort that a man's moral character is just the sum of his free actions. A man's good acts do not come from but are his goodness. The proposition that a man cannot be responsible for his acts unless they flow from his character loses what appearance of obviousness it has when it is translated into a proposition to the effect that he is not responsible unless his actions follow necessarily according to causal laws from his sequence of previous actions (together with any past external events relevant). As we have just seen, there is good ground for holding that the truth of this proposition would be incompatible with being under moral obligations and so with his responsibility in the moral sense for not fulfilling them, and I cannot see any ground for saying on the contrary that responsibility entails its truth. No doubt in thinking of a man's character we are thinking of his acts as systematized in some way and not just as an aggregate, but that is very different from saying that they are totally determined. I think the determinist argument under discussion confuses the proposition that a man's acts must issue from, express, be determined by the self and the proposition that they must be determined by his previous character. As I have insisted, the former statement is true and must be true if he is to be responsible for them, and it is not really the intention of a sensible indeterminist to deny its truth, but this is not to say that the latter statement is so too. As I have said, the indeterminist ought indeed to agree that no man's action could have been different from what it was, his character and circumstances being the same, for his free act in choosing what he did choose formed part of his total character. The sting of the determinist theory lies not in this but in the word 'previous' applied to character, which makes all he does determined by the past.

It may be objected that we cannot argue from 'I ought to do *A*' or 'to have done *A*' to 'I can' or 'could have done *A*' because while ought does imply can, we cannot use this argument without a vicious circle since we are not in a position to say that a person ought to do something unless we already know that he can. Kant made a definite mistake when he said that he knew he could refuse to give false evidence against an innocent man even if subjected to the severest tortures in the event of his refusal because he knew that he ought to and ought implies can. That it would not have been psychologically impossible for Kant to resist more than a certain degree of agony is something that could not possibly be known a priori like this. But we can argue: It is incredible that the moral ought should have no application at all, but if it is to have application there must be some cases where a man is free to choose between alternatives. If this is not so, one whole basic section of indubitable beliefs will have to be abandoned, as much so as if we admitted that physical things did not exist. It does not follow that we can know a priori which these cases are any more than we can know a priori what physical things exist, though very often I can be practically certain in my own experience that I had no desire so overwhelming that I could not have overcome by an effort of will and there was no physical obstacle to prevent me. Further, since we cannot know beforehand how much torture we could resist, we can say that, even if we were placed in the unfortunate position depicted by Kant, we know that we ought to try our hardest to resist though we could not know that we should succeed.

It has been objected to indeterminism by, for example, Ross,[1] a thinker whose desire to safeguard ethics was second to none, that a freedom to do something whether we wanted to do it or not would be a freedom that was not worth having and nobody would seriously claim. But a word is omitted which makes all the difference to what the indeterminist does seriously claim. He does not say 'I can do this whether I want to or not', at least if 'wanting' is used to include wanting on moral grounds, but 'I can do it whether I predominantly want to or not'. What most philosophical indeterminists at any rate claim

[1] *Foundations of Ethics*, p. 241.

is not that we can do things which we do not want to do at all for any reason but that a man can do A rather than B in some cases where he has some desire to do either but the desire to do B is stronger than the desire to do A. That this is so seems by no means such an implausible view. It does indeed raise the question what is meant by 'the strongest desire',[1] and these words can be used in such a sense that it is an innocuous tautology to say that we act according to the strongest, for the sole measure of the strength of a desire may be found in our actions. It may however also be found in the degree of felt force attached to a desire, and in that sense of 'strongest desire' action against the strongest desire, as was recognized by Hume,[2] though unfortunately not by most determinists or their opponents, is quite compatible with determinism. Determinism merely says that our acts are determined by some causal laws and does not specify what these laws are; we cannot tell a priori that there is a law to the effect that the causal efficacy of a desire is always in proportion to its felt strength (or to the psychological difficulty felt in resisting it) and the empirical evidence which would be needed to establish such a law is not available. On the contrary the empirical evidence we have strongly supports the opposed view that action against the desire felt most strongly does occur, not indeed nearly as often as would be desirable but still pretty frequently. Some of the cases in which we do not do what we desire most in this sense may be explained without denying determinism. It seems to me that even apart from any specific moral effort, desires on which one has made it a rule habitually to act may prevail against a more keenly felt desire. A man will not necessarily have to make a special effort to continue his regular work every time a holiday strikes him as a more attractive alternative, even in cases where there would be censure or dismissal if he succumbed to the temptation, and a man may from inertia continue a habitual form of recreation even at moments when he is more attracted by a new. But this does not cover all cases; conscious moral effort (or a parallel effort on prudential ground) is surely a phenomenon which occurs, and I should now commit myself to an indeterminist interpretation of it. If so, one must recognize action against the strongest desire in a third sense to cover cases where

---

[1] Since there may be several reasons for desiring to do the same act, 'strongest desire' should in this discussion be understood as including 'the strongest group of desires'.

[2] In his distinction between 'calm' and 'violent' passions.

as free beings we act against a desire which is not only felt more keenly than the desire on which we do act but is causally more powerful in the sense that it would lead to the act prompted by it if we did not perform an act of free will to stop it. Such a distinction would not be possible for the determinist. So there is a sense in which indeterminism does and determinism does not allow of action against the strongest desire, though there are at least two other senses of 'action against the strongest desire', one in which this is compatible even with determinism and one in which it would in any case be absurd.

McTaggart thinks that if our free acts are held to be undetermined, 'there cannot be the slightest probability' that any man will choose the right rather than the wrong or vice versa so that all possibility of prediction would disappear,[1] and I suppose many determinists would agree. This would obviously make complete chaos of practical life, and the indeterminist can only meet the objection by admitting partial determination. This is certainly what indeterminists mean to do, but it is not too easy to think out how the two are to be combined. The usual line taken is to maintain that undetermined choice occurs only in a very limited class of cases, namely those cases where the agent believes something to be his duty but has a stronger desire to do something else which conflicts with his duty or what he thinks to be his duty.[2] Causal factors, external or internal, limit a man to certain alternatives, and the past determines the strength of his desires (though no doubt many of the events which exercised this determining causation were affected themselves by human free will in the past, including his own). Free will is exercised simply in choosing between the objects of conflicting desires, and indeed it is commonly thought by indeterminists that there is only one single desire, the desire to do what is morally right as such, which enables a man to escape the determination that governs all his other acts and states without exception. Obviously such an account still leaves a lot of scope for prediction, but the difficulty remains how it is that we can rationally predict with much probability not only how a particular man will act in those cases where is no such clash between desire and duty but in cases where there is, for we can say with an excellent chance of

---

[1] *Some Dogmas of Religion*, p. 183.
[2] I should not myself wish to limit freedom so narrowly, but I have no space to go into the matter here.

being right that a particular man will resist a temptation of a certain kind. No doubt in many cases the indeterminist may just answer that we can make the prediction simply because it is not a temptation to this particular man, though it would be to many others. It is not a case for him of going against the strongest desire, because he desires, for example, to be honest in making tax returns or to help his friend more than to gain an advantage for himself, so he is not exercising his free will. But prediction is surely not limited to such cases. It has been suggested by indeterminists[1] that all we can predict in cases where there is a real temptation is that a man who has succumbed often to similar temptations in the past will find it harder to resist in the future so that he will be less likely to do so. But this is not enough; if it were all, the overcoming of temptation would not make one any more likely to be a better man morally in the future, at least in any sense that the indeterminist would allow; it would merely make the temptation less severe. One would be less likely to do wrong things, but one would not be any more likely to overcome an equally strong temptation than one was before, so the elementary and universally accepted generalization that to act rightly improves one's moral character would have to be discarded. It could not be predicted that a saint in the future would be any more likely to resist an *equally* strong temptation than that a man who had behaved as a scoundrel would do so. To meet this objection the indeterminist would have to admit that the willingness to do one's duty under temptation is itself directly increased by exercise over and above any effect on the strength of the tempting desires. He must in any case admit some causal influence on free acts at some point or other, and if he admits it as at least limiting the alternatives between which the man can choose and making it more or less difficult to choose one rather than another I do not see why it should not also be true that use or abuse of free will in the past directly makes a man more or less likely to take the moral course in the future even where the temptation is in fact the same in degree as before.

An argument for determinism that I used to find forceful was that God himself would always be determined by his nature to do what is best, and if determinism is good enough for God why should we regard it as beneath the dignity of man? There is a very important

[1] See C. A. Campbell, *In Defence of Free Will*, p. 47.

difference however. The objection to determinism for men – that it implies that what we are and do is determined inevitably by something other than ourselves – would not apply in the case of God. Determinism for God would be completely self-determinism. Further, the objection that the present is determined by the past also disappears if God is not in time in the sense that we are, as is usually thought. It might also be replied that indeterminism is necessary for the type of moral values we realize but not for the kind of values a perfect being would realize. We may recall Kant's distinction between the moral will and the holy will and the objection of theologians to applying the term 'ought' or duty' to God.

If determinism were true, our attitude to our moral defects and the overcoming of them could, rationally, only be very different from what it naturally is for a man sensitive to moral considerations. It is surely plain that the attitude *ought* to be: I shall at least try to do better in future; but on the determinist view it could only consistently be: I may hope that I shall try to do better, since I do not know all the conditions, external and internal, and they may for anything I know turn out better in the future than they have done in the past, so that the fact that I have not tried much to overcome my fault in the past does not prove that I shall not make more effort in the future. This is certainly not the attitude to take up if one wants to improve morally. And the determinist could not consistently feel the bitterness of remorse because he has done something bad which he could very well have avoided but only the very different feeling which might be expressed by saying 'what a pity I was made like this'. For however much the determinist may work on an analysis of 'could', the analysis can only be an account of what he would have done if he had been in some way different.

We must however remember that we have not denied and cannot deny that the free acts of the self are causally determined by the self. All I deny in denying 'determinism' is that they are caused in such a way that they could be inferred on principle in full detail or in all morally significant detail with certainty from the past or that it is settled prior to the free decisions of myself what I shall decide. This implies not the denial of causation but the admission of a particular kind of causation different from that recognized in natural science. Indeterminists normally state their views in terms of the pure ego

THE PROBLEM OF FREEDOM

theory, as it is commonly called – i.e. the view of the self as a substance over and above its experiences – and it has not, so far as I know,
been stated in terms of the theory of the self as a series of events. How
it could be so stated I am not clear, though I should not dismiss it as
impossible. I think many of the contemporary thinkers who reject
determinism would also reject the pure ego theory and therefore ought
so to state it, but they have shirked this difficult task, the fulfilment
of which would alone enable them to make a distinction between
mere uncaused chance and a free action. That it seems to require a
pure ego theory may be regarded as an objection to indeterminism,
but I have already taken my decision in favour of such a theory on the
basis of arguments unconnected with the question of freedom.[1]

The 'indeterminist' view thus conceived is the view that the self
as subject can determine (decide) what it does *to some extent* independently of any characteristics which it had before making the
decision and any past events. It is not necessary for a person who
holds such a view to maintain that the self as substance is the *whole
cause* of its free acts, as C. A. Campbell does,[2] and I agree with Broad[3]
that this cannot be true. What the indeterminist can say is that it is a
part-cause, for the free acts could not take place as and when they
do without certain other causal conditions being satisfied. In an earlier
work[4] I brought against this view the objection that a bare substance
apart from its properties could not be intelligibly conceived as producing any effects; but it is not necessary for the indeterminist to
suppose that it could. What happens is rather that in the cases cited
by the indeterminist as typical there are at least two qualities (felt
states of desiring), or at any rate a state of felt desiring and a consciousness of moral obligation (if we refuse to call the moral motive a
desire), present in the agent which tend in reverse directions, and a
vital role in the decision is played by at least one of them, that with
which the man as such identifies himself. The self as substance is not
acting apart from its present (or immediately past) qualities but deciding through which of them it will act. (The situation is no doubt
complicated by the fact that in most cases the moral decision is also
backed by some other desire, though maybe one by itself much weaker
than the opposing desires.)

<hr/>

[1] See p. 81 ff. [2] *Selfhood and Godhood*, p. 178.
[3] *Ethics and the History of Philosophy*, p. 215. [4] *Second Thoughts*, p. 185

This account may seem paradoxical, but we must remember that, even if I had decided in favour of determinism, I should have had to admit that we cannot form any idea whatever even in general principle of the way in which the decisions of men are determined in detail by the past. We know of certain causal laws about the genesis of human desires, for instance that prolonged absence of food tends to produce a strong desire to eat, but how could it be predicted with certainty which of two or more conflicting desires will lead to action? If, as the determinist will suppose, it is settled by the relative strength of the desires, the determination in advance which desire will prove stronger will require some quantitative way of measuring desires that admits of mathematical calculation, and it is doubtful whether this is even conceivable. It may be contended that 'intensive quantity' could be measured by physical correlates or by taking as unit each perceptible difference threshold. But to measure its physiological correlates is not to measure the quality itself, and except on a purely physiological form of determinism it will not be the physiological correlate but the desire itself which produces the effect. We should also have to assume that there is a complete correlation between differences in the physiological correlate and differences in the intensive quantity of the desire, which could hardly be established. If we adopted the threshold system suggested instead, the objection would arise that we should have to assume that the difference between each of the series of feelings perceptibly just different and the next is always equal, which again could not be established. There is the further well-known difficulty that the axiom of equals does not hold in these cases, which differentiates them sharply from instances of spatial quantity. There are other conditions which would have to be fulfilled before we could see even in principle a way in which determinism could be worked out in the psychological sphere. For us to see how a physical event is determined by the past in full detail we should have to be able to divide it into a number of isolable factors and connect each of these by general causal laws with a causal factor present in earlier events; and further, the results of all the factors have to be capable of summation in such a way as to make it possible to deduce the total event on principle from them; but we have no idea whatever how these conditions could be fulfilled in dealing with the self. In *Second Thoughts*[1]

¹ P. 184.

I suggested that these might be objections only to the notion of predictability and not to determinism, but they at any rate exclude complete determination in any way conceivable by us in even the most general terms, and it looks very likely that at least the first point, the one about intensive quantity, makes it a priori impossible. The indeterminist merely says that the self decides between conflicting desires in a way which would not follow with certainty from any statements about past events together with causal laws. But why have we any right to expect that it should?

It is a not unplausible metaphysical guess that the limits of determinism might coincide with the limits of causation by the qualities which used to be called 'primary' and alone admit of exact measurement in themselves. Beyond these limits there would still be causal influence, but it would either only incline and not necessitate, as is the case with the causal influence of desire on free acts according to the indeterminist view, or determine in a way that as in the case of a free decision by the self was incapable of prediction beforehand. If it be true, as used to be supposed almost universally, that apart from conscious beings the physical world is a sphere where complete determinism reigns, and that, as seems to be generally still assumed, all physical causation is by primary qualities which are measurable in themselves, that would agree with the theory I have just suggested. But it would make indeterminism extend much further than most indeterminists want. I think myself however that they do limit it too narrowly.

The indeterminist, while denying that free acts can be predicted with certainty, must hold that they can be rightly said in advance to be more or less probable, and in *Second Thoughts*[1] I made it a serious objection to indeterminism that it was incompatible with the general and reasonable view that the concept of probability is simply the concept of a relation to certain data and not of something which an event could have in itself. But the indeterminist can still hold a relational view of probability. The probability of a free act will consist in its relation to the sum-total of earlier events. The only difference here from the determinist view is that, while on the latter the occurrence of the earlier events probabilifies the occurrence of the latter to the maximum degree (100 per cent) which we call certainty, on the

[1] Pp. 185–6.

I

former it probabilifies it to a lesser extent. We may note that if the objection I mentioned be valid against the doctrine of free will it will be equally valid against the admission of indeterminism in the inanimate world now commonly allowed by scientists, for this admission is certainly not regarded as inconsistent with the making of probable predictions, and the possibility of science as well as our whole practical life depends on this.

How is the indeterminist view to be fitted into our concept of causality? It does not fit in intelligibly with either of the extremer views, the regularity theory on the one hand and the pure entailment theory on the other. As I have insisted, the self must cause our free acts if responsibility is to be saved, but to say the self causes a free action certainly does not mean that the act follows regularly on a certain state of the self. I could not be held responsible for an act if it just followed a previous state of myself and was not connected with the self in a more definite way which we express by saying that the self brought it about. If on the other hand we adopted a pure entailment theory, all the acts caused by the self would have to be held to follow a priori from its nature together with its circumstances, and we should have a determinism all the more rigid or at least even more unwelcome to the believer in freedom because of the logical a priori character of the postulated causation. I have indeed defended what I called an entailment theory of causation,[1] but I never maintained that causation was simply reducible to the entailment. All I maintained was that there was a factor in causation at least analogous to logical entailment. In support of this view I brought two main arguments: (1) that the admission of such a factor is implied in any belief that we can reason from cause to effect and so in the whole of induction; (2) that the very extensive occurrence of regularities we empirically encounter requires it for explanation if this is not to be regarded as a fantastic coincidence of the most improbable kind. But, even if I am right, this entailment factor is only present in so far as the causation can be expressed in terms of universal, or at least statistical, laws, since it is only in so far as this is so that induction is possible and that we can explain what would otherwise be coincidences by causal laws. It is not relevant to that element in our life which, though it is in a

---

[1] See *Non-Linguistic Philosophy*, pp. 139 ff.

wide sense causation by the self, is called undetermined because it could not be predicted by laws.

A further point which it is very important to make is that what psychological causal laws we know almost always express tendencies, **x** i.e. they do not lay it down that something will always happen under certain conditions but that there is a tendency for it to happen under these conditions, for example, there is a tendency for a man to be displeased by insults or to feel grief at the death of one he loves. The man may be in such a state of mind that he wants to be humiliated or he even may be so distracted by other things that he is not distressed by the death of his friend, but in the vast majority of cases the events I have mentioned will follow, and we can see that they result from the inherent nature of insults and of love respectively (whether we think this proposition empirical or, as I have suggested elswhere, a priori) and only fail to follow if the tendency to produce them is counteracted in some way. After all even the law of gravitation only expresses a tendency. It asserts that everything in our neighbourhood tends to fall on to the surface of the earth (limiting for the sake of simplicity of exposition its application to terrestrial conditions), but this tendency is constantly counteracted by circumstances such as support by an intervening heavier object or the presence of an engine in motion propelling the body in question. In referring to tendencies I am not saying merely that something generally happens, but asserting that there is a positive force tending in a certain direction, though it may be held in check by other factors. If we admit that the existence of certain properties in a thing may entail such causal tendencies, we can reconcile an entailment theory of causal laws with the now commonly held view that the laws should be usually, or conceivably even always, regarded as involving only statistical and not completely universal regularities.

It must not be said that in asserting the existence of such positive tendencies we are asserting univerifiable properties. Who has not verified empirically the force of gravitation when he has lifted a heavy load, or the force of a desire which he was anxious to resist, whether on moral grounds or because it conflicted with other non-moral desires that he wished to gratify or both? What he feels is something quite positive and definite, not merely a probability. It is a causal tendency which entails that it will be fulfilled if nothing to counteract it happens, but something that counteracts it may well happen. It is

I*

on these positive causal tendencies that the probability of a particular not fully determined event happening must depend. The stronger the tendencies for and the weaker the tendencies against it, the more likely it is to happen, but they do not make its occurrence certain but only probable. We are free, hard though it may be, by an act of free will to bring about the improbable.

The question of free will has been a very tiresome one not only from the ethical but also from the theological point of view. The usual conception of God as omnipotent and omniscient has seemed to clash with human freedom. But the difficulties raised by the former property may be met by maintaining that God's omnipotence includes the power voluntarily to renounce his power so as to allow his creatures to have that freedom which was necessary if they were to be moral beings and have a life higher than that of animals. We cannot indeed say that the intrinsic value of freedom is so great that a free sinful act is in itself better than a determined right act. I am not sure whether undetermined freedom in itself is an intrinsic good at all irrespective of the way in which it is used, but it does seem to be a condition without which we could not attain some of the greatest goods known to us, perhaps the very greatest. The attainment of such goods may be well worth the risk, even the practical certainty, of our freedom sometimes being abused, provided the moral evil thus incurred is eventually overcome and redeemed. It has been asked whether an omnipotent being could give a freedom which he could not take away; but the question is not whether he could but whether he would in his goodness take it away. Obviously if he has given it to us he has seen that it is very much limited by circumstances and natural laws.

As regards God's omniscience, it has been said to be no contradiction of this to maintain that God does not know what it is logically impossible could be known, and if indeterminism is true it is logically impossible to have certain knowledge in advance of events affected by free will. More frequently it is said that God does know them but does not know them by causal inference, the only kind of knowing which would imply determinism. It is thought that God is 'out of time'[1] and can thus know events at all times directly, but this need not imply that the future is predictable from the past and therefore settled before it has happened.

---

[1] See p. 279 ff for a further discussion of this very difficult concept.

Any difficulty about human freedom has, however, been grossly increased, it seems to me quite gratuitously, by certain schools of Christian theology with their exaggerated insistence on human depravity and impotence.[1]

It has been objected that, if people sometimes freely choose to do what they ought, there could be no logical impossibility in their always having done so, and therefore God might have made them so that they always freely did so.[2] But the fact that there would be no contradiction in their always doing what they ought freely does not by any means imply that there would be no contradiction in their being made so that they always did it freely. To make them such that they always did it would be to fix beforehand what they did, and then they would not be free. It could only be interpreted as meaning that prior to their acts their character was made such that they would do them, and that is determinism. It also has been argued that God might have left men free to will but intervened whenever they started to will wrongly; but there would be no temptation to will wrongly and therefore no undetermined freedom if we knew that willing wrongly would be completely inefficacious because we were always prevented from carrying out what we willed.

Would determinism make the problem of evil completely insoluble? There are other ways of mitigating the difficulty besides indeterminism, as I mentioned in the last chapter: the principle of organic unities, the fact that it may easily be best for A to stand in a certain relation to B but not best for B to stand in the converse relation to A, the plausible supposition that causal laws involve necessary connection; but even so would not the acceptance of determinism increase the gravity of the problem to a point at which ethical theism would become quite untenable? There are strong reasons for saying it would. For God would then have to be admitted to have deliberately himself caused all the crimes of which history is so full. His causation would indeed be not direct but indirect (we need not adopt Berkeley's theory on this point), but the guilt of a murderer is not decreased by the fact that he has not killed his victim with his own hands but merely laid a mine, lighted a fuse and waited for it to go off. The determinist

---

[1] As pointed out by H. D. Lewis in *Morals and the New Theology*, chapters 5–7.

[2] See J. L. Mackie, *Mind*, no. 254 (1955), pp. 208 ff.; for reply see A. Plantinga in *The Philosophy of Religion*, ed. Basil Mitchell, pp. 105 ff.

might indeed like Leibniz reply that God might justifiably produce moral evil for the sake of a greater good. He points out that the objections to a man doing this would not apply to God since they depend on the fact of human ignorance, which normally (Leibniz apparently thinks always) prevents our being sure enough of the good consequences to be able to count on their outweighing the immediate evil of the means used to attain them. It is thus not, I think, absolutely self-contradictory to hold that this universe was created by a perfectly good and omnipotent God even if determinism be true. But there is a corollary which it is really quite impossible to accept. If God is perfect and everything is determined by God, everything that happens without exception must be the very best thing that could possibly have happened in the circumstances or at least there could have been none better. This would apply to all the crimes of a Nero, a Hitler or a Stalin. The intrinsic evil of these acts would be outweighed by their consequential good or by the fact that they were necessary consequences of something which carried with it outweighing consequential good. A God who would deliberately bring about the deeds I have mentioned could not possibly be called good unless at least he also knew that the ultimate resulting good either of the acts themselves or of something from which they necessarily followed outweighed the terrible evil involved. He could not have brought about the torture and massacre of the Jews by Hitler unless it would have been even worse if they had not been tortured and massacred.

Further, a serious ethical attitude could not possibly be combined consistently with the view that whatever in fact one does will always necessarily be the very best thing to do under the circumstances, everything else considered, or at any rate something which even God could not better.

GOD AND MAN: FURTHER POINTS

Having been at a loss for a title to this last chapter I eventually with some hesitation chose 'God and Man'. In one respect this is very unsuitable because, while it is inevitable that we should think of God as though he were primarily concerned with men as the only finite personalities known to us, this is really incredible. When we consider the vast number of stars it seems immensely improbable that many others will have not given rise also to planets containing intelligent life. And the beings inhabiting them will be as much objects of God's concern and love as ourselves. The possible variety of beings is immense, and it is to be hoped that a very large proportion of them behave better than humanity at the present day. Nor must we assume that the whole of God's purpose is concerned with created beings. We should expect God to be concerned too with his own development, or its non-temporal equivalent, which we cannot so much as conceive. But we are inevitably limited to talking about God in relation to man.

The view that I have put forward as regards our destiny will be considered far too optimistic for these days. But it seems to me that nothing less is required if the fundamental assumptions of the religious attitude are true. The specific religious attitude cannot be rational unless we may view the object of religious experience as supremely good. This object is either God conceived more or less personally or Reality as a whole, and it seems to me that either view gives a guarantee of ultimate universal salvation. The first does so because otherwise we should defeat God's purpose; the second because Reality could not be regarded as good as such unless all the evils in it are part of a total process making a good organic unity, and this can only be if they will ultimately be so for the person himself who has suffered and sinned. Otherwise we could not say that Reality is good but only that there is good in Reality. The claim of the mystic is an absolute one. I have suggested that there are two distinct kinds of religious experience with different objects, the experience of God as personal and the mystic's experience of the Whole, and if they can both be trusted this will give a dual ground for believing in universal salvation. The temporal vicissitudes of the present day are of very little relevance to answering the question whether good will ultimately triumph, perhaps as little as one particular day's bad work at school will usually have to one's whole future career. It is quite as unjustifiable to be led by the two world wars and the other evils of the present day into thinking that there can be no God or that his purpose will fail of achievement as it was for our fathers or grand-fathers to have let the experiences of Victorian days (which incidentally had a much more substantial quota of evil than many realize, as our days still have of good) often lead them into thinking that progress was inevitable, God or no God. With the world still habitable as far as we can foresee for many millions of years this is not a matter to be settled by our empirical evidence. There may well still be some time something like an earthly utopia, and indeed we may say there *will* be *if* people learn how to use science aright and there is no cosmic catastrophe; but religion can guarantee only the ultimate triumph of good in some form, not necessarily in this planet. And as for the problem of evil, there has always been so much of this as to make it unreasonable to think that any extra increment of it which men think they find in these days appreciably adds to the difficulties of theism. I say nothing to minimize evil in the intermediate stages except that, as religion and ethics teach, there is a way to win some good out of even the worst evils.

I have suggested that certain differences in the religious experience of mankind might be explained by the experience being directed to two different objects, God as a personal or quasi-personal being and the Absolute or Whole. It seems to me that some of the difficulties and controversies in the theological field might be explained by a conflation of the demands of these two kinds. The former kind has been much the most common, since even in those eastern religions where the religion of the great sages has been of the latter kind the less educated men have worshipped rather a plurality of personal gods. But there has been a strong tendency among Christian teachers and still more philosophers whose religion was primarily of the first type to claim for God a kind of 'perfection' he could only have if we identified him with the object of the more characteristically mystical experience. On the ordinary Christian view human beings were indeed ultimately created by God but not part of, or in Spinoza's phrase 'modes' of God, yet there has been a strong recurrent tendency towards pantheism among Christian mystics and philosophers. It has been felt difficult to see how one mind could be part or a mere 'mode' of another, but the chief objection to pantheism is that it is incredible that beings so bad as Hitler or Stalin, or indeed the writer of this book, could be actually part of God. This is very different from saying that they were created by God and then abused their freedom. On the other hand it is obvious that they are parts of the Whole, and if we look on the Whole as including the whole time-process this will not exclude the possibility of admitting the goodness of the Whole provided they will ultimately be redeemed. But we ought to face the fact that from the more orthodox view it follows that there is at least one perfection which we cannot ascribe to God, namely the fullest completeness. God is less than the Whole. We should indeed add that this is a self-limitation; God need not have created the world if he had not chosen to do so. However, if it is better that a world should be created than not there must be a sense in which God could not have omitted to create a world because it would have contradicted his nature to do so. I have also suggested that there are other perfections which God could not possess because they presupposed evil in the person of the being who had them or at least limitations that we could not ascribe to deity. I am referring to the good of victory over evil in oneself, the good of religious faith, the good of worshipping something supremely above oneself, the good of temporal progress. These are values which are to be found somewhere in the whole of things but not in God. We must then think of God not as the being who has all possible perfections but rather as the most perfect possible single being. To ascribe to him all the values there are as part of his nature would be to make him imperfect in a way much more serious than is done by saying he has not the metaphysical perfection of absolute completeness. That does not debar one from saying that since he created the world the realization in existence of all values is absolutely dependent on him. Nor are we debarred from describing God as immanent as well as transcendent as Christianity commonly does. The artist can be thought of as immanent in his work; but further the doctrines of the immanence of God and of the Holy Spirit suggest agreement with the mystic that religious experience at its highest indicates the possibility of a relation to its object even closer than can be expressed by 'love', whether this be regarded as a relation which we all really have but commonly do not consciously realize or a relation which none or a very few have yet but which will sometime be realized. In any case what I have said suggests the desirability of an attempt to work out a philosophy of religion which will do justice both to the concept of a personal God and the concept of the Absolute. It may be that a satisfactory philosophy of religion requires both the retention and the separation of the two concepts, not an attempt to merge them into one. Personally I find more value in the former concept than in the latter, I must add, but I am certainly not a mystic.

I shall supplement this discussion by putting together what I have already said or implied on the subject of the personality of God. There is no doubt that this for God must mean something very different from what it does for us, for whom it is bound up very much with our limitations. But it does seem to me that the arguments for God, if they show anything, show the existence of a being who has at least thought and will and therefore may be called personal without qualification in one most important sense of the term. The same consideration is supported by an appeal to religious experience. For God to Love us in any but the most Pickwickian sense or to realize in himself the ideal of ethical goodness he must be a separate centre of consciousness, and not merely a characteristic abstracted from the world-order as a whole. The same is implied if there is to be any purpose behind the world: I cannot understand what purpose could be without the thought of an end and the devising of means to it, and that implies mind, i.e. a being with thought and will. And if we think of God in terms of perfection, we must admit that plainly a being who has consciousness is more perfect than a being that has not. No doubt there may be beings who have consciousness without having personality, as we suppose to be the case with animals; but while we can conceive beings which are sub-personal we cannot conceive what it is like to be super-personal except in the negative, formal sense that we can understand in some kind of way what is meant by saying that for God the sense of limitation which we all have is not present. Some mystics have claimed that they had in their mystical experience some sense of what it was like to transcend personality, but the vast majority of men, even religious men, have not. This does not show that God is not super-personal in the sense that it is misleading to say that God is personal as well as to say that he is not. But, at any rate for us, the former statement is much less misleading than the latter, even if it might not be for an archangel if there are such beings.

St Thomas taught that any affirmative statement we can make about God must be analogical in character. His ground for this, namely that 'God's existence is identical with his essence', lacks meaning for me, but there is no doubt a sense in which the analogical doctrine of theology is true and important. We have no idea what it feels like to be the kind of person God is. It may well be the case that God's attributes are related to him in a generically different way from that in which the attributes of any finite being are related to that being, though I do not see how we could know this to be so. We certainly cannot form any concrete idea of how God's mind works except (and this is an important exception) that we know the laws of logic to which even God's thinking must conform. God must know them at least as well as we do, however much else he also knows. But once we have assured the fundamental conditions without which the religious attitude would be as inappropriate as a Kantian ethics without objective moral principles, a reverent agnosticism as to further philosophical questions in theology is perhaps the only possible attitude. Yet for a philosopher, as we shall see, there does seem to be some scope for speculation on further points, and I think some ground favouring tentative conclusions, and some people may feel driven to it by theoretical difficulties and difficulties also in their practical religious life. But in this chapter, except in so far as I am negative, I shall be navigating through still more tortuous channels than before in uncharted seas, not that it would be right of me to take a dogmatic attitude as to my conclusions either in earlier chapters. What I feel at least fairly confident about is that reality is in some way dominated by value and that there is a being capable of satisfying the religious aspirations of mankind. That I have justified this view in quite the best way or given a fully correct account of the mysteries of religion it would be outrageous for me, or any other human philosopher, to claim; but the human mind has been given the power of speculation about these matters to a surprising degree, considering our extreme finitude, and if we are to progress in understanding we can only do it by individual philosophers trying to work out the views which seem to them the least difficult to maintain. We are certain not always to be right, but by putting forward what seems to us most reasonable or least difficult to accept we may still make a contribution.

My view of God, as will have already been noticed, involves the admission that God does not include all values or even all different kinds of value in himself because some values presuppose imperfection and even evil in the beings to whom they belong. God cannot achieve the value of victory over sin in himself, as can a human being. But he may be conceived as realizing in himself values which presuppose evil in other beings. In this category falls the value of a sacrificial love directed towards other beings who are in dire need of help. Here I should agree with Hartshorne that God, if he loves us, must feel something of the nature of pain when we suffer or go wrong. This is in agreement with Christianity as mostly preached popularly, but save for one important exception not with the usual metaphysical view which attributes 'impassibility' to God. The exception to which I refer is admitted in the doctrine of the incarnation. It is held that God as incarnate could and did suffer with us. But surely if God loved us so much as to die on the cross for us as incarnate in Jesus Christ he must also suffer for us in sympathy when not incarnate; and it seems to me that if he is to be conceived as loving us in any true sense this much is implied whether the doctrine of the incarnation is true or not. It is likewise implied in the doctrine, supported strongly by the experience of religious men, of God's immanence. If we recognize the existence of 'organic unities' in the realm of value, this need not be inconsistent with the supreme goodness of God's total state. For we must suppose that the sympathetic suffering, though a real element in God's experience, is somehow transcended so that his experience as a whole is one of inconceivable bliss, especially if we think of the evil in the world as eventually becoming *sub specie temporis* part of a good organic unity of supreme value as a whole. But we cannot think of a righteous loving God as feeling no concern for our suffering and our sin. This involves the further paradox that what we do can produce effects on God's experience, as is indeed already implied by the mere admission that God can know what we do. It is of the essence of knowing that the state of mind of the knower should be affected by what he knows, otherwise he would not know it at all.

This is no derogation from God's perfection. One must admit, I think, that God would be in an even happier state if human beings had never abused their free will by, for example, going to war, but God may still be absolutely perfect in his inherent nature. The defect lies not in God but in his experience, and is due to the action on him of beings who, even if they abused their freedom to a certain extent, it was better should be left free. And the possibility of their acting on God would only arise because of a voluntary limitation of God's omnipotence. We certainly need not suppose that God's state would have been better if he had never produced any human beings: we may well hold that he would have been less and not more perfect if he had not been willing to expose himself to the risk of loving free finite, and so potentially sinful, beings.

A difficulty that has worried many is the supposed impossibility of creation *ex nihilo*, but I do not see how we can know a priori that a substance, even a pure ego, could not be so produced, even if we have no idea how it could be done. I do not see any self-contradiction or logical absurdity in the notion. Indeed there is one kind of entity, namely images, which even human beings can produce *ex nihilo*, for though they must be in some way derived from our previous experience they are not made of pre-existing matter in the sense in which artificial physical objects are. Nor do we know enough to deny that it is possible that the world might depend for its existence on a being that was himself non-temporal. Of course I am not envisaging the different selves as being specifically created by God. It seems to me that for anything I could see it might well be the case that according to natural causes when the experiences which constituted a living being had attained a certain degree of complexity they, so to speak, crystallized into a pure ego, a self-substance.

The reader has already seen what a very important part is played in my metaphysics by what I have called the value principle. This principle I do not claim to be self-evident to us or logically proven, but it may be defended, it seems to me, as a metaphysical hypothesis which fits in excellently with various lines of thought. It is the only terminus of the cosmological argument that can give the latter real force, for it provides the only possible way of explaining rationally the universe as a whole. It solves the antinomy between the ethical arguments for God and the objections to making the moral law dependent on the existence of some being. While the conviction that ethics is in some way bound up with the central nature of reality has usually led to the derivation of the ought from the is, and so implied conclusions which carried out logically would have destroyed the autonomy which is essential to the proper understanding of ethics, it has not been noticed that the difficulties of making ethics dependent on theology could be avoided and the cosmic significance of ethics yet maintained by reversing the argument and making reality dependent on values. And the hypothesis resolves the conflict between the natural religious way of thinking about God and the principles of modern logic by making the existence of God necessary without its being logically necessary so that his non-existence entailed a self-contradiction, which Kant rightly made an objection to the concept of a logically necessary being. I am not of course the first person to have assumed the value principle. All the thinkers who have supposed that the perfection of God necessitated his existence assumed it implicitly, and the principle has been explicitly stated by many writers. It was a generally accepted doctrine of medieval philosophy that the degree of value of a thing was in proportion to its degree of being, but the degree of value was regarded as dependent on the degree of being rather than vice versa; yet in so far as God was regarded as necessarily existent just because he was perfect, the principle acquired the status which I have given it, except that the distinction between logical and metaphysical necessity which I have maintained was not usually made. The principle played a large and explicit part in the philosophy of Leibniz, who did make such a distinction, though I think in an inconsistent way, and the ramifications and history of the principle have been traced by Lovejoy in *The Great Chain of Being*.

But a further question now arises. If the value principle holds at all, will it not supply a ground also for the existence of beings who still have value but less value than God? If God must exist because of his absolute perfection, will not all possible beings tend to exist, the degree of force of this tendency being proportionate to the limited degree of perfection they possess? Will not in consequence each degree of perfection between God and zero value be realized in some existent being in so far as such beings are compossible, if they are not always so? Such a view was put forward by Leibniz and a number of other philosophers. It has however been usually held that the principle resulted *directly* only in the existence of one being, God. This was clearly Leibniz's view. The value principle was indeed still conceived as indirectly determining the existence of imperfect beings, but this was only because God's perfection led him to create the best possible universe and the best possible must include the greatest variety as well as the greatest unity compatible with the variety. (Leibniz held that no being could exist whose value was less than zero). It was not because of an inherent tendency on the part of these beings to exist, as it was in the case of God. The reason for the difference was that in the case of God alone is there no possible competitor for existence since God surpasses all other beings in perfection. The value principle, having determined the existence of God, thus becomes in relation to other beings not a principle which itself brings about their existence but an ethical principle governing the action of God.

But, if the value principle holds at all, might we not think of it as having a direct as well as an indirect effect in bringing about the existence of finite beings? I was tempted to hold such a view for the following reason. There is much to suggest the hypothesis of a God not limited indeed in goodness but limited in power. Such a view may be supported, though not decisively established, by the problem of evil, and the argument from design with its emphasis on means to ends has often been held more congruous with a God limited by material external to himself of which he had to build the world than by an omnipotent creative God. Now an important objection to such a view is constituted by the fact that the existence of other beings supposed to limit God's power would itself require explanation. This point will not indeed affect a person who thinks that things can exist without any ultimate reason to explain their existence or that there is no sense in asking such questions, but it should appeal to anybody inclined to believe both in a limited God and in the cosmological argument for God. For the cosmological argument to be valid the existence of everything must have some explanation, but for the existence of beings independent of God it could in its ordinary form give no explanation. If the value principle could however be conceived as directly leading to their existence as well as God's, there would be an explanation. It might be thought indeed that, since the value principle could only produce what was good, this would not help with the problem of evil, but different beings good on the whole can, we well enough know, come into conflict to such an extent as to produce great evil, and if all conceivable beings on the scale of values were produced this would not necessarily make for the best possible universe since those of lesser value conflict with those of greater, as we see when we think of criminals, harmful animals, disease germs. There thus might well be a discrepancy between the will of God and the value principle as bringing into existence beings other than the deity. But I see no way of working out such an explanatory theory satisfactorily.

I had better now say something about my own attitude to authority in religion and in particular to Christian orthodoxy, though I am afraid I shall in doing so give pain by quarrelling with and criticizing a doctrine that will be very sacred to many of my readers. I feel I must do so in the interests of what I take to be the truth. I accept the Christian faith myself in that I believe in God and the supreme goodness of God and in the ethical ideals laid down by Jesus Christ, but I am not prepared to accept what is commonly regarded as the central doctrine of Christianity, namely the incarnation, at any rate unless it be interpreted simply as signifying that God is revealed and in some sense immanent in all good men in so far as they are good and so in a special degree in Christ as the best man we know, in so far as we can tell. This interpretation has been given to the doctrine not only by members of the Unitarian Church, to which I now belong, but even by some very prominent members of the Church of England, for example the philosopher Rashdall, Dean of Carlisle, but this watered-down form is certainly not considered sufficient by the vast majority of Christians. I am fully and even painfully aware that, because I cannot hold the doctrine in a stronger form, a great many people would refuse me the title of Christian. The doctrine of the incarnation has been of very great value if even only as a myth conveying effectively to men the idea of God's love and of sacrifice as the chief way of overcoming evil. It is at the very least a beautiful story that God in order to redeem the world took on human form and in this form lived and died among and for humanity with all the sacrifice that involved, but I do not think there is anything like sufficient evidence for the tremendous conclusion that this really happened in the person of Christ. The incarnation would be a miracle of the most extraordinary kind, and without going so far as Hume and ruling out all miracles a priori on the ground that a miracle being by definition more unlikely than any natural event, it must be always less unlikely that there was something wrong with the evidence for it than that the miracle took place, we must admit that belief in a miracle requires for its validation far stronger evidence than belief in an ordinary event, and it seems to me that in this case no very strong evidence is forthcoming at all. There is no evidence that Christ ever directly claimed to be God in so many words, and even if some of his phrases suggest this I do not see any great difficulty in supposing that they bear the same sort of significance as the statements which many mystics have made about the presence of God in themselves and their sense of the identity between their deeper selves and God, at least if we admit that, as is commonly held by scholars, the fourth gospel, which contains the most far-reaching of these utterances, was intended not to give the actual words of Christ but the interpretation put on them by its author. Even the Jewish prophets, who were not characteristically mystical, regard God as speaking through them, so that their message is not their own but God's. Unless we carry biblical criticism to what seems a pretty unreasonable extreme of scepticism, we must admit that Christ made a claim for himself which was not made by the Jewish prophets or by any ordinary mystic, namely the claim to be the Messiah. But to claim to be the Messiah was not to claim to be God. No doubt the Messiah was not regarded as merely human but in some way supernatural, but he was certainly not identified with God but was rather God's messenger to man. That he was such a special messenger Christ can well have believed and, if we believe in God at all, when we consider the enormous and unique effect of Christ's message on the world, we need have no compunction in adding 'truly believed'. This is not to say that Christ was the Messiah in the sense of having the precise characteristics ascribed to this being by the Jews. Christ himself did not think this since he refused to come as a conquering king in the military sense of the word and, at least in the end, regarded his mission as directed to all mankind and not merely to the Jewish people. That is, he rejected the elements in the orthodox Jewish conception of the Messianic mission which conflicted with his ethical insight. If he believed that he was Messiah at all, he would naturally apply to himself the supernatural ideas connected with Messiahship by Jewish tradition such as that he would come to judge the world, rejecting those elements in the tradition against which he had positive objections, as with that I have just mentioned. 'Liberal Christians' have commonly committed the error of underrating the extent of the supernatural elements in Christ's teaching as expounded in the New Testament, but it does not follow that because they are present there these beliefs are right. The fact that his disciples came to regard him as not only the Messiah but as actually divine leaves me quite cold when put forward as evidence for his really being so. They were not expert philosophers, and anyone who has studied philosophy much knows the enormous scope for misunderstanding there is when concepts of an unfamiliar philosophical nature are involved. Further, the tendency of religions to glorify their founder is well known, and the fully fledged doctrine of the incarnation only appeared centuries after Christ.

The only real argument for the incarnation in any case seems to be that, if Christ had been under such a delusion as that he was God when he was not, he would be insane; and he certainly was sane. But in view of what I have said I do not see any difficulty in supposing that a man with such extraordinary a religious experience as Christ's said things which were subsequently interpreted by disciples in a way which led to the orthodox incarnation doctrine. We are by no means forced to choose between the supposition that the orthodox doctrine of the incarnation is true and the supposition that he erroneously held such a doctrine himself. There are two important sources of uncertainty here. In the first place biblical criticism leaves it at any rate decidedly dubious what were the actual words of Christ or whether any of his actual words on this topic have come down and what we have concerning it does not merely consist of interpretations. In the second place there are some elements in the biblical account which seem to me to tell strongly against the incarnation doctrine. I am referring to Christ's saying to one who called him good 'Call no man good but only God';[1] Christ's cry of despair 'My God, my

[1] St Mark x. 18 f.

God, why hast thou forsaken me', a cry which should be strictly nonsensical on the orthodox view; and the fact that Christ always prays to God as though he were some being other than himself. What evidence there is would leave the issue distinctly dubious even if we were dealing with a type of event which was known to occur frequently but, as I have said, we should need extraordinarily strong evidence to justify belief in such an extraordinary miracle, and this evidence is not forthcoming. Nor can I see what possible reason could be given for saying that, though there was not adequate evidence for it, it was our duty to believe it on faith. We must also remember that every saying attributed to Christ was a paraphrase of another language, Aramaic, and that the original is unknown to us.

There is a further grave difficulty about the view which has been commonly overlooked. It is this. There is no doubt that on any interpretation of Christ's teaching it has often been misunderstood in ways which produced the most grievous evil. On a narrow old-fashioned type of view a great number of heresies have arisen which involved vast numbers in the eternal agony of hell, and even though the more educated have gradually dropped this view and do not any longer believe that a man will be consigned to hell for holding wrong theological beliefs – for instance most Roman Catholics must presumably still believe that people who are not Roman Catholic but Protestant at any rate suffer grievous spiritual loss. Now, even if Roman Catholicism should be the true religion, it would have to be admitted that it has not been made at all clear and explicit in the Gospels that this is so, and it is plain that without performing any sort of miracle but merely by the adoption of simple precautions in the way of presenting his teaching Christ could have made it so clear that the alleged heresies of Protestantism would never have arisen or at any rate never spread so widely as they did. The same will apply *mutatis mutandis* if we hold that some form of Protestantism is much superior to Catholicism. If the Roman Catholics are not right, why was Peter told that the Church had the keys of life and death? If they are right, why was it not made clear that the Roman Catholic Church was the type of Church meant? In either case it would seem that Christ must have made serious mistakes in the way in which he stated his gospel, for it is not possible to regard either the Catholic or the Protestant interpretation as sheer inexcusable perversity. On a 'narrow' interpretation of Christ's teaching why did he not make crystal clear which of the narrower types of Christianity was right when man's eternal salvation was at stake? On a broader interpretation, on the other hand, why did he utter those sayings which have been used to support the narrower creeds? From narrow interpretations have stemmed the wars of religion, horrible persecutions and great mental anguish for vast numbers of people troubled as to whether they had the right beliefs and practised the right kind of observances to avoid the unspeakable torment of eternal hellfire. It was not beyond human wisdom, let alone divine, to foresee that some of the sayings attributed to Christ would be liable to be interpreted in these misleading ways. It might indeed be said by either side that all the passages which made against their view were interpolations or interpretations and not Christ's actual words, and this may be so, but somebody could say so equally about the passages on which the incarnation doctrine is based.

It has been urged – for example by Hick[1] – that the message of Christ was not made completely unambiguous because otherwise there would be no room left for the virtue of faith, but this to my mind implies a quite wrong interpretation of what faith ought to be. I cannot see that there is any virtue in believing doctrines on insufficient evidence, however edifying these doctrines may be. I do indeed attribute a value to faith, but I think in so far as commendable it consists in holding steadfastly to what one has judged to the best of one's ability to be probable (not necessarily certain) when this is rendered by emotional factors a very difficult thing to do. It is difficult for most people to hold to the belief in God (or for that matter the incarnation) in any way that makes it an effective influence on their state of mind when overwhelmed by the evil in the world or by a weight of dull care, and it is a virtue still to hold to these beliefs in such a mood if one has considered them carefully on other occasions and then been convinced of their rightness. We ought not to let our beliefs be dictated to us by passing moods and circumstances, though this does not exclude the duty of sometimes reconsidering them on intellectual grounds. It would also be a virtue on the part of a convinced agnostic who had decided on his position after careful reflection not to fall back into theism just because he was impressed by the

[1] *Faith and Knowledge*, p. 185.

beauty of a service or felt in a mood in which he longed for divine help or because owing to a bereavement he had an intense desire to meet the one he had lost in a future life. But there is no virtue in holding a belief to be more probable on the evidence that it is. And I cannot believe that an incarnate God would deliberately make things in his teaching less clear than he might with results such as the horrors of the Inquisition and the loss of faith in vast numbers who would have believed if their religious teachers had not insisted on irrational doctrines which would in their turn not have been widely spread if they had not been supported by misinterpretations of ambiguous passages in Christ's teaching, still less if they had been definitely and clearly excluded.

I am well aware that most theologians teach the doctrine of kenosis according to which God as incarnated in Christ did not retain omniscience but only moral perfection, and that from that doctrine it would follow that one need not expect Christ to foresee all the effects of the words he used; but we must at least expect that an incarnate God would have wisdom to make the best use of all knowledge he could have by ordinary human means, and it would not have needed superhuman foresight to see that many of the sayings of Christ would be liable to be misjudged with disastrous results in ways that could have been corrected by a wisdom well possible for a human being and not requiring any kind of miracle. To expect Christ to foresee this is not like expecting him to know the theory of relativity or any scientific doctrine that was quite out of the ken of thinkers of his day. No premise and no mode of inference would be required that was not available in the first century A.D. If Christ was not more than a man, such mistakes need not necessarily be a ground for moral blame. A man may without moral blameworthiness be liable to the error of expanding his doctrines ambiguously, but it is a very different matter if God himself is regarded as the author of the words. No doubt it must be metaphysically impossible for God to express his nature fully in human form, but at least a wise God without giving Christ-as-human omniscience, would surely have seen to it that a being who was both very God and very man did not in expounding his teaching make mistakes of such a kind as to impair its benefits most gravely. It was quite possible to see that many such things as were said would be liable to be misinterpreted with dire results without having the supernatural ability to predict exactly what would result from the misinterpretation. We can recognize that what is set forth as Christ's teaching, wonderful for a man not exempt from fallibility, is not the perfect product we should expect in a man who was also God, if indeed that combination be possible.

If the doctrine of the incarnation in an orthodox sense is abandoned, I see no reason left for holding Christianity to be *the right* religion for all time. (Indeed even if the incarnation be a fact, I do not see how it follows that there could not be another incarnation later even on this earth.) It seems to me to be unreasonable and arrogant in the sense in which 'apartheid' is unreasonable and arrogant to claim that Christianity is the only religion by which men can be 'saved'. If 'to be saved' means 'to have attained perfection' no man is or can be saved, at least in the course of his earthly life, but it is outrageous to say that a non-Christian cannot live a good and even religious and saintly life. Except as regards the doctrine of the person of Christ there is no appreciable difference in the concept of God held by many Jews, Mohammedans and Hindus and that which a Christian may well hold. Christianity may well be the finest religion that has yet developed on earth, but it is utterly without a shadow of justification to claim as Barth did that *the only* word of God to man is Christ. Nor are we entitled to assert that Christianity is final in the sense that it cannot be added to or even amended. Progress is not indeed incompatible with finality in certain respects. It is inconceivable that any further progress will lead to the amendment of our conviction that $2 + 2$ is equal to 4 (though conceivably to some reinterpretations of some applications of the principle in recondite spheres), and I think that some ethical principles are in a similar position. That we ought to concern ourselves not only with our own happiness but with the welfare of others is an example, and much of Christ's ethical teaching falls into this category (though it should be added that it is not peculiar to Christ). We may say the same about some at least of his religious teaching if we believe in religion at all. But to say that no teacher will ever arise in the millions of years which may lie before the human race who will supersede Christ in the sense of teaching even more effectively all the truths he taught and also adding to and in some respects rightly amending his teaching is a prophecy which I see no ground to make. Actually the ethical outlook of

Christianity has already been improved long before being carried out in practice by the addition to it of an appreciation of the Greek ideal of the value of knowledge and thought, a valuation which was not indeed repudiated but not as far as we know expressly made by Christ, and of the importance of freedom of thought and of toleration, which were very much discouraged by certain sayings of Christ as interpreted commonly by the Church (though I trust not as really meant by Christ).

Nor does my view leave any place for revealed religion in the most usual sense of the phrase. Not only the rest of the Bible but the New Testament and even the sayings attributed to Christ himself must be treated as subject to criticism and not necessarily exempt from error. Such a line has been by now adopted by a very large and increasing proportion of Christians on the ground that, even if Christ was infallible, it is not clear whether he has been reported or interpreted correctly, so that his actual words cannot be just accepted without further reasoning; but we must on my view add to the possibility of misinterpretation the possibility that Christ may actually have been mistaken sometimes, not only as to points later discovered by science – a possibility very generally admitted by Christians – but even as regards ethical and religious matters. Revealed theology in the sense of a special set of propositions miraculously communicated and guaranteed by God I can see no ground for accepting, but 'revealed religion' in the sense of religious discoveries made wholly or partly by intuitive religious insight I have shown that I have no inclination to deny.

Let us now pass to the very difficult question of time. God is commonly held to be 'out of time', and it is even widely supposed among religious people that we shall attain a timeless state when we die. Yet timeless existence seems utterly inconceivable to us, though this does not necessarily prove it impossible. Hartshorne has quite a case for his view that God himself is in time.[1] For if God is not in time, must not time be unreal, since reality must be just as God sees it to be, a view which would make all our supposed knowledge not only of the physical world but of ourselves illusory? For Kant, when denying the reality of time, is, I think, unsuccessful in his attempt to soften the blow. He claims that we still have real knowledge of

---

[1] See *Man's Vision of God*, pp. 98 ff.

appearances, meaning that we know our experiences at least; but our experiences are in time. Now experiences exist, if anything does, so something really temporal exists, we may reply, therefore time is real. The only alternative to this would be to say that our experiences are not really in time even as experiences but only appear to be so, in which case all or practically all our introspections are illusory. Time is such a central factor in our life that our experience would be quite unrecognizably altered if *per impossibile* it could be conceived removed. We must be complete sceptics even about our own experiences if time is strictly unreal, and our moral life, on which Kant laid so much stress, would seem to lose all point without the notion of time.

Or could we meet the difficulty by dividing reality into two parts, one temporal and one non-temporal? Possibly, but if God is not in time is it possible for the world process to appear to him successively? Must it not appear to him in some super-temporal form? And then we can still argue that the world must really be not as it appears to us but as it appears to God.

I shall now be bold and venture a tentative theory in a field which one might expect to lie beyond the bounds of human capacity. Nobody could hope that his speculations on such a subject would be right just as they stand, but I shall at any rate put forward a way of thinking about these difficult topics which has recently occurred to me and suggests to me a method for removing its worst difficulties. The Cambridge philosopher, McTaggart, in dealing with the question of time, made a distinction between what he called the A and the B series, and though I do not in other respects agree with McTaggart's theory of time I think this is a very important distinction for dealing with the topic in question. The B series is a function of the relations before and after, the A series of the relations (I should rather say states of being) past, present and future. A differentia between the two is that if one experience occurs before another it will always be the case that this particular experience has occurred before the other, and similarly with the converse relation after, but if it is now future it is not the case that it will always remain future. It will on the contrary become first present and then past. The A-series distinction is always relative to a particular time. Further, we are aware of what is present in a sense in which we cannot be said to be aware of what is past, as can be easily seen by comparing pain I now feel to pain I felt a year or even an hour ago. The anticipation of future pain is usually more disturbing than the remembrance of past pain, but apart from the possible exceptions alleged in paranormal psychology the future is not the object of immediate awareness but only of probable inference. We have a strong sense of the present as being really real in a sense in which neither past nor future is and the past as being real in a secondary sense but still a sense in which the future is not. But this leads to the paradox that the only thing really real seems to be an infinitesimal moment, and it may be asked whether something infinitesimal is real at all. Still less can it be the only reality, as it seems it should be from the point of view of the *A* series. This seems to me a stronger reason for doubting the reality of the *A* series than the reason, as I think fallacious, which McTaggart produced. To avoid this paradox psychologists and philosophers have had recourse to the notion of the specious present. But the distinction between past and present again obtrudes itself within this specious present so that the literal present becomes a mere mathematical line, an abstraction not experienceable by itself. We have to admit then that we are aware of a certain short stretch of past time with a present immediacy that must be sharply distinguished from mere memory and that this and not the exact present is to be regarded as the real present of experience. If we admit this we can admit, as has been often suggested, the possibility of the specious present being for some minds widely extended, so that there might conceivably exist a being for whom the whole time series was present and there was no such thing as future or past as distinguished from earlier or later, at least if the difficulty of there existing an infinite series can be overcome, as the experts of mathematical logic now think is the case. Now for such a being time would obviously not constitute an *A* series as it does for us. But it would still be a *B* series, for an event would be apprehended as before or after another, as my typing the first line in the letter *A* might be apprehended as preceding my typing of the second line even if the two events were for me part of the same specious present. In a sense we could indeed say that the distinction of the past, present and future still held for such a being, but it would not be absolute but relative to different events in the time series, as for a being who was non-spatial considering the spatial world as a whole Manchester would still be such and such a distance from Moscow, though no place in the world would for such a being be 'here' or such and such a distance away, meaning by 'away' distant from the place where the being was. But then to say an event was present, past, or future relative to another would only be to say it was simultaneous with, preceded or followed it. Tenses would lose their function, though not temporal prepositions.

It seems plain that a perfect being would not experience the world-process as an *A* series in the way we do. For he would then be incomplete in a way which is quite incompatible with perfection. He would never be more than a minute fraction of his total being, and each such minute fraction would be lost for ever as it was succeeded by the next. Yet he might well experience time under the form of the *B* series. In fact he must if he is to experience the world as it is, and if the world and our own experience is not a complete illusion. An omniscient or even a tolerably knowledgeable God must be aware that the battle of Hastings took place before the world wars. I am not saying that God is in time, I am saying that the content of his experience (or at least part of it) must be. As I have pointed out, since what we experience is always a period, however short, there can be temporal relations of before and after in the specious present between experiences experienced together.

This view enables one to deal with the argument of Hartshorne, who contends that many religious practices and beliefs are senseless if God is not in time. Hartshorne insists that if God loves us he must be affected by sympathy when misfortune befalls us and grieve when we act wickedly, that is, he must be affected by events in time, and though he is changeless in the sense that he will never falter in his central purpose he therefore cannot, if he takes any interest in human affairs, be literally always the same. Again if there be any truth in the belief in the objective efficacy of petitionary prayer through God's action,[1] we must suppose that God sometimes acts differently because someone has prayed. Indeed he could not even know an event in time without that event affecting his conscious experience. But it seems to me that these requirements might be met provided the relations of before and after occur in God's experience, even if time does not take for God the form of the *A* series. There obviously can be causal relations within the specious present, and

[1] I am not intending to commit myself either for or against this doctrine of prayer.

certainly are in ours. Even if God is only aware of two events together, he could be aware of one event as coming before and affecting another. We might further think of relations of before and after as falling rather in the content of God's experience than in his experiencing itself.

Now the conception that I have put forward has the great advantage of not making time an illusion, as even Kant, though he denies it, in practice really does. For what is it to perceive time under the aspect of the A series instead of only under the aspect of the B series? It is not to perceive anything positive that is not there but merely to fail to perceive more than a very small part of the time-series which is really there. It does not make our perception that one experience of our own comes before another some sort of a mistake. It does really come before the other. No doubt because we only experience at once or even remember such a small part of our experience as we do and are not able to foresee the future we miss a great deal of the significance of the present events we do experience, but our introspections may still be completely correct in so far as they are not mixed up with judgements as to the causes of our experience or of their ultimate role and value in our life-process, which we may expect to be partially mistaken. It is not that God does not perceive something positive which we perceive; it is only that he perceives whole where we perceive part. Further, just as God though he does not sin must be aware of what it is like for a man to sin, so God must be aware what it is like for us to have this limitation of temporal perception, though he does not himself have it. My conception would still involve admitting that an omniscient God would apprehend an event in my life in a very different way from that in which I do, without missing anything that is included in my apprehension. For he would know its ultimate effects and place in the whole world-process and this would make his view of it very different, at least in many, perhaps all, cases. What we see as for example, an almost unmitigated disaster might be seen by God, and later even by ourselves as a part of an organic unity that was as a whole good.

If time *qua* A series is unreal as I suggested but as B series real this removes the most serious objection to the entailment theory of causation, a theory for which there seems to me to be strong positive ground, as I have indicated earlier. The strongest objection to it is the difficulty of seeing how C could entail E without E being always present when C is, whereas the cause has ceased to be present when it produces its effect. But obviously this way of talking presupposes the A series view; if the past has not really lapsed into non-existence it does not apply.

But, especially if the Berkeleyan argument I used earlier is correct, the whole temporal process depends on God's mind in a way which seems to put God himself outside time, though the *content* of his experience would include the temporal relations involved in the B series. We may instance as an illustration that has some analogy the fact that, though my ego is not spatially spread out, its images are so. Now the objection has often been made that a non-temporal being could not create – or affect when created – the temporal world because for him to do that his causation would have to be in time. But this objection impresses me little. Causality is a relation and therefore it could not be in either of its terms in the sense in which their qualities are. It seems to me like asking whether the distance between London and Manchester is in London or Manchester and because I cannot answer this question concluding that I am wrong in thinking that there can be such a relation as distance between them at all.

There remains a last hurdle to be surmounted by any view which does not put God in time. It seems at first sight that it must lead to determinism. I have objected to determinism on the ground that, if what I do today is fixed from all eternity, it cannot be said, whatever I may do today, that I ought to have acted differently; but does not the view of time I have just put forward imply that what I do is fixed timelessly, i.e. from all eternity? But I think this idea is due to one or both of two fallacies. (1) We may be confusing foreknowledge based on immediate insight with foreknowledge based on prediction from causes. Complete foreknowledge of the latter kind would imply determinism, events being all fixed by preceding causes, but if some events are undetermined this kind of knowledge of them is impossible even for God, and to know them in advance directly is not to infer them from causes. But (2) it may be objected that I am still involved in the difficulties of determinism because in any case I have admitted that God can know what I shall do today from all eternity and therefore it is fixed from all eternity and I could not have omitted to do it. But this argument commits another, if less obvious, fallacy. It puts God both outside and inside the series of temporal events. What is incompatible with freedom is the notion that all events are fixed before they happen, but I am not suggesting that God knows them before they happen. That would be putting him in the time-series after all. If my suggestion is correct, it is not true that God knew in 1000 B.C. that Hitler would start war on Poland in A.D. 1939, because God does not exist in the time-series; he knew it timelessly if at all. And supposing it was an act of free will on Hitler's part, as I imagine it was, he only knew it because he was immediately aware of Hitler as doing it. What determinism there is would lie in the opposite direction in the limited degree in which Hitler was free; God would know it because Hitler did it, not vice versa.

At the same time we must naturally admit that we cannot conceive what God's consciousness of time is really like, even if we may be fairly confident that it includes awareness of temporal relations in the *B* series without God's experience taking the form of an *A* series as does ours. But we cannot form the slightest notion of what timeless experiencing is like (unless some mystics are right in thinking they have had experiences which give them the idea). To think of it as a simultaneous experiencing of everything in the time process is already to introduce the temporal relation of simultaneity, and we cannot think of the experience without giving it some duration, itself another temporal category. But the fact that we can form no idea of a certain mode of experience is far from proving that it does not occur, or even that we 'in heaven' may not eventually experience it in some degree, though not in its completeness, since this would be incompatible with our finitude. I am, however, much more inclined to think with the orientals that this is a state which we shall only attain, if ever, after an agelong advance than that we shall, even the best of us, attain it directly this present life ends. There is nothing more central to our experience than time, and if it were by some miracle removed suddenly from us, we should be completely and unrecognizably transformed. We should also lose all chance of progress and we are far from being ready for that yet.

Why should there be time? Might I be bold enough to suggest two possible complementary answers to this apparently fantastic question, one for time as viewed in the *A* series and one also for time as viewed in the *B* series? May the first not be simply that a finite being could not from the nature of the case see everything at once, otherwise it would be infinite? This should account for our experience falling into the *A* series. And might a further reason not be found in the realm of values? With free finite beings who may misuse their free will a good organic unity is not achieved at once. I cannot at the same moment sin and overcome my sin. If the sin is to be redeemed and a good organic unity achieved, this must occur *after* the sin has been committed, therefore the relations before and after must figure in both *A* and *B* series, if the purpose of the universe in regard to finite beings is to be achieved. To a being who could see the whole process at once the redemption must be seen as still related to the sin, the overcoming of evil to the evil by the relation of after, otherwise the process is not being perceived correctly; and for the finite being who sins or incurs misfortunes which he cannot at the moment convert into a good organic unity he must experience them in the *A* series without being aware at all at the time of the ultimate victory he will achieve over them. Yet the overcoming of evils and temptations is a value without which the whole would be poorer, though it would be better still if they were always overcome at the time they occurred so that there was no sin.

INDEX